D0222538

A Guide to the Global Business Environment

This book is dedicated to:

Derek Braddon, Richard Emery and John Thomas

and

Rick Barichello, James Gaisford and Kurt Klein

A Guide to the Global Business Environment

The Economics of International Commerce

William Kerr

University Distinguished Professor, University of Saskatchewan, Canada

Nicholas Perdikis

Professor of International Business, Aberystwyth University, UK

Edward Elgar

Cheltenham, UK • Northampton, MA, USA

© William Kerr and Nicholas Perdikis 2014

All rights reserved. No part of this publication may be reproduced, stored in a retrieval system or transmitted in any form or by any means, electronic, mechanical or photocopying, recording, or otherwise without the prior permission of the publisher.

Published by
Edward Elgar Publishing Limited
The Lypiatts
15 Lansdown Road
Cheltenham
Glos GL50 2JA
UK

Edward Elgar Publishing, Inc.
William Pratt House
9 Dewey Court
Northampton
Massachusetts 01060
USA

A catalogue record for this book
is available from the British Library

Library of Congress Control Number: 2014932634

ISBN 978 1 78347 667 1   (cased)
ISBN 978 1 78347 669 5   (paperback)
ISBN 978 1 78347 668 8   (eBook)

Typeset by Servis Filmsetting Ltd, Stockport, Cheshire
Printed and bound in Great Britain by T.J. International Ltd, Padstow

Brief contents

**SECTION V   INSTITUTIONS THAT
              FACILITATE INTERNATIONAL TRADE**

**SECTION VI   FUTURE TRENDS IN INTERNATIONAL
               TRADE AND COMMERCE**

Full contents

Figures

Tables

Preface

The evolution to the true globalization of commercial activity over the last 50 years has made it essential that business people and those pursuing business studies courses understand the economic forces that shape the international business environment.

Our experience, gained on both sides of the Atlantic from teaching economics to business studies students, led to our dissatisfaction with existing texts. While the standard international economics books are excellent in themselves, the theoretical approach adopted by them is largely inappropriate for business students. On the other hand, the texts on international business, while being less theoretical than their economics counterparts, tend to include areas such as accounting, human resource management, marketing and strategic management. As a result, international economic issues and institutions are not dealt with in sufficient detail. Our aim in writing this book was to provide business studies students with a text that deals with these issues both rigorously and in depth, but in a way that is sympathetic to their needs. For the convenience of readers a glossary is included at the end of the volume. Words included in the glossary are indicated in **bold** font in the text.

Saskatoon, Canada, 2014
Aberystwyth, United Kingdom, 2014

Section I

Introduction

1

Why study the economics of international business?

1.1 One executive's story

BOX 1.1

1.1 ONE EXECUTIVE'S STORY

It had all been so easy. It had all gone so wrong! Ryan had finished cleaning out his desk and was waiting, as he had been told, for security to come and escort him out of the building. Until they had told him just over an hour ago, Ryan had been manager of the international division of a medium-sized British manufacturer of patient monitoring equipment used in hospitals. He had joined the firm ten years ago after completing an MBA in the US. In his first eight years he had been in domestic sales and worked his way up to be one of four assistant managers. Then one day, two years ago, he got the call.

The purchasing manager in a large Latin American company wanted to know if Ryan's firm would be interested in providing monitors to re-equip their hospital chain. The potential order was large, but his firm had never had any export dealings. After a meeting with senior management it was decided that the company should pursue the order, and Ryan was put in charge of the project. He flew to Latin America, met with the hospital chain's management, and was wined and dined, after which a deal was sketched out. The order was too large for the company's existing manufacturing capacity, and new investment would be required. Back in the UK, Ryan drew up a formal business plan. The price the company would have to charge after accounting for all the additional transportation and insurance charges would make a competitive bid difficult. Ryan was, however, able to find an Asian company which could supply a costly and crucial computer component at a far lower price than their local British supplier. He was also able to secure a local government grant which was available to assist new exporters. The lower-cost Asian component and the grant would allow the exported monitors to be profitably sold at a price less than monitors sold in the British market.

➡

←

The imported component would also improve profit margins on monitors sold in the domestic market.

Ryan presented his plan to the board of directors, and the expansion in manufacturing capacity was approved. After a successful bid, a lucrative formal contract was negotiated in Latin America. Ryan was made manager of a new international division, which was to be responsible for fulfilling the contract and searching out other foreign markets. The expansion of manufacturing facilities was completed on schedule, and regular shipments of monitors to Latin America began. Ryan began travelling the world seeking out additional sales, while his division waited for the profits to roll in.

It was then that things began to go wrong. The first inkling was that the profits did not begin to roll in. The payments from Latin America were always late and were never the amount agreed in the contract. A stream of complaints that the monitors were defective upon arrival was used to justify the reduced payments. Ryan and the company's engineers had to make a number of expensive trips to Latin America to check the state of the equipment. The engineers could find no faults, but the hospital chain's management still insisted that the monitors were not performing to the specifications in the contract. On the advice of the company's British law firm, Ryan reluctantly hired legal counsel in the hospital chain's country to sue for payment. Negotiations with the hospital chain continued while the lawyers prepared their case. Legal bills began to roll in.

The legal counsel in Latin America was informed by the country's government that the imported monitors were now the subject of two trade actions. A manufacturer of competing monitors located in the country was bringing an anti-dumping suit with the government's dumping tribunal. The suit was based on the imported monitors being sold at lower prices in Latin America than in the UK. Further, the country's unfair trade practices commission was conducting an 'export subsidy' investigation into the grant Ryan's company had received. If either investigation found against Ryan's company, large import duties would be applied to any imported monitors. While the lawyers thought the investigations were instigated largely for their nuisance and political value, good cases would have to be prepared for both hearings. Legal costs increased.

Back in the UK, there were other problems. The switch to the Asian supplier of computer components had led to job losses at the company's former British supplier. The union representing the workers who had been made redundant was accusing Ryan's company of exploiting low-paid Asian workers and contributing to the demise of British manufacturing. Ryan remembered one particularly difficult session when the press asked him about this point – he did not have any good counter-arguments and, in fact, he wasn't sure

➡

←

that he didn't agree. The chairman of the board had made it known that he thought the adverse publicity was damaging the firm's reputation.

The management of the former British supplier had obtained one of the Asian company's components. Their computer people suspected that the Asian manufacturer had pirated their technology. The British government was being asked to take action against imports from the Asian supplier on the basis of patent violations.

Back in Latin America, the country was going through a period of sustained inflation, and the value of the local currency was falling dramatically against the pound. As the contract price had been specified in the local currency, those payments that were received from the hospital chain could be exchanged for fewer and fewer pounds. Meanwhile, the legal wheels were grinding slowly, and the case for non-payment was finally going to court. The Latin American law firm sent an e-mail suggesting that the case be dropped, because the judge appointed to hear the case was the cousin of the doctor who headed up the company which owned the chain of hospitals. That had been this morning.

An emergency meeting of the board of directors had been called and a decision taken to cut the company's losses and abandon the Latin American contract. The international division was to be wound up and Ryan let go. Ryan wondered what he could have done differently. He did not have long to ponder, as the company's security escort had arrived.

While Ryan, and his company, might have been particularly naive, the catalogue of woes listed above are all real problems that must be addressed by business people who wish to engage in international commercial activity. If such problems are not anticipated, or are dealt with without careful investigation, they can sour even the most lucrative foreign business opportunities. Most of these problems – and many others – can be effectively dealt with if the workings of the international economy are well understood. Specialized institutions, both public and private, often exist which can lower the costs and reduce the risks associated with international business. This book is an attempt to provide a guide to the complex system which constitutes the international commercial environment within which companies operate. The intent is to prepare business people – or future business people – and others interested in international commerce to anticipate problems like those faced by Ryan, our fictional executive. The book also lays out the choice of options that can be used to eliminate or at least mitigate the costs and risks associated with the problems anticipated. International business will never be as easy as Ryan thought, but a good understanding of the economics of international business can prevent it from going wrong.

It is said that no man is an island, and in international business and commerce this is no less true for nations, companies or individuals, whether they are located on one of the world's largest continents or even one of its islands. When looking at news bulletins on the internet or watching television one is struck by the way individuals, companies and national leaders appreciate that fact. Reactions, however, often vary from the 'We should keep all foreign goods out and meet our needs from home production' kind to the 'An open world economy is best for business because trade increases our standard of living' kind. There are many variants in between these extremes. Often those commentating on trade perceive a need for other countries to open up their economies to foreign competition but never see the case for opening their own markets. Nowhere have the arguments been better rehearsed than in the multilateral trade negotiations that take place in Geneva or in bilateral discussions such as those between the US and China. China's formal integration into the international trading system since it opened its market has highlighted the importance that domestic factors, such as the organization of distribution systems, credit and labour supply, have on international trade and business. It is no longer solely economic policies that affect, and are being affected by, changes in international competitiveness – countries' social policies are also impacted. Hence businesses, whether directly involved in, or only indirectly affected by, international commerce, cannot afford to ignore international economic issues and how they will impinge on the businesses' activities.

1.2 International trade in the post-Second World War period

The end of the Second World War ushered in a new era in international trade. New institutions were put in place in post-war conferences which, while they have been considerably altered over time, still provide the framework within which international trade takes place. The most important of the institutions were the **General Agreement on Tariffs and Trade (GATT)**, which defined the environment for trade in goods, and the **International Monetary Fund (IMF)**, which regulated the exchange rate environment. In 1994 the GATT became part of the newly negotiated **World Trade Organization (WTO)**. While the influence of these organizations has grown or declined over time, they have presided over the greatest increase in international commerce ever seen.

Table 1.1 Growth in global trade

2003	2004	2005	2006	2007	2008	2009	2010	2011	2012
4.9%	10.6%	7.7%	9.5%	7.1%	2.7%	−9.2%	12.5%	6.5%	3.9%

Source: Global Economic Outlook Database, Development Policy and Analysis Division, United Nations, New York.

1.2.1 The growth of world trade

World trade in goods and services has grown rapidly in the period since the end of the Second World War. In value, trade has increased from US $53 300 million in 1948 to US $23 406 500 million in 2012. This growth has been characterized by several phases. In the period between 1948 and 1960 trade grew on average at the annual rate of 6 per cent, between 1960 and 1973 it grew by 8 per cent annually, between 1973 and 1980 there was a period of slower growth of 4 per cent, and there was even lower growth, averaging 2 per cent, between 1980 and 1985. The period 1985 to 1993 saw a resumption of more rapid growth, approximately 6 per cent. This average rate was sustained in the decade leading up to 2003. As can be seen in Table 1.1, since 2003 there have been considerable year-to-year fluctuations, which dampened somewhat the positive contribution of international commerce to the general process of economic growth and development. In particular, there was a significant retreat from the long-run expansion in global trade in the wake of the financial crisis of 2008 – but growth in trade has subsequently recovered.

A further important and consistent feature of the post-war growth is that in volume terms the growth in world trade has outstripped the growth in world output. As a result, the world's trading nations have become more integrated.

What caused this rapid increase in trade? Three post-war phenomena are largely responsible:

1. the rise in **real incomes** and, hence, demand for goods and services in the world's leading economies;
2. technological improvements in transportation and communications;
3. a general reduction in the restrictions imposed on trade.

Since the end of the Second World War in 1945 the global economy has experienced an unprecedented period of economic growth. This does not mean that this growth has followed a straight-line trajectory. There have been a number of serious economic downturns and periods of inflation without economic growth, but despite these 'bumps along the way' the world is a much richer place than it was 60 years ago. While the growth in income has been widespread, there are still areas of the world that have languished in poverty and not benefited from the general global rise in standards of living. To a considerable degree, however, these are countries that have not been willing, or able, to integrate into the modern international economy. In part, this is because some countries have chosen not to integrate and have used trade policies to isolate their economies to a considerable degree. For example, many developing countries attempted to spur their economic development by following a policy of 'import substitution industrialization' whereby local industries were encouraged by higher-than-international prices arising from tight restrictions on industrial imports. After an initial period of success, import substitution was found not to lead to sustained economic growth, and it was largely abandoned as a development policy. Communist countries also attempted to develop in isolation from their capitalist rivals, but have opened their markets since the end of their 'command economy' experiment in the early 1990s. Other countries have not been able to join the global economy because they are too impoverished or badly governed to put the appropriate infrastructure in place to engage in modern international commerce. Large sections of the African continent, for example, remain relatively isolated from the modern global economy.

It is also true that the benefits of generally rising global incomes have not been spread evenly to all members of relatively rich societies. Pockets of relative poverty remain in many countries. Individuals with poor or inappropriate skills and/or those who are trapped in areas with declining industries have not reaped the benefits of rising incomes.

Part of the reason that there has been a long-term general increase in income globally is that governments in developed economies have done a much better job of managing their economies than in previous eras. Up until the end of the Second World War the economies of developed countries were characterized by severe 'boom and bust' cycles where **recessions** were common, and severe, and where those who found themselves unemployed or on farms had too little personal wealth to prevent their descent into poverty and little or no assistance available from government or society as a whole. Economists of the time thought business cycles were the norm and that governments could do little to influence them. In many cases government macroeconomic management practices based on the prevailing economic wisdom actually contributed to the economic malaise experienced during recessions. In the 1930s, what has become known as the global 'Great Depression' led to widespread unemployment and low agricultural prices over much of the decade. Governments offered no real solutions except simply to 'wait it out'. Governments exacerbated the deepening recession by putting trade barriers in place in desperate attempts to save jobs – but simply kicked off a 'beggar-thy-neighbour' trade war whereby international trade plummeted to a greater degree than the faltering economies of developed economies. The absence of a credible plan to deal with the Great Depression and the continuing very high levels of unemployment were unacceptable to voters, and they chose governments offering alternatives.

The continuing economic malaise also spurred economists into looking for the means to better manage the economy. One economist in particular, Britain's John Maynard Keynes, put forth a new theory of macroeconomic management that garnered widespread interest among economists and government policy makers. Keynes suggested that in a recession neither consumers, strapped for cash, nor investors, facing flat or declining markets, would be willing to increase their expenditures to pull the economy out of its malaise. Keynes surmised that only governments could add the spending power needed to 'kick-start' the economy out of recession. Some governments accepted Keynes's theory and began to tentatively implement some of his recommendations, but their experiments were cut short by the start of the Second World War. Keynes's ideas on economic management took root, however, and were well entrenched in economic circles and among policy makers by the time the war ended.

Faced with managing their economies as they made the transition from wartime production to peacetime endeavours, policy makers began following what became known as **Keynesian** economics, which was a greatly embellished theory based on Keynes's original ideas. A central focus of Keynesian economics was that governments accepted responsibility for keeping the economy near to **full employment**. Hence, in the face of impending economic downturns, governments would intervene with increased spending (or lower taxes) to offset declining spending by consumers and private sector investors. In a similar way, governments were expected to intervene by reducing their expenditures (and/or raising taxes) when the economy showed signed of overheating – when rising rates of inflation were observed. In short, governments began intervening in the management of their economies in ways that attempted to counter cyclical tendencies and bring a considerable degree of stability.

These efforts had a significant degree of success; for example, there have been no cyclical declines such as that of the Great Depression since the Second World War. While governments accept a major role in economic management, the tools they have chosen to use to provide economic stability have evolved. In the 1970s an alternative to Keynesian economics gained popularity with some economists and government policy makers. Instead of changes in government spending and taxation, the new focus was on using the ability of the central bank to control the availability of credit – through manipulation of the money supply – to stimulate or slow spending. This approach is known as **monetarism**. As with the Keynesian approach to economic management, monetarism was not able to consistently produce full employment and low inflation. The governments of developed countries still accept responsibility for managing their economies in countercyclical ways but now are likely to use a combination of credit manipulation through the central bank and changes in spending and taxation.

The increase in economic stability produced by proactive government intervention in their economies led to considerably reduced risks for investors. This led to increases in investment that expanded productive capacity and improvements in productivity. Incomes rose, fuelling increased consumer spending and general increases in prosperity. Rising incomes allowed increased investments in both education and research and development, which led to further increases in productivity. All of this led to increased demands both for foreign sources of resources and for foreign-produced goods – fostering increased international trade. Some of the investment in research and development went into technological improvements in transportation that facilitated trade. Even more important were the investments in communications technology – satellites, computers, the internet, mobile phones, etc. – which significantly lowered the costs of conducting international business.

Countercyclical management of the economy works best during times of relative stability – near an economic equilibrium. Governments have been much less successful in dealing with unanticipated shocks to the economy. Sometimes these shocks arise from natural disasters such as earthquakes, droughts, hurricanes or floods, but they also arise from economic sources that create an economic disequilibrium that forces costly adjustments. For example, in the 1970s, after decades of low oil prices, an important group of oil-exporting countries got together and agreed to reduce the global supply of oil to raise its price. The **Organization of the Petroleum Exporting Countries (OPEC)** succeeded in shocking the global economy twice in the 1970s, leading to painful economic adjustments and recession despite the best efforts of governments to stabilize their economies. After years of impressive economic growth through the 1960s and 1970s, Japan's urban real estate market entered an unsustainable boom and, when prices eventually collapsed, the shock created a disequilibrium that the government of Japan was unable to contain, leading to no or low rates of economic growth for decades. In a similar fashion, the bursting of the dot.com investment bubble at the beginning of the twenty-first century brought disequilibrium to investment markets that governments had difficulty overcoming, again leading to an economic downturn. Another source of disequilibrium was the integration of low-cost China into the global economy after it ended its 30 years of self-imposed isolation under the economic policies espoused by Communist Party leader Mao Zedong. While the arrival of low-cost consumer goods from China was a benefit for consumers, it also meant that many long-established industries in developed and developing countries were no longer competitive, meaning that they experienced a period of costly adjustments. In 2008, poor regulation of the financial sector and an unwillingness to restrain a 'boom' led to a major banking crisis requiring large government bailouts of banks. The financial crisis spilled over to the rest of the economy as banks were forced to reduce the availability of credit, leading to the most significant global economic downturn since the Great Depression. Hence, while the record of government countercyclical management of economies in times of relative calm is fairly robust, they have considerably less success dealing with major shocks.

International business has also benefited from the international institutions – particularly the WTO – that have reduced the risk of governments imposing trade barriers that threaten successful investments in international business opportunities. The rules of international trade agreed by the member countries of the WTO and the reductions in trade barriers negotiated among the members have allowed trade to become an international 'engine of growth'. Since 1947, and the negotiation of the GATT, the number of member countries where the trade-liberalizing rules apply has risen from less than 20 to over 150 – which in itself provided a great boost to world trade (Kerr, 2010).

1.2.2 The structure of world trade

Table 1.2 shows the composition or structure of world trade. In contrast, in 1955, agricultural products constituted 35 per cent of world trade and manufactures 49 per cent. It is clear that trade in manufactures has increased its domination of international commerce. The trade numbers reported in Table 1.2 are values, so, over the decade leading up to 2011, the relative share of manufactures has fallen because, with China joining the community of trading nations, the price of manufactures has fallen. At the same time, the prices of fuel and food have risen. The fastest-rising category of manufacturing trade is office and telecoms equipment, reflecting the computer and internet communications revolutions. It also includes the shift to mobile phones from a much more static market for landline phones.

Table 1.2 World merchandise exports by product, 2011

	Value 2011 US $ billion	Share		Annual percentage change		
		2001 %	2011 %	2005–11	2010	2011
All products	17 849	100.0	100.0	11	22	20
Agricultural products	1 660	9.1	9.3	12	16	21
Food	1 356	7.3	7.6	12	12	21
Raw materials	304	1.8	1.7	n.a.	n.a.	n.a.
Mining products	4 008	13.2	22.5	14	33	34
Fuels	3 171	10.3	17.8	14	29	37
Manufactures	11 511	74.8	64.6	8	20	15
Iron and steel	527	2.2	3.0	10	30	24
Chemicals	1 947	9.9	11. 2	10	18	16
Automotive products	1 287	9.4	7.2	6	29	17
Office and telecoms equipment	1 680	13.8	9.4	5	22	4
Textiles	294	2.5	1.6	6	20	17
Clothing	412	3.3	2.3	7	11	17

Source: WTO International Trade Statistics 2012.

The 2011 and 2001 snapshots of international trade, however, obscure the effects of the major world recession that started in 2008 in the wake of the major crisis in the financial industry, which required governments in a number of developed countries to bail out many of their banks. As credit tightened, demand declined, and international trade declined to a much greater degree than domestic economies – in the 25 per cent range. The strong growth rates in 2010 and 2012 indicate a strong resurgence in trade after declines in 2008 and 2009.

What forces have brought about the long-term changes in the composition of trade? The continued upsurge in manufactures at the expense of other categories can be attributed to the fact that consumers spend relatively more on these goods as their incomes rise – in economists' terms they have higher **income elasticities**. As incomes have risen in the world economy, the demand for manufactures has risen at a faster rate than for other groups such as agricultural products that have lower income elasticities.

So far only the trade in goods, or what is also called visible or merchandised trade, has been discussed; however, invisible goods or services are also traded. Trade in services constitutes approximately 25 per cent of the value

Table 1.3 The composition of world services trade

	2003 US $ million	2004 US $ million	2005 US $ million	2006 US $ million	2007 US $ million	2008 US $ million	Average annual change 2004–08 %
Transportation exports	404 291	504 414	570 367	635 587	761 616	881 161	3.49
Travel exports	535 095	638 013	691 178	751 275	866 934	945 734	2.96
Other services exports	893 097	1 078 533	1 218 863	1 423 695	1 742 372	1 944 180	3.60
Government services exports	56 907	64 450	69 562	77 853	83 548	87 505	2.71
Total services exports	1 889 390	2 285 410	2 549 970	2 888 410	3 454 470	3 858 580	3.37

Source: OECD (2010).

of the trade in visible goods. The growth of trade in services has roughly matched that of manufactures. Table 1.3 shows the composition of the trade in services for the period 2003–08 and their annual average rate of growth. The principal causes of the overall growth in services can be attributed to the substantial growth seen in some of the component parts.

For example, travel services have been influenced by the rapid growth in tourism and are a function of the growth of real incomes in the richer countries of the world. A rapid rise in royalties and fees accruing to the owners of **patents**, copyrights and trademarks reflects the increasing proportion of the value of goods which can be attributed to inputs of intellectual property, leading to the growth in the 'other services' category. Other private services, which include amongst other things the use of telecommunications equipment (mobile phone services, satellite and computer networks), underline the importance of the revolution in information technology and the move toward knowledge-based economies in developed countries.

1.2.3 The distribution and concentration of world trade

Trade is not distributed evenly across countries, and it is highly concentrated amongst the so-called developed or industrial countries of the world. Trade has also grown faster for these countries than the growth of world trade. As a result, these advanced nations now account for approximately three-quarters of world trade. The principal explanation for this dominance of the industrial countries in the distribution of trade is that they are the most efficient producers of the goods that are in greatest demand.

Those developing countries that have been able to industrialize – the so-called newly industrialized countries (NICs) – have also benefited from the growth in world trade. Their export performance since the 1980s has been particularly strong. Originally utilizing their abundant resource of cheap labour, they produced and exported mainly labour-intensive goods such as textiles and clothing. As their skill base has developed they have moved on to include electronics components, electronic goods and communications equipment as major exports. Their ability to break into markets where trade barriers were high makes their achievements even more remarkable. The precise grouping of NICs varies, but they usually include Singapore, Taiwan, Hong Kong, South Korea and Malaysia – the Asian Tigers – as well as Thailand. Brazil and Chile have also more recently joined the list.

Perhaps the most important recent development in international trade has been the appearance of China as a trading nation. After the communist revolution in China in 1949, the government s goal was self-sufficiency. Starting in the late 1970s, the opening up of the Chinese economy to world trade has been an integral part of its development strategy. It has achieved an annual average growth in trade of 15 per cent, with exports currently accounting for over 20 per cent of GNP. Over three-quarters of its exports are manufactures going primarily to the developed economies of Japan, the United States and Europe. China's long process of integration into the international economy took a major step in 2001 when it joined the WTO.

In Latin America and the Caribbean, trade has also expanded, largely as a result of economic liberalization and an abandonment of the trade-restricting development strategy of import substitution, which attempted to foster manufacturing industries by restricting imports. The region's impressive growth in trade reflects the rapid expansion of Brazil, Chile and some of the countries of Central America and the more moderate and less consistent expansion in trade experienced by Argentina, Uruguay and Mexico. The principal trading partners of this area are still the developed market or industrialized economies, which account for just over 60 per cent of its exports and 70 per cent of its imports. Intra-area trade, however, constitutes only 15 per cent of total trade. In recent years, agricultural and mineral exports to Asia have increased.

Africa's export trade is dominated by **primary products**, with over 70 per cent coming from agricultural and mining products. This concentration has had its drawbacks, since the demand for primary products grows at a slower rate than the growth in world incomes. Debt problems, falling commodity prices, stagnant economic growth and inept governments have contributed to keeping African import growth in check. Africa has, to a considerable degree, been bypassed by the trend to globalization.

The participation of the former communist countries – or command economies – in the international trading system prior to their economic transformation can be said to be minimal. With the widespread change in regimes and accompanying ideologies following the fall of the Berlin Wall, a major shift has taken place in trade relations. Since then, these countries have been increasingly integrated into the global economy. This integration has been particularly strong in the countries of Central and Eastern Europe, a number of which joined the European Union (EU) after 2000. Countries of the old Soviet Union such as Uzbekistan and Kyrgyzstan remain relatively isolated and less integrated into the global economy. Russia joined the WTO only in 2012.

It is clear that over the post-war period international trade has been increasing rapidly and much faster than world output. This period has also seen a relatively steady increase in the share of manufactures and decline of primary products traded in the world economy. Latterly, services have increased their share of total trade. The world economy has become much more integrated – sometimes referred to as globalized. The major growth has been experienced by the developed, market or industrial countries. Other economies that have shown spectacular success in the trading area are the so-called NICs, particularly those in South and East Asia. China has also become a growing market and a major exporter. In the last years of the twentieth century, long-reticent India began to view trade in a positive light and began to open its markets. Other developing countries, particularly those in Africa, burdened by major economic difficulties, have not participated fully in the growth exhibited by international trade. The former Central and Eastern European countries, which initially experienced difficulties in their period of transformation, are becoming increasingly integrated into the international economy.

1.2.4 Foreign direct investment

The last 60 years have seen not only the rapid growth of trade both in goods and in services but also the growth of foreign investment. This has been of two types:

1. indirect, made up of equity investment (the purchasing of shares in foreign companies), private debt investment (the acquisition of foreign

bonds and other debt instruments) and intergovernmental transfers principally made up of loans, gifts and economic aid;

2. **foreign direct investment (FDI)**, whereby firms extend their operations into foreign countries.

The major objective of FDI is to gain or maintain access to markets and/or resources. Manufacturing and the extractive industries such as oil, coal and minerals have been the most important areas for FDI, but it is also prominent in the services sector – banking and finance, legal services, marketing and distribution. The bulk of foreign direct investment is carried out by the US, Japan and the countries of the EU, which together account for over 80 per cent of the total value of these investments.

The reason for the rise in FDI is a subtle combination of both push and pull factors. As the world economy grew and national incomes rose, the increase in the size of foreign markets enabled companies to set up facilities abroad which could attain the same cost structures as could be achieved in the home country. In many cases, the simplification of production procedures – which reduced the need for skilled labour – enabled firms to transfer production abroad to countries where labour costs were lower.

Trade barriers have also played their part in the expansion of FDI. By acting as a brake on trade, trade barriers have encouraged firms to set up production facilities abroad in order to break into or maintain their foothold in foreign markets even if the size of production facilities required to service the local market in the initial phases of development have not been of a size necessary to be internationally competitive.

The formation of **regional trade associations** has acted as a stimulus to FDI not only because of the possibility that an association might wish to restrict its external trade in the future but also because with the adoption of free trade amongst member states the potential market increases. As a result, one often sees substantial FDI into regional associations such as the EU from other rich nations such as the US and Japan.

It must not be forgotten that some nations have actively encouraged FDI, in an attempt to fulfil industrialization plans, to improve the efficiency of domestic firms through competition and/or in the hope that foreign firms with their perceived superiority in organization and production will spur domestic firms to copy their example. Foreign countries have often encouraged FDI by offering a series of incentives linked to tax breaks, allowances and rebates, grants, guarantees to allow the repatriation of profits, the provision of land for development, and the improvement of infrastructure.

1.3 Plan of the book

World trade is, therefore, important both for the countries that participate in the international economy and for the businesses that engage in international commercial activity. The rest of this book is devoted to explaining the determinants of trade and trade patterns and the institutions that shape and influence the international trading environment.

In Section II we discuss the determinants of trade patterns from the perspective of economic theory. We examine the concepts economists use to explain why nations trade and show how the resources available to be used in production, whether natural resource endowments or the results of past investments in physical facilities and people, influence the types of goods a country trades. We also discuss the factors that can lead some countries to be more successful traders than others. The factors that shape the international trading system are also examined. Emphasis is placed on the reasons for openness in trade and the political and economic factors that might lead to restrictions on the movements of goods and services internationally.

Section III examines the nature of the international trading system. Chapter 4 concentrates on the role of the nation state, especially in the development of trading relationships via bilateral agreements. Chapter 5 explores the formation of regional trade associations. Multilateralism is dealt with in Chapter 6. Particular emphasis is placed on the role of the WTO, as well as its predecessor, the GATT, in overseeing the trading system. Chapter 7 deals with the various arrangements that contribute to orderly trade, such as commodity agreements, voluntary export restraints and countertrade. Chapter 8 provides a detailed discussion of the policy measures available to countries to restrict trade, while Chapter 9 explains how the multilateral system attempts to control the use of trade restrictions. The means of addressing problems considered 'unfair' trade are the subject of Chapter 10.

The role and function of the major participants in international commerce are studied in Section IV. Emphasis is placed on the rationale for growth and development of transnational companies, although other players such as trading houses are not neglected. The role of state trading organizations is also discussed.

Section V examines closely the system that facilitates international commercial transactions. These largely private sector institutions reduce the risks involved in trade by providing and guaranteeing finance and payments, providing insurance and organizing the transportation of goods. Since trade involves buying and selling across frontiers with countries having different business ethics, cultures and legal systems, disputes between the parties involved are bound to arise. We, therefore, examine closely the means available to businesses to settle international disputes.

Finally, Section VI examines some of the likely future developments in the trading system. While the future appears to hold further growth in trade and closer economic integration, we would not be performing our duty as dismal scientists if we did not emphasize some of the potential difficulties that might arise and impact adversely on international business.

 REFERENCES

Kerr, W.A. (2010) GATT-1947: A living legacy fostering the liberalization of international trade. *Journal of International Law and Trade Policy*, 11(1), 1–11.

OECD (2010) *OECD Statistics on International Trade in Services 2000–2008*, Organisation for Economic Co-operation and Development, Paris.

What insights does trade theory provide?

Introduction to Section II

Why should those interested in international business study the trade theories of economists? In the economics profession, the pure theory of international trade has a reputation for being extremely abstract. It is considered by many outside the economics profession as being more of a rigorous intellectual exercise than useful in solving real-world problems. While these perceptions are to some extent correct, being familiar with the major trade theories is important for anyone interested in being involved in international commerce. The foremost reason is that the influence of trade theory on government attitudes toward international trade is considerable. The conclusions of some of the major theories are used (and misused) to support a wide variety of international political initiatives, trade policies and lobbying positions. Some popular theories have not withstood the tests of close intellectual scrutiny or empirical investigation. Others are not theories at all but, rather, the well-disguised propaganda of particular vested interests.

Technological advancement, particularly the revolution in communications, is fostering greater economic integration. Debates over trade policy will continue. Business people will increasingly be drawn into those debates. Hence, a basic understanding of the theories upon which many of the arguments are based is important. The input which business people can have on trade policy will be enhanced if they are informed participants in trade discussions. This section attempts to provide an introduction to the insights which trade theory provides.

2

International trade and economic theory

2.1   What determines competitiveness?

The purpose of this chapter is to briefly outline the theories that economists have used to explain the pattern of world trade. The models presented will appear simple. They will be framed in terms of two countries or two products or two inputs to production. Those engaging in international commerce are typically faced with a complex world with many countries, an industry producing a wide range of goods, and production processes using enough inputs to justify employing a department full of cost accountants. It is often difficult to see the relevance of the simple models of economists.

Models, however, are by their very nature simplifications. Economists justify their simple models in two ways. First, while more complex systems can be modelled, they require sophisticated mathematical treatment which only specialists can understand. For the sake of communication, the models are kept simple. This would not be a valid justification if adding complexity altered the conclusions generated by the models in a fundamental way. The second reason that economists use to justify the use of simple models is that adding complexity, at least in terms of more countries, products or inputs, seldom changes the conclusions of the simple models. Economists say that the results of the simple models can be 'generalized'. The models presented in this chapter will continue the tradition of simplicity. What is important is the insights generated by their conclusions.

Since Adam Smith's day it has been assumed that nations trade because it will bring them some advantage. (Adam Smith was professor of moral philosophy at the University of Glasgow from 1752 to 1763 and is commonly thought of as the father of modern economics. His famous book *The Wealth of Nations* was originally published in 1776 (Smith, 1961).) This issue will be discussed in greater detail in Chapter 3. The differences in what countries trade is determined by their competitiveness in producing goods, which in turn is determined by the productivity of the inputs used in the productive process. What trade theories try to do is explain how this competitiveness comes about. The views of the 'classical' economists on this topic are outlined before we proceed to the more modern theories and explanations for trade in differentiated products.

2.2 Classical trade theory

The classical approach to trade was mainly concerned with showing that trade was beneficial to the parties that undertook it. These theories still provide much of the popular intellectual underpinnings for the belief in **trade liberalization**.

2.2.1 Absolute advantage

Adam Smith's proposition was simple. He argued that if two nations voluntarily traded with each other then both must gain if each country specialized in the production of the good in which it had an **absolute advantage** and exchanged this for the commodity in which it had an absolute disadvantage. Advantage is defined by relative efficiency in the use of resources in production.

Absolute advantage can best be illustrated numerically by referring to Table 2.1.

Here we have two countries, I and II, and two goods, A and B. By expending 1 unit of labour (per hour, week, month, etc.), country I can produce 1 unit of A and 5 units of B. For the same outlay, country II can produce 6 units of A and 4 units of B. From this we can see clearly that country I has an absolute advantage in producing good B, while country II has an absolute advantage in the production of A.

Assume that country I will exchange B for A on a one-for-one basis. If country II specializes in the production of A and can trade 6 units of it for 6 units of

Table 2.1 Absolute advantage

Goods	A	B
Country I	1	5
Country II	6	4

Note: Output per unit of labour.

B produced by country I, it will gain 2 units of B (i.e. by moving 1 unit of labour from its own production of B, 4 less are produced but 6 are gained from trading). Alternatively, if it only wanted to produce 4 extra A for trade it would save itself one-third of the labour time expended. Under a situation of **autarky** (no trade), country II produces either 6 A or 4 B or alternatively it can trade and exchange 6 A for 4 B. The 6 units of A that country I receives would have required it to expend 6 units of labour time if it had produced these domestically. If country I had used this labour time in the production of B it could have produced 30 units of B. By specializing and trading, country I can make a net gain of 24 units of B or save 5 labour units.

Our example has shown that by specializing in the production of the good in which it has an advantage and engaging in international exchanges – trade – a country can make gains. What should a country do, however, when it is more efficient than other countries in the production of all goods? To answer this question the nineteenth-century economist David Ricardo developed the concept of comparative advantage (Ricardo, 1951).

2.2.2 Comparative advantage

The theory of **comparative advantage** concentrates not on the absolute differences in countries' efficiency in producing goods but on the differences in relative efficiencies. The law of comparative advantage states that a country with an absolute advantage in the production of both goods in a two-good world should specialize in the production and export of the good in which its absolute advantage is greater. Consumption of the other good would be satisfied by importing it from the other country, which in turn would specialize in the good in which its absolute disadvantage would be less. This can be numerically illustrated in Table 2.2.

Here again we have two countries, I and II, each producing two goods, A and B. In this example, country I has an absolute disadvantage in the production of both good A and good B, while country II is more efficient in producing both of them. Country II is six times more efficient at producing good A and

Table 2.2 Comparative advantage

Goods	A	B
Country I	1	2
Country II	6	4

Note: Output per unit of labour.

twice as efficient at producing good B. Its major advantage, however, clearly lies in the production of good A, and so it can be said that its comparative advantage lies in the production of A. Compared to country II, country I is less inefficient in the production of good B, producing only half of B per unit of labour (2:4) compared to one-sixth of A (1:6). Thus, country I can be said to have a comparative advantage in the production of good B. If both nations specialize in and export the good in which they have a comparative advantage they will both benefit from trade.

To illustrate the gain from trade let us assume as in our previous example that country II can exchange 6 units of A for 6 units of B. Once more, it would gain 2 units of B compared to its autarkic position. Country I would also gain in that it would receive 6 units of A in exchange for B, which would have taken it 6 units of labour time to produce. Country I could now use that labour effort to produce 12 units of B and change 6 of these for 6 units of A. Under autarky it could produce only 6 units of A with 6 units of labour time, so by trading it has gained 6 units of A. Again, country I gains more than country II, but they have both gained by specializing and entering into trade with one another.

It should not be assumed that mutually beneficial trade arises only when 6 units of A are exchanged for 6 units of B. Exchange rates other than this 1:1 ratio can also lead to gains. As long as country II can achieve more than 4 units of B by giving up 6 units of A it will gain. Similarly, if country I can give up less than 12 units of B for 6 units of A then it too will gain. Thus, the range within which advantageous trade can take place lies between 4B < 6A < 12B. When the two countries trade 6 units of A for 6 units of B, country II gains 2 units of A and country I 6 units of A, 8 units in total. As the ratio of exchange moves closer to 4 units of B to 6 units of A the smaller is the share of the gain occurring to country I. Conversely, the closer the ratio of exchange approaches 6A for 12 units of B the greater is the gain for country II. For example, if country II exchanged 6 units of A for 8 units of B then both countries would gain 8 units of B. If country II exchanged 6 units of A for 10 units of B it would gain 6 units of B but country I would gain only 2 units of B. Thus, differences in the ratio of exchange would determine the actual as opposed to the possible gains from trade and, more relevant to our discussion, the type and quantity of goods trade, that is, the pattern and volume. The determination of the ratio of exchange was, however, not addressed by the theory of comparative advantage, and it was able to describe the conditions of supply and the benefits only once demand was known.

While the classical economists' focus was on the benefits to be gained from trade, their analysis did not answer the question 'What determined comparative advantage?' The classical view suggested that climate and differences in the quality of natural resources led to differences in the productivity of labour between countries. As a result, nations would have different comparative advantages and, hence, they would export different products to one another. This may well have been a reasonable explanation in a period when the products traded were agricultural and/or when labour was the predominant input. Many of the goods that are actually traded require inputs other than labour and natural resources. In a world where labour skills can be learned and production know-how is widely available, the classical view loses a great deal of its explanatory power. Economists of the 'neo-classical' school attempted to address the issue by relating comparative advantage to the productive factors with which a country was endowed. The major contribution of the classical theory was, however, to prove that, if a difference in productive efficiency existed, gains could be expected from engaging in trade.

2.3   Neo-classical trade theory

The **neo-classical** theory of international trade was developed by the Swedish economists Heckscher and Ohlin (Ohlin, 1933). It is also known as the factor proportion theory.

2.3.1   The basic 2 × 2 model

Neo-classical theory still accepts as its starting point the two country–two commodity world that the classical economists assumed, but differed on a number of points. Firstly, more than one factor of production was assumed. **Capital** was included along with labour. Secondly, the two goods produced were assumed to have different **factor intensities**, one using relatively more capital than labour, while the reverse was the case for the other. Thirdly, while factor intensities differ between products, the production technologies used to produce each of the goods are assumed to be the same in both countries. In other words, a good that requires relatively more capital than labour in its production in one country can therefore be said to be capital intensive. It is also produced capital intensively in the other country.

Given the above production conditions, how does the theory operate or what does it predict? Let us take two countries that are distinguished from one another by an inequality in the distribution of resources between them. That is, one country is capital abundant, while the other is labour abundant. In this way the capital-abundant country has a higher capital-to-labour ratio than the labour-abundant country. If demand conditions are the same in the two countries, then the price of the factors is determined by their supply as reflected in the quantities the countries are endowed with. In the capital-abundant country, capital becomes relatively cheaper, while in the labour-abundant country labour is relatively cheaper. By linking these relative prices to the production conditions outlined above, neo-classical theory produces the conclusion that goods which use capital intensively in their production will be produced at lower cost in the relatively capital-abundant country. The opposite will be the case in the labour-abundant country, which will have a comparative advantage in producing labour-intensive goods. Thus, countries that are relatively well endowed with capital will produce and export goods that use capital intensively in their production, while labour-abundant countries will export labour-intensive goods.

The neo-classical theory went deeper than the classical approach in that it not only predicted trade patterns but also could account for the differences in comparative advantage between countries. Classical theory would suggest that labour productivity would determine what goods a country would produce and export. Heckscher–Ohlin went beyond this and gave a reason for the difference in labour productivity. For example, in capital-abundant countries, labour productivity would be high, because it had more capital to work with than in labour-abundant countries.

2.3.2 The Leontief paradox

The neo-classical explanation held sway in economics until mathematical and statistical tools were developed which could test it empirically. Examining the trade patterns of the US, which was considered to be a capital-rich country, **Leontief** (1953) – who was to go on to win a Nobel Prize in economics for his work – discovered that its exports were in fact labour intensive while its imports were capital intensive. This paradoxical result was also found for other countries and was furthermore confirmed for the US by later studies (Leontief, 1956). This led economists to re-examine the assumptions on which neo-classical theory was based and either to modify it so that it explained the facts or to seek alternative explanations (Perdikis and Kerr, 1998).

A number of justifications were put forward to reconcile the empirical results with the theory. One of the first, which was proposed by Leontief, was that US labour was roughly three times more productive than its foreign counterpart as a result of superior management, better training and greater motivation. By taking US labour superiority into account one could recalculate the figures to show that the US was, in fact, a labour-abundant country.

The second influence to be examined was the impact of the US restrictions on imports. It was argued that labour-intensive industries in the US were highly protected so that imports were biased in favour of capital-intensive goods (Travis, 1964).

Neo-classical theory's concentration on only two of the many factors of production was also suggested as a possible explanation. For example, it was pointed out that the US was really an importer of natural-resource-intensive goods which also happened to require a great deal of capital but little labour. On a straight capital/labour measurement they would show up to be capital intensive, whereas they would really be natural resource intensive (Vanek, 1953).

A further explanation of the paradox was the possible influence of demand factors. It was suggested that US demand was heavily biased in favour of capital-intensive goods, which raised their price, hence neutralizing the comparative advantage of home-produced goods while enforcing that of imports (Valvanis-Vail, 1954).

2.4 Alternatives to neo-classical trade theory

These and many other explanations were put forward to explain the paradox and rehabilitate the neo-classical theory of trade. Other economists, as we have pointed out, took a different view and tried to explain trade patterns by expounding alternative theories. These were usually developed by holding constant the factors that Heckscher–Ohlin assumed variable and assuming variable the factors they held constant! For example, **economies of scale** (an economic concept which suggests that, over at least some range of production, efficiency will improve as the quantity of output a factory is designed to produce increases) were allowed to exist, whereas under Heckscher–Ohlin there were only **constant returns to scale** (where production facilities are equally efficient no matter what their size), labour was no longer assumed to be homogeneous but had different skills, factor intensity was allowed to vary over the life of the product, and so on. We will now examine some of these so-called alternative theories and the light they shed in determining a country's comparative advantage and, in turn, its trading pattern.

2.4.1 Human skills

More as an extension of the Heckscher–Ohlin theory rather than a true alternative, economists have suggested that skilled labour inputs are an important source of comparative advantage and, hence, trade patterns (Keesing,

1966; Appleyard et al., 2006). It has been argued that countries that are well endowed with professional personnel and highly skilled labour will specialize in the export of skill-intensive goods. The converse is also true, as countries that have abundant supplies of unskilled labour concentrate on the production and export of goods employing untrained labour. By defining skills in terms of either educational attainment or the average wage rates in the industry (since wages are assumed to reflect training and professionalism), empirical support has been found for this theory. This evidence is particularly strong from tests where labour has been 'decomposed' into its various skill components and has been used along with capital to explain trade patterns (Baldwin, 1971).

2.4.2 Economies of scale

One of the assumptions on which the factor endowments theory was based was that of constant returns to scale. Firms, however, are known to achieve economies of scale, and a large home market has been said to contribute positively in bringing these about. As a result, large countries would be expected to benefit over small countries in the production of goods whose methods of production allowed them to reap economies of scale. Although ostensibly at a disadvantage, small countries could achieve economies of scale and gain comparative advantage if they concentrated on the production of goods conforming to international standards that do not rely on national characteristics as a selling feature (Drèze, 1960; Bhagwati et al., 1998).

One interesting aspect of the economies of scale argument is that trading patterns could be determined by historical accident, depending on which countries' firms had established an early lead over their rivals in one or a range of industries. By gaining a lead, a country would achieve lower costs and would therefore make it potentially difficult for rival countries to compete successfully. Under these circumstances it becomes possible for a country to export a good or a range of goods that are contrary to those expected from an examination of its factor endowments.

2.4.3 Technological theories

While explanations of trading patterns were sought by incorporating static economies of scale into trade analysis, another approach incorporating dynamic economies of scale and technical progress was also put forward. This group of theories assumes that there is a link between high national income levels and innovativeness or dynamism. The argument made suggests that industrially advanced countries are the initiators of new products, in the production of which they are able to reap both static and dynamic economies of scale given their large and expanding markets. As long as identical innovations do not take place simultaneously between countries or imitation is instantaneous, then one country will gain a lead or comparative advantage over another in the development and production of a specific commodity (Posner, 1961; Hufbauer, 1965). In this way, trade will be generated between countries. Each country will exchange, with the other, goods that it has not yet been able to imitate and produce at home. Once the importing country's firms have succeeded in reproducing the good at a comparable cost, trade in the commodity will cease. Studies have shown that this technological approach to trade can explain some of the trade between developed countries and between developed and developing countries (Hufbauer, 1970; Dinopoulos et al., 1993).

2.4.4 The product cycle

Although a link between income and dynamism or innovativeness can be established, it is not so clear why the production of new goods should be located in advanced countries. An answer to this question was, however, provided by Vernon (1966, 1979), who suggested that as a good matures its characteristics change, which also leads to a change in the location of its production.

In the initial phase of a product's development there are major uncertainties regarding styling and the appropriate production process. These uncertainties can be reduced if changes in the market's mood can be translated quickly into alterations in the product or the production process. The first can be acted on if production is carried out close to the market, while the second can be achieved if flexible skilled labour is substituted for machines. As the product matures and becomes standardized, marketing and production uncertainties are reduced and competitive pressure increases. This will, in turn, encourage firms to find cheaper locations for their production, and comparative advantage moves from the innovating country to those with the lowest production costs.

2.4.5 Income similarity

As well as encouraging the development of new goods, income can also be looked upon as shaping tastes and, hence, demand patterns. Income similarity was put forward by Linder (1961) to explain the increasing volume of trade between advanced countries with similar factor endowments. His argument went like this: Entrepreneurs initially concentrate on supplying the home market, but once this has become saturated they seek new outlets, principally in countries or social groups within those countries that have similar incomes and, hence, tastes to those in their own country. Trade will, therefore, be greatest in intensity between countries that have similar national incomes. Again, there is a great deal of evidence to suggest that these demand factors have played an important role in the determination of trade patterns between countries. This hypothesis has, however, been very useful when coupled with the notion of increasing **returns to scale** in explaining the phenomenon of intra-industry trade or trade in similar products (Perdikis and Kerr, 1998).

2.5   Intra-industry trade

During the late 1950s and early 1960s it became obvious that trade was growing fastest between the advanced industrial countries and that this trade was in similar – from the same industry in the other country – but differentiated products (Verdoorn, 1960; Balassa, 1975). Both orthodox neo-classical theory and the alternative theories predicted that trade would take place between countries with dissimilar factor endowments and, hence, in dissimilar goods, so this new phenomenon needed an explanation. To place the role of this intra-industry trade in context, one merely has to examine the following figures. For example, it has been estimated that over 60 per cent of world trade is in manufactured goods, and half of this is accounted for by intra-industry trade (Greenaway and Miller, 1986). Trade in non-manufactures is also subject to this phenomenon. Other researchers have concluded that, for some individual countries, up to 70 per cent of their trade in manufactures is subject to intra-industry trade (Aquino, 1978). It has, furthermore, been increasing over time (Hesse, 1974).

2.5.1   The measurement of intra-industry trade

There are a variety of ways to measure intra-industry trade, but the simplest is to measure the extent of overlapping trade in a particular commodity or good and express this as a proportion of overall trade, that is, exports plus imports.

Intra-industry trade can then be expressed as:

$$Bi = \frac{(Xi + Mi) - /Xi - Mi/}{(Xi + Mi)} = 100\%$$

where Bi stands for intra-industry trade in commodity i, and Xi and Mi the level of exports and imports respectively in that commodity.

Thus if exports equal $200 and imports $120, then $240 is overlapping trade (i.e. $120 of imports and $120 of exports), while $80 does not overlap. Intra-industry trade would thus be 75 per cent of the total.

Using our formula this can be deduced from:

$$Bi = \frac{(200 + 120) - |200 - 120|}{(200 + 120)} \times 100$$

$$= \frac{320 - 80}{320} \times 100$$

$$= \frac{240}{320} \times 100$$

$$= 75\%$$

2.5.2   The aggregation and classification of goods

When discussing intra-industry trade, it is essential to know what is meant by similar goods, because the extent of this type of trade can be affected by their definitions. Let us take chocolates as an example and let us say that Belgian chocolates are totally different to British chocolates. With this definition, no intra-industry trade can take place. This would, however, be stretching the point, since in another sense chocolate is chocolate all over the world. It may differ in colour, texture and taste, but its basic make-up is the same. At the other extreme, we could say that all manufactured goods could be defined as a single product, in which case exporting advanced medical equipment in return for bicycles would make all trade resemble intra-industry trade. Thus, the degree to which we aggregate and disaggregate goods has important implications for intra-industry trade and has led some economists to regard it as nothing more than a statistical artefact (Pomfret, 1986). Other researchers, however, discovered that, as trade was disaggregated into finer classifications and intra-industry trade declined, it nevertheless remained at levels that still required an explanation (Grubel and Lloyd, 1975).

At this juncture it may be pertinent to explain how commodity trade is classified. Most countries present their trade statistics in the form adopted by the World Customs Organization and known as the Harmonized System. It is a numerical classification, with each commodity being allocated a classification. Each section is then subdivided into division groups and subgroups,

Table 2.3 An illustration of the Harmonized System

Section V1 (06)	Chemicals and allied industries
Subsection (06.29)	Organic chemicals
Group (0629.01)	Hydrocarbons
Subgroup (062901.10)	Saturated acyclic hydrocarbons

Source: Harmonized Commodity Description and Coding System, World Customs Organization, Brussels.

with each of these being given a number prefixed by that allocated to the section. Table 2.3 illustrates this clearly.

Thus the first digit refers to the section number (i.e. 06) and the second to the subsection (i.e. 29), the third to the group (i.e. 01) and the fourth to the subgroup (i.e. 10).

2.5.3 Explaining intra-industry trade

The first explanations of intra-industry trade began with the work of Grubel and Lloyd (1975), who emphasized **product differentiation** and economies of scale as potential causes. It soon became evident, however, that differentiation also required some explanation and that intra-industry trade also existed among non-differentiated or homogeneous products.

Homogeneous goods

Intra-industry trade in homogeneous goods can be explained fairly easily by three factors. The first is the existence of **entrepôt** or re-export trade. A considerable proportion of the trade of Singapore and Hong Kong is of this type. A country may import goods in bulk, which are then shipped out to other neighbouring countries, possibly having been broken down into smaller consignments. In this way, one would see the simultaneous importing and exporting of goods. The second explanation is seasonality, where products are exported during one part of the year and imported during another. This is quite common for agricultural products where the production season is different in the northern and southern hemispheres – grapes from Chile and apples from New Zealand sold in Canada in the winter. The third explanation is the cost of transport, which may encourage users of a particular good to import it from a bordering country rather than a domestic producer who is located at the other end of a large country. For similar reasons, the domestic producer may export a good to another country that is located nearby. It is quite common to see this type of cross-border trade take place between land-locked countries such as those found in Europe.

Differentiated goods

For differentiated goods, a more sophisticated explanation is required, based on differences in tastes amongst consumers and economies of scale in production. As suggested earlier, taste is, at least in part, determined by income (Linder, 1961). As people become richer, the more they will demand better-quality goods and greater variety. If we assume that domestic producers cater only for dominant domestic tastes, then, under autarky, choice will be limited. Consumers could buy their preferred choices from abroad but would be limited in doing so by high transport costs and other barriers that add to the purchase price of the import. As incomes rise, however, consumers may well be able to afford the premiums required to acquire imports (Barker, 1977).

The opening up of trade between countries and the expansion of markets will allow firms to specialize in the production of varieties. Under autarky, domestic firms will concentrate their production on one or a few varieties. To expand on the number of varieties produced would lead to increased costs and lower profits for the firms concerned. Once trade is opened up, however, market segments appear which are large enough for suppliers to reap economies of scale and, as a result, they are able to produce more varied goods. Which country achieves a lead and, hence, a comparative advantage is very much a matter of chance and can be the result of company strategy or government policies which promote particular industries (Krugman, 1979). The latter is known as industrial policy. Major policy debates take place over whether governments can improve on market signals by identifying future leading industries – pick winners – thus attempting to ensure they secure the comparative advantage (Davies and Kerr, 1997).

A further explanation of intra-industry trade has been suggested which builds on the Heckscher–Ohlin framework (Pomfret, 1986). This approach suggests that different varieties require different factor inputs and, as a result, each country will specialize in the product that uses its abundant factor intensively. It will then exchange this variety in return for the other. What this theory suggests is that a product, say chairs, can be produced from different materials (e.g. wood and plastic). Those countries that are abundant in wood will produce wooden chairs, and satisfy their demands for plastic chairs by selling wooden chairs abroad to finance imports. What this theory suggests, however, is that products are being misclassified, in that chairs should really be sub-categories of the wood and plastics industries and not grouped together. While this explanation of intra-industry trade is plausible, a number of writers do not feel that it explains the phenomenon of intra-industry trade fully (Lloyd, 1989).

How do the theoretical explanations of intra-industry trade measure up in practice? As with all empirical work, methodological problems arise when one tries to identify theoretical concepts in practice. Data for the variables that need to be used to model homogeneity, product differentiation, market structure and scale economies are sometimes not available, and the proxies available are often at best rough approximations. Without minimizing the problems involved in estimating the relationships, the principal empirical works show that variables such as overlapping tastes, product differentiation, market structure, technology and economies of scale have a positive influence on the level of intra-industry trade between countries (Greenaway and Miller, 1986). Other factors that were found to have a negative influence were trade barriers and foreign direct investment. Neither of these needs much explanation, as one restricts the volume of trade and, hence, the opportunity for intra-industry trade to take place, while the other acts as a replacement for trade.

2.6   What do trade theories tell us about trade patterns?

Probably the first thing to note is that it is unlikely that any one particular theory can account for the observed pattern of world trade. The economics profession tends to conduct analyses on the basis of the Heckscher–Ohlin model despite its limitations and its poor showing in empirical tests (Perdikis and Kerr, 1998). There are several reasons for this. Firstly, it is a simple theory whereby, with a few assumptions concerning the use of abundant resources and knowing the factor endowments of a country, one can make predictions about its trade pattern. Secondly, the tests that tend to refute the Heckscher–Ohlin model are not without their own flaws. For example, they rarely take into account trade policies and distortions and, hence, cannot be said to refute the neo-classical theories directly. Thirdly, if Heckscher–Ohlin is modified to include human capital, as some researchers have done, then this modified version gives reasonable results (Baldwin, 1971). Finally, empirical evidence for the alternative theories is not strong enough for any one of these to be regarded as an adequate alternative. It has been suggested that the **product cycle** theory is probably better at explaining changing trade patterns over time than explaining trade at any one point in time.

As the issue of a general trade theory has not been totally settled, some trade economists have, however, suggested that trade theories are useful at explaining trade patterns in certain groups of goods (Hufbauer, 1970; Hirsch, 1974). Those that require heavy natural resource, climatic or unsophisticated labour inputs could be classed as '**Ricardian-type goods**'. Thus, trade in goods coming from the extractive industries (i.e. coal, petroleum, minerals) or food products such as wheat or corn, or industries that process these goods, can be explained adequately by classical Ricardian trade theory. Typically, one would expect the flow of these products from developing countries, although in the case of food grains and some minerals many of the developed countries, for example the US, Canada and Australia, also export these goods.

Those goods that require standardized technologies and no single specific factor inputs will be located in countries that offer the best combination of factor prices. In other words, industries such as textile manufacturing and ferrous metal production would be regarded as 'Heckscher–Ohlin type goods', and the neo-classical theory would describe the location of those industries and their pattern of trade. In particular this theory would explain the trade between developed and developing countries.

Following the classification of trade theories outlined above one would, therefore, expect that trade in technologically advanced goods would be explained by the technology theories. Given that these theories emphasize the generally advanced nature of the economies involved in producing such goods, in terms of both income level and innovative skill, we can expect that these goods will be produced in advanced countries and exported to either other advanced and/or developing countries. Thus, exports of micro-electronic goods and sophisticated transport equipment such as aircraft will usually emanate from the developed economies. That is not to say that this will always be the case, for, as we have seen above, once the production technologies become standardized these goods can come under the Heckscher–Ohlin category.

Several country studies testing this approach have found that the US exports are concentrated in the technology group as well as the Ricardian group. Japan's exports are found predominately in the Heckscher–Ohlin group, while the Ricardian group is virtually non-existent. The EU is fairly strong in both the Heckscher–Ohlin and technology groups but weak in Ricardian goods (Hirsch, 1974). Studies on individual countries have found that the pattern of the UK's exports was shifting away from technological goods to Heckscher–Ohlin varieties (Katrak, 1982). In contrast, the evidence from Japan suggested a movement into technological goods (Heller, 1976).

One question that might be asked is what role do the theories of intra-industry trade play in this analysis? The answer is that countries whose industries had gained substantial economies of scale, and hence had specialized in particular product lines, would export these lines to countries with similar income levels and tastes. Thus, Heckscher–Ohlin type goods such as cars can be traded between countries with similar factor endowments, as can technological goods such as medical equipment and sophisticated computer components.

Assuming that we are able to categorize goods by the inputs required in their production – which should not be too difficult – then our trade theories enable us to explain trade patterns and to be more precise in answering the question: which countries will produce and export which goods? A question that still remains to be answered is, however, why are some countries more prone to trade than others? This topic is discussed in section 2.7.

2.7 The determinants of trade intensity and competitiveness

Economists have tried to identify the factors that determine:

1. trade dependency, that is, the ratio of imports to GDP;
2. net exports.

Leamer (1974, 1984) related these measures to three groups of variables:

1. the state of development, that is, GDP and population;
2. resistance variables such as trade restrictions and transport distances;
3. variables that reflect resource endowments such as capital intensity, research and development expenditure, skills and education, and the consumption of electricity.

This last variable was used as a proxy of the industrial complexity and sophistication of a country's economy.

The results showed that there was a close link between trade dependency and the development variables, while resource endowments contributed little. In other words, countries with high GDPs and large populations are the major traders. The results for net exports, however, were contrary in that resource variables were more important. In Leamer's 1974 study, research and development was the most important factor, while in his 1984 study the factor intensity variables predominated.

An approach that attempted to explain why some nations were more successful than others in exporting is that of Porter (1990), in particular an explanation for why some countries' industries continued to be successful even when factors like exchange rates, resource endowments and so on worked against them. The answer, Porter suggested, lay in the maintenance and growth of national productivity and, in particular, how companies formulate their strategies. More precisely, five major determinants of international competitiveness or **competitive advantage** were identified. These were:

1. factor conditions (land, labour and capital);
2. demand conditions (the size and composition of the home market relative to foreign demand);
3. the existence of related and support industries, especially if these are internationally competitive;
4. firm strategy, structure and competitiveness;
5. government policy, which also had a role to play in influencing competitiveness, education, research capability and infrastructure investment.

How well these factors interact determined not only which industries were established in which countries, but how successful they were in the international marketplace. Evidence from one hundred case studies drawn from ten leading industrial countries, among them the US, the UK, Italy, Germany, Japan, Sweden and Switzerland, supported the hypothesis. In many ways this hypothesis supported the earlier work mentioned above but also departed from it in that it emphasized the strategic behaviour of companies. (See Figure 2.1.)

In the first decade of the twenty-first century some economists became interested in the effect on patterns of trade and competitiveness arising from the interaction of the existence of very large firms engaging in international trade and the rise in intra-industry trade. In part, the success of large firms can be attributed to their ability to access larger markets through trade and, in particular, intra-industry trade driven by consumers' *love of variety*. Melitz and Trefler (2012) identify three sources of gains from trade arising from the dynamic interaction of intra-industry trade and large firms: 1) through increased incentives to innovate; 2) from the shifting of resource use to efficient – *winner* – firms from less efficient firms; and 3) as a result of the ability to access foreign markets for reasons of intra-industry trade, leading to opportunities to achieve the efficiencies arising from economies of scale. In the first case, larger international markets allow the substantial fixed costs of research and development to be spread over greater sales. If larger, more efficient firms can access foreign markets then they may replace less efficient firms in the importing country, leading to rising productivity in the use of inputs. The empirical evidence presented by Melitz and Trefler (2012) suggests that all three of these dynamic interactions have been important in generating global gains from trade.

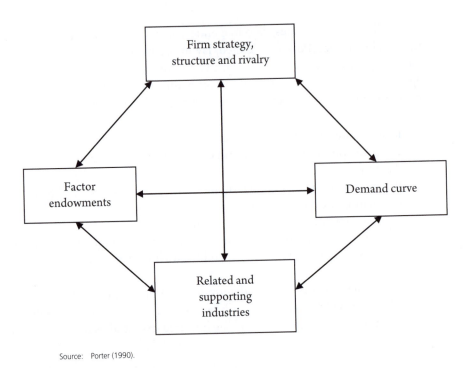

Source: Porter (1990).

Figure 2.1 Porter's diamond and national competitive advantage

2.8 What can be concluded?

Since Ricardo's time, economists have sought to explain the pattern of trade by making use of the concept of comparative advantage. Countries will export those goods in which they have such an advantage and will import goods in which they do not. They will gain by doing so. The question that later economists sought to answer was what factors determine comparative advantage? The Heckscher–Ohlin approach emphasized a country's factor endowments as being the key to this. Hence, a relatively capital-abundant country exported goods that used capital intensively in their production process, while it imported labour-intensive goods. The Leontief paradox highlighted the limitations of this approach and encouraged not only a recasting of the original theory to take into account factors such as land and human skills/capital but also the development of alternative theoretical models (Perdikis and Kerr, 1998). In this way, the influence of technology, innovativeness and research and development was brought to the fore, as were economies of scale and income similarity.

While these theories enriched the explanations of trade patterns, they did not, at least directly, explain the growing phenomenon of intra-industry trade.

This phenomenon needed the interaction of income similarities and economies of scale in production to provide theoretical insights. This was especially so for differentiated goods. Intra-industry trade in non-differentiated goods could be largely accounted for by the existence of entrepôt trade, seasonality in the production of goods, and transport costs.

Trade theories also allowed economists to isolate the factors that encouraged a country's trade intensity and competitiveness. Trade dependency was closely related to the stage of an economy's development as shown by GDP and population. Success in exporting, though, was linked closely to innovativeness as measured by research and development and factor intensity.

Which countries did best at exporting, especially in areas in which they did not apparently have a comparative advantage, led some researchers to identify explanations other than factor endowments and research and development expenditure as important determinants. These included inter-industry linkages and support, the competitive environment, socio-economic factors, infrastructure and government policy (Appleyard et al., 2006).

Theoretical explanations of trade patterns lead directly into policy debates regarding what governments can do to improve a country's competitiveness. Some policy prescriptions are fairly straightforward. If labour skill levels or expenditures on research and development improve competitiveness, then governments should make and also encourage these investments. However, the returns on these expenditures will depend upon whether the types of goods that can take advantage of these improvements are important to a country's trade. Other, more dynamic theories may suggest to governments that they get involved in trying to identify potential growth or 'winner' industries. Their record has been mixed at best.

The importance for business is clear. At the most basic level, the theories should improve planning through being able to classify the type of industry the company is in. If domestic markets are not growing, insights can be gained into the likely prospects for exporting.

Dynamic theories such as those based on the product cycle may provide insights for the future. Which markets are likely to grow? Should investments in research and development take place and into which product lines? Of equal if not more importance, the dynamic theories may point to likely sources of future foreign competition. Finally, business will be called on to advise governments on industrial policy. Trade theory can improve the impact firms can exert on the direction of policy. It can provide powerful arguments that may be particularly useful in preventing governments from following inappropriate industrial policies. In other words, while trade theory may not be able to precisely identify future 'winners', it can help identify potential 'losers'. Japan's orderly restructuring of its once pre-eminent export-oriented shipbuilding industry and its no longer internationally competitive steel industry are obvious examples.

The main classical conclusion – that countries gain from trade – has also been the subject of considerable theoretical effort. This work contributes to the long-standing debate on trade liberalization and protectionism, and is the basis for the discussion in Chapter 3.

 REFERENCES

Appleyard, D.R., Field, A.J. and Cobb, S.L. (2006) *International Economics*, McGraw-Hill, Boston, MA.

Aquino, A. (1978) Intra-industry trade and intra-industry specialisation as concurrent sources of international trade in manufactures. *Weltwirtschaftliches Archiv*, 114(2), 275–96.

Balassa, B. (1975) *European Economic Integration*, North Holland, Amsterdam.

Baldwin, R.E. (1971) The determinants of the commodity structure of US trade. *American Economic Review*, 61, 126–46.

Barker, T.S. (1977) International trade and economic growth: An alternative to the neo-classical approach. *Cambridge Journal of Economics*, 1(2), 153–72.

Bhagwati, J., Panagariya, A. and Srinivasan, T.N. (1998) *Lectures on International Trade*, MIT Press, Cambridge, MA.

Davies, A.S. and Kerr, W.A. (1997) Picking winners: Agricultural research and the allocation of public funds. *Review of Policy Issues*, 3(3), 39–50.

Dinopoulos, E., Oehmke, J.F. and Segerstrom, P.S. (1993) High-technology-industry trade and investment. *Journal of International Economics*, 34(1 and 2), 49–71.

Drèze, J. (1960) Quelques réflexions sereines sur l'adaptation de l'industrie belge au Marché Commun. *Comptes Rendus des Travaux de la Société Royale d'Economie Politique de Belgique*, 275, 3–37.

Greenaway, D. and Miller, C.R. (1986) *The Economics of Intra-Industry Trade*, Blackwell, Oxford.

Grubel, H.G. and Lloyd, P.S. (1975) *Intra-Industry Trade: The Theory and Measurement of Trade in Differentiated Products*, Macmillan, London.

Heller, P.S. (1976) Factor endowment change and comparative advantage: The case of Japan 1956–1969. *Review of Economics and Statistics*, 58, 283–92.

Hesse, H. (1974) Hypothesis for the explanation of trade between industrial countries, 1953–1970, in *On the Economics of Intra-Industry Trade*, ed. H. Gierch, J.C.B. Mohr, Tübingen, pp. 39–59.

Hirsch, S. (1974) Hypotheses regarding trade between developing and industrial countries, in *The International Division of Labour: Problems and Prospects*, ed. H. Gierch, J.C.B. Mohr, Tübingen, pp. 65–82.

Hufbauer, G. (1965) *Synthetic Materials and the Theory of International Trade*, Duckworth, London.

Hufbauer, G. (1970) The impact of national characteristics and technological trade in manufactured goods, in *The Technology Factor in International Trade*, ed. R. Vernon, National Bureau of Economic Research, New York, pp. 145–231.

Katrak, H. (1982) Labour skills, R & D and capital requirements in the international trade and investment of the UK 1968–78. *National Institute Economic Review*, 101, 38–47.

Keesing, D. (1966) Labour skills and comparative advantage. *American Economic Review*, 56, 249–67.

Krugman, P.R. (1979) Increasing returns, monopolistic competition and international trade. *Journal of International Economics*, 9, 469–79.

Leamer, E.E. (1974) The commodity composition of international trade in manufacture: An empirical analysis. *Oxford Economic Papers*, 26(3), 350–74.

Leamer, E.E. (1984) *Sources of International Comparative Advantage*, MIT Press, Cambridge, MA.

Leontief, W.A. (1953) Domestic production and foreign trade: The American capital position re-examined. *Proceedings of the American Philosophical Society*, 97, 332–49.

Leontief, W.A. (1956) Factor proportions and the structure of American trade: Further theoretical and empirical analysis. *Review of Economics and Statistics*, 38, 386–407.

Linder, S.B. (1961) *An Essay on Trade and Transformation*, John Wiley, New York.

Lloyd, P.J. (1989) Reflections on intra-industry trade and factor proportions, in *Intra-Industry Trade*, ed. P.K.M. Tharakan and J. Kol, Macmillan, London, pp. 15–30.

Melitz, M.J. and Trefler, D. (2012) Gains from trade when firms matter. *Journal of Economic Perspectives*, 26(2), 91–118.

Ohlin, B. (1933) *Inter-Regional Trade and International Trade*, Harvard University Press, Cambridge, MA.

Perdikis, N. and Kerr, W.A. (1998) *Trade Theories and Empirical Evidence*, Manchester University Press, Manchester.

Pomfret, R. (1986) On the division of labour and international trade: Or Adam Smith's explanation in intra-industry trade. *Journal of Economic Studies*, 13(4), 56–63.

Porter, M.E. (1990) *The Competitive Advantage of Nations*, Free Press, New York.

Posner, M.V. (1961) International trade and technical change. *Oxford Economic Papers*, 13, 323–41.

Ricardo, D. (1951) On the principles of political economy and taxation, in *The Works and Correspondence of David Ricardo*, ed. P. Sraffa, Cambridge University Press, Cambridge.

Smith, A. ([1776] 1961) *An Inquiry into the Nature and Causes of the Wealth of Nations*, ed. E. Cannan, reprint, Methuen, London.

Travis, W.P. (1964) *The Theory of Trade and Protection*, Harvard University Press, Cambridge, MA.

Valvanis-Vail, S. (1954) Leontief's scarce factor paradox. *Journal of Political Economy*, 62, 523–8.

Vanek, J. (1953) The natural resource content of foreign trade, 1870–1955, and the relative abundance of natural resources in the United States. *Review of Economics and Statistics*, 41, 146–53.

Verdoorn, P.J. (1960) The intra-block trade of the Benelux, in *Economic Consequences of the Size of Nations*, ed. E.A.G. Robinson, Macmillan, London.

Vernon, R. (1966) International investment and international trade in the product cycle. *Quarterly Journal of Economics*, 80, 190–207.

Vernon, R. (1979) The product cycle hypothesis in a new international environment. *Oxford Bulletin of Economics and Statistics*, 41(4), 255–67.

3

The great debate – free trade versus protectionism

3.1 The middle ground of managed trade

The background against which international trade and commerce take place is neither one of free trade nor one of total restriction. The bulk of trade is carried out somewhere in between, in what can be called a managed environment. This middle ground is not fixed and can change over time and oscillate between a more and less open system. As we will see, theory suggests that a free trade system leads to an increase in trade, which of course is beneficial to firms engaged in international commerce and, furthermore, maximizes all countries' welfare. It might then seem surprising that some of the main proponents of protective measures are firms. Business people, nevertheless, are heard to claim that they face 'unfair' foreign competition and want their home governments to do something about it (Culbertson, 1986). Politicians, while accepting the arguments for free trade, will ignore such requests for protection against foreign goods at their peril if the power of these interests and their supporters is strong. The ability of governments to provide their firms with protection from imports represents a major risk for firms wishing to engage in international commercial activities. Participating in international business requires firms to undertake heavy investments, so an understanding of the forces that lead to increased liberalization or protection and their consequences is fundamental to managing risk.

This chapter outlines the theoretical arguments for liberalism and protectionism and the pressures that bring these trade regimes into being. In the previous chapter, to gain insights into the underlying reasons for engaging in trade and the effects of engaging in trade, what economists call a general equilibrium approach to trade was employed. This approach is useful for examining the changes that arise as resources move from one sector to another. To understand the appeal of both trade liberalization and the vested interests in having a market protected from foreign competition, a different approach is developed in section 3.2. This approach is referred to by economists as the partial equilibrium approach. The partial equilibrium approach is the 'workhorse' of the economic analysis of trade policy (Kerr, 2007). This is because trade policy is carried out on a product-by-product basis where the inter-sector movements of resources are dispersed and of less interest than the direct effect of trade policies on the market being analysed. The case for free trade, however, can be illustrated using the partial equilibrium approach. Once the partial equilibrium case for free trade has been made, alternative approaches to trade restriction and the political factors that foster them will be explored. General equilibrium approaches to trade policy are explored further in the appendix at the end of the chapter.

3.2 The case for an open trade regime

The economic behaviour and equilibrium relationships that constitute the partial equilibrium trade model are developed in this section. Following Gaisford and Kerr (2001), there are three key behavioural components of the partial equilibrium trade model. These are the demand behaviour of domestic consumers, the supply behaviour of domestic producers, and the trading behaviour of foreigners who are located in the rest of the world.

We begin by examining the optimal behaviour of domestic consumers. Panel (a) of Figure 3.1 shows the demand curve, D, for a commodity such as potatoes. As the price of potatoes, P, rises, consumers are willing to purchase less and less. Consequently, the quantity demanded, Qd, declines and the demand curve for potatoes is negatively sloped. There is another way to view the demand curve. The height of the demand curve indicates what consumers are willing to pay for each successive tonne of potatoes. We call this the marginal willingness to pay, or marginal benefit. Suppose that the price is $P0$. If less than $Qd0$ tonnes is purchased, the marginal or extra benefit from purchasing another tonne of potatoes is higher than the price, so it makes sense to purchase more potatoes. Contrariwise, if more than $Qd0$ tonnes is purchased, the marginal or extra benefit from purchasing the last tonne of potatoes is lower than the price, so potato consumption will fall. Consequently, the optimal purchases of potatoes are equal to $Qd0$ tonnes when the price is $P0$ dollars per tonne.

We measure the total benefit of $Qd0$ tonnes of potatoes by adding up the marginal benefits of each successive tonne purchased up to $Qd0$. This total benefit, or total willingness to pay, for $Qd0$ tonnes of potatoes is given by the monetary value of the sum of areas $a + b + c + e + f$ in panel (a) of Figure 3.1. Actual consumer expenditure, however, differs from this total willingness to pay. Since the price is $P0$ dollars per tonne and domestic consumers choose

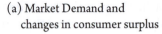

(a) Market Demand and
changes in consumer surplus

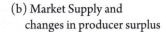

(b) Market Supply and
changes in producer surplus

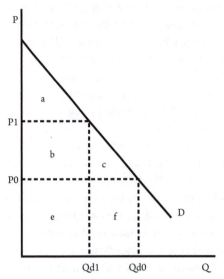

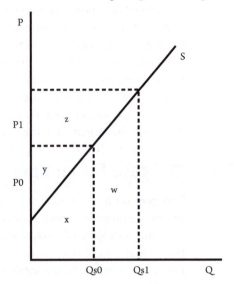

Figure 3.1 Model components

to buy $Qd0$ tonnes, they will spend a total of $P0 \times Qd0$ dollars. Thus, the actual expenditure on potatoes is equal to the sum of areas $e + f$ dollars in panel (a) of Figure 3.1. Consequently, there is a net benefit or consumer surplus of areas $a + b + c$ dollars when $Qd0$ tonnes of potatoes are purchased at $P0$ dollars per tonne. The presence of this consumer surplus makes sense, since consumers were not coerced into purchasing potatoes. The reason that people voluntarily purchase $Qd0$ tonnes of potatoes at a price of $P0$ is that it is beneficial for them to do so.

Now suppose that the price of potatoes rises from $P0$ to $P1$ dollars per tonne of potatoes. This gives rise to a reduction in the quantity from $Qd0$ to $Qd1$ tonnes. Total willingness to pay for $Qd0$ units falls from the sum of areas $a + b + c + e + f$ dollars to $a + b + e$ dollars in panel (a) of Figure 3.1. Actual expenditure changes from $e + f$ dollars to $e + b$ dollars. (The final expenditure on potatoes will be less than or greater than the initial expenditure depending on whether the percentage reduction in the quantity demanded is less than or greater than the percentage increase in price. In the former case, where the percentage reduction in the quantity demanded is less than the percentage increase in price, demand is said to be inelastic, while in the latter case it is said to be elastic.) Whereas the initial consumer surplus was the triangle-like area above the $P0$ price line and inside the demand curve, comprising

$a + b + c$ dollars, the final consumer surplus is the smaller triangle above the
$P1$ price line, consisting of a dollars. Thus there is a loss, or negative change,
in consumer surplus consisting of $b + c$ dollars. This not only reflects the
obvious fact that consumers are made worse off by a price increase, but also
allows the damage that they suffer to be quantified – a monetary value equal
to area b. We emphasize that the change in consumer surplus or consumer
welfare can typically be represented by the area lost or gained between the
two price lines and inside the demand curve. (The assessment of changes in
consumer surplus becomes somewhat more complicated if policy measures
force consumption to take place off the demand curve.)

Now consider the supply behaviour of domestic potato producers shown in
panel (b) of Figure 3.1. As the price of potatoes rises, production becomes
more profitable and the outputs supplied by firms increase. Thus, the quantity supplied, Qs, increases, leading to a positively sloped supply curve, S, for
potatoes. We assume that the industry is competitive in the sense that there
are many potato producers, each with a small market share and an impercep-
tible effect on the market price. In such a competitive industry the price is
equal to the extra or marginal revenue that a producer obtains from selling an
additional tonne of potatoes. There is, of course, a cost of obtaining resources
or inputs to production that are necessary to supply potatoes. We call the
cost of bidding production inputs away from alternative uses the opportunity
cost of producing potatoes. The height of the supply curve measures the
extra opportunity cost or marginal cost of supplying each successive tonne
of potatoes. As more potatoes are produced, the marginal cost typically rises,
reflecting the fact that it becomes more difficult to obtain the underlying
inputs from competing economic uses. Again, we see that the supply curve is
positively sloped. Further, in the short run there are constraints that preclude
adjusting fixed factors such as capital or land use.

Indirectly, the presence of fixed factors prevents the entry or exit of firms in
the short run. Thus, the relaxation of fixed factor constraints – both directly
and indirectly by allowing new firms to enter or exit the industry – makes
increases in output less costly in the long run than in the short run.

Suppose that the price of potatoes is $P0$ dollars per tonne in panel (b) of
Figure 3.1. On the one hand, if the quantity supplied were less than $Qs0$,
the marginal or additional opportunity cost of the last unit produced would
be less than the marginal or extra revenue obtained, and producers would
expand production. On the other hand, if the quantity supplied were more
than $Qs0$, the marginal cost of producing the last unit would have exceeded
the marginal revenue and producers would reduce output. Consequently,

the optimal supply of output is $Qs0$ at the price of $P0$. The total opportunity cost of output $Qs0$ is obtained by adding up the marginal opportunity cost for each successive unit of output up to $Qs0$. This gives a total opportunity cost of the area beneath the supply curve or x dollars. On the other hand, the total revenue obtained by producing $Qs0$ is $P0 \times Qs0$ or $x + y$ dollars. Thus the total revenue exceeds the total opportunity cost and there is a net benefit to firms or a producer surplus of y dollars. Since potato producers voluntarily sell their product, the presence of such a producer surplus is hardly surprising.

If the price now rises from $P0$ to $P1$ dollars per tonne in panel (b) of Figure 3.1, the industry output rises from $Qs0$ to $Qs1$ tonnes of potatoes. The total opportunity cost rises from area x dollars to $x + w$ dollars, while the total revenue rises from $x + y$ to $w + x + y + z$ dollars. Although the opportunity cost of obtaining the necessary resources to increase potato output from $Qs0$ to $Qs1$ is area w dollars, the additional revenue from the price increase is $z + w$ dollars. Thus, there is a gain of z dollars in producer surplus stemming from the price increase. Not surprisingly, an increase in price is beneficial to producers. Trade is now introduced to the model in Figure 3.2.

When domestic consumers and producers both have access to international markets, then we refer to the price in international markets as the world price. To clarify the essential issues, assume that there are no transport or transactions costs and, for the moment, ignore the wide array of policy measures that create differences between domestic and world prices. At high world prices, there will be an excess of supply over demand for potatoes that will lead to potatoes being exported. Thus, when the world price is $Pw1$ in panel (a) of Figure 3.2, $X1$ or $Qs1 - Qd1$ tonnes of potatoes will be exported. Conversely, at low world prices there will be an excess of demand over supply that will necessitate importation. In panel (b), $M0$ or $Qd0 - Qs0$ tonnes of potatoes are imported when the price is $Pw0$. If the world price happened to be equal to P_A, the quantities demanded and supplied by domestic residents would balance and trade would be unnecessary.

The more potatoes foreigners import, the lower the world price they will be willing to pay. In other words, as the domestic economy exports more, the world price will fall. Conversely, as the domestic economy imports more, the world price will rise. The determination of the world price is considered in detail below. Generally, the rest of the world is much larger than any one domestic economy. Consequently, changes in the domestic market tend to cause only minor variations in the world price. Indeed, for small countries, these world price changes would be negligible. For most of the issues that

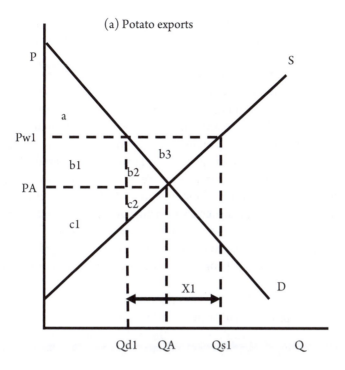

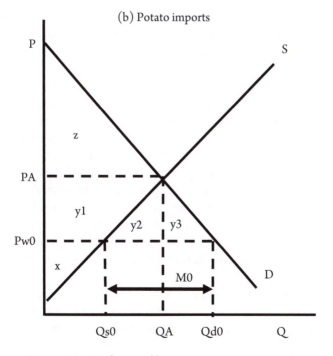

Figure 3.2 Trading equilibria

will be examined here, we need only mention the world price changes rather than explicitly incorporate them into the diagrammatic exposition.

The position of the domestic demand curve for potatoes is affected by the preferences and incomes of consumers and by the prices of related products. For most goods, an increase in incomes generates additional consumption and thus shifts the demand curve to the right. For such *normal goods,* an increase in consumer incomes, due say to an economic upturn, generates higher consumption at any given world price. This will reduce exports, cause a switch from exports to imports, or generate an increase in imports. In an economic downturn, when incomes tend to fall, these effects are reversed. However, some staples such as porridge are *inferior goods* where consumption declines in response to an increase in income. For such goods an increase in incomes would reduce consumption at the going world price and thereby increase exports or reduce imports (or cause a switch from imports to exports).

If the world price of a substitute product such as rice were to rise, the demand curve for potatoes would shift to the right. Potato consumption would rise at the prevailing world price for potatoes, and the domestic economy would export less or import more. However, if the world price of a complementary good that is consumed together with potatoes were to rise, the demand curve for potatoes would shift to the left, consumption would decline, and exports would rise or imports would fall.

The position of the supply curve is affected by the underlying input or factor prices. Consider an autonomous increase in the price of an input, such as domestic labour, which is not caused by a variation in the market output of potatoes. Costs will rise, shifting the market supply curve to the left, lowering the output of potatoes at the prevailing world price and making farmers (producers) worse off. Further, exports will fall and imports will rise (or the country will switch from importing to exporting). Since labour is not very mobile internationally, the impact on the world price is likely to be negligible. If we consider an increase in the price of an input that is internationally tradable such as oil, however, the world price of potatoes would tend to be pushed up as well. This would partially offset the impact on domestic producers.

Technological improvements have been a hallmark of, for example, agriculture over the last century. The green revolution of the 1970s and 1980s and current developments in biotechnology are but recent examples. Technological changes typically affect both domestic supply and the world price. Since a technological advance in potato production – such as the introduction of a new genetically modified variety – would reduce costs, output would increase and exports would rise or imports would fall at the initial world price. Further, those producers who were able to adopt the successful new technology would be very profitable, while producers who were committed to the old technology would be hurt and might ultimately go bankrupt. Since the new technology would be available throughout the world, however, the world price would be likely to fall. This would at least partially reduce the increase in output and the overall producer benefits. In the case of genetic modification, for example, consumers may not be indifferent, which would cause further complications associated with a demand reduction.

The model can now be utilized to analyse changes in trade policy. In subsection 3.2.1 we consider changes in trade policy caused by the implementation of tariffs and export subsidies. Following that, we consider more drastic policy changes where a market that was initially closed to trade is opened up to unrestricted trade.

3.2.1 Using a model for policy – tariffs and export subsidies

Here we put the partial equilibrium trade model through its paces to examine two important types of policy intervention in international markets. First, we will analyse the impact of a tariff imposed by an importing country. Thereafter, we will consider an alternative situation, where an exporting country implements an export subsidy.

Suppose that South Africa imposes a tariff (tax) on its imports of maize. For simplicity we assume a simple flat rate or per unit tariff of T rand per tonne (the rand is the South African currency). While the tariffs are also often assessed on an *ad valorem* or percentage basis, the substantive economic effects are the same. These effects are summarized in Figure 3.3. The world price, Pw, is the price at which imports of maize can be secured on the international market. To clarify the essential relationships, we continue to assume that there are no transport or transactions costs. Prior to the implementation of the tariff, therefore, the domestic price or landed price is equal to the world price. At Pw, domestic consumers are willing to purchase $Qd0$, while domestic firms are only willing to supply $Qs0$. The difference, $Qd0 - Qs0$, is met by maize imports.

After the tariff is imposed, the domestic price of imports rises to Ph or $Pw + T$. This becomes the price at which domestic firms must compete with imports. The higher domestic price affords profit-maximizing firms the opportunity to expand output. In the market, domestic output expands from $Qs0$ to $Qs1$

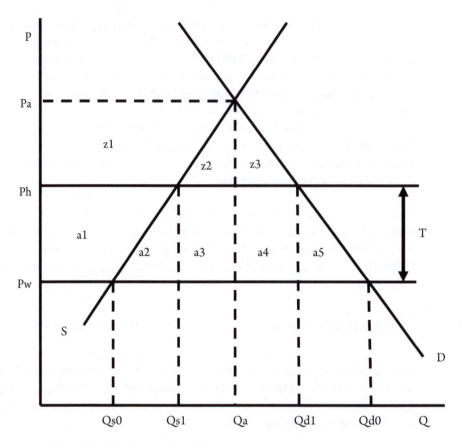

Figure 3.3   The impact of a tariff

as resources are drawn away from other sectors of the economy. However, the higher domestic price leads to a decline in consumption from $Qd0$ to $Qd1$. Consequently, imports fall to $Qd1 - Qs1$.

As the loss suffered by consumers due to higher prices is greater than the combined gain reaped by producers and the government, the change in trade regime is also assessed to be welfare reducing for South Africa's domestic economy. The higher domestic price causes a gain in producer surplus and a loss in consumer surplus. In particular, the change in the value of consumer surplus is equal to a loss of $a1 + a2 + a3 + a4 + a5$ ($a1 + \ldots + a5$) rand, while the change in producer surplus is a gain of area $a1$. The loss in consumer surplus exceeds the gain in producer surplus by $a2 + \ldots + a5$ rand. The change in government revenue arising from the tariff is a gain of $a3 + a4$ rand, which amounts to the height of the tariff multiplied by the quantity imported. Thus, there is an efficiency loss or a decline in real income from the tariff. This is represented as a change in total surplus that is a *dead-weight* or *distortionary loss* of $a2 + a5$ rand. Thus, relative to the case of non-restricted trade, the imposition of the tariff is what economists term *welfare decreasing* – it makes the economy worse off.

Increases in the height of the tariff always serve to increase production but reduce consumption and imports at the given world price. Consequently, there are inevitably further gains in producer surplus (i.e. area $a1$ becomes larger), further losses in consumer surplus (i.e. the sum of areas $a1 + \ldots + a5$ gets larger) and further distortionary losses (i.e. areas $a2$ and $a5$ each increase). Tariff revenue given by areas $a3 + a4$ is subject to conflicting pressures, however, since more revenue per unit is collected on a smaller volume of imports. Thus, as the tariff is slowly increased from zero to a height that prohibits trade, tariff revenue will initially rise but eventually declines.

When a smaller country implements a tariff, the change in world price is typically negligible. Consequently, no further analysis is needed. Suppose, however, that Japan implemented a tariff on rice. Since Japan is a large trading country, the fact that Japanese rice imports are reduced leads to a lower world price for rice (i.e. the reduced Japanese imports must be absorbed in other markets). Thus there is a favourable terms of trade effect for Japan that arises at the expense of the rest of the world as a whole in addition to the distortionary loss. If the tariff were kept sufficiently small, the terms of trade gain would outweigh the distortionary loss, resulting in an overall gain for Japan. Since the rest of the world suffers from an exactly corresponding terms of trade loss, there remains an overall efficiency loss affecting the world as a whole. Even large countries, however, rarely conduct trade policy to try to obtain such national welfare gains. In fact, Japan's tariff on rice is set so high that it most definitely results in an overall reduction in welfare even though it is beneficial to Japanese producers.

We now turn to the case of a policy intervention in a market where the commodity is exported. Suppose, for instance, that South Africa imposes an export subsidy on beef. It might do this if it believes the world price is too low for its beef producers to survive. An export subsidy – like a tariff – will raise the domestic price above the world price, because domestic consumption in the exporting country is not subsidized. It is noteworthy that a tariff must be implemented in conjunction with the export subsidy to prevent cheap beef from the world market entering (or re-entering) the high-price domestic market. Thus a tariff equal to ES rand per tonne would raise the domestic price from Pw to Ph in Figure 3.4. The subsidy becomes effective when product surplus to the domestic market arises at Ph. Since producers

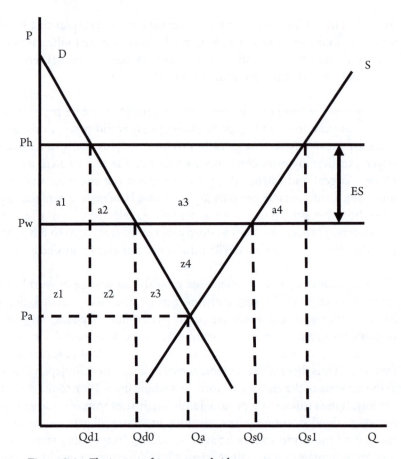

Figure 3.4 The impact of an export subsidy

must earn *Ph* on this excess product, the government must spend *ES* per unit exported to make the product competitive at *Pw*.

The export subsidy is similar to the tariff in terms of the impact on domestic producers and consumers. The increase in the price from *Pw* to *Ph* increases output from *Qs0* to *Qs1* as resources, once again, are drawn away from other sectors of the economy. As a result of the higher domestic price, consumption drops from *Qd0* to *Qd1*. Since the country is initially an exporter, these changes serve to increase exports rather than reduce imports. The export subsidy raises exports from *Qs0* − *Qd0* to *Qs1* − *Qd1*. As in the case where a small country imposes a tariff, the overall impact on domestic welfare is negative. Producers gain *a1* + *a2* + *a3* rand in producer surplus, but consumers lose *a1* + *a2* in consumer surplus and the treasury loses $(Qs1 - Qd1) \times ES$ or

$a2 + a3 + a4$ rand in subsidy outlays. Thus, there is an efficiency loss of $a2 + a4$ rand.

Increases in the height of an export subsidy cause further increases in output and exports, and further reductions in consumption at the given world price. Consequently, there are, inevitably, further gains in producer surplus (i.e. area $a1 + \ldots + a3$ becomes larger), further losses in consumer surplus (i.e. the sum of areas $a1$ and $a2$ gets larger) and further distortionary losses (i.e. areas $a2$ and $a4$ each increase). Unlike raising tariffs, where the impact on government revenue is ambiguous, total outlays on export subsidies are certain to rise as export subsidies are increased. This is because of the combination of higher subsidies per unit and larger export volumes (i.e. area $a3$ increases).

As in the case of the tariff, there is a negligible impact on the world price if a small country such as South Africa implements an export subsidy. In the case of a large trading entity such as the European Union, however, the reduction in the world price arising from additional subsidy-induced exports can be significant. In the case of an exporting country, this would represent a terms of trade deterioration that would add to the negative impact on overall welfare. Clearly, the observed widespread use of export subsidies on agricultural commodities, for example, cannot be explained on the basis of attempts to improve national welfare. The underlying rationale for such export subsidies is investigated below.

Tariffs and export subsidies share the common feature of increasing domestic prices and generating producer benefits at the expense of consumers. Price floors or support prices that apply both to producers and to consumers afford similar protection to the domestic industry. We have seen that a tariff or like measure is an integral element of an export subsidy policy, since it is necessary to deny consumers access to cheaper products on the world market. Similarly, a tariff will be required with a price support system. If the country remains on an import basis, as in Figure 3.3, a tariff is the only auxiliary policy that is necessary. However, if the country comes to be on an export basis, as in Figure 3.4, further auxiliary measures are necessary to deal with the surplus product that arises at the floor price. In the case of food, for example, government must intervene to buy up the surplus; thereafter, its options include storage, subsidizing exports and/or providing domestic or overseas food aid. Figure 3.4 shows a situation where South Africa is an exporter of beef prior to the implementation of an export subsidy programme. It is certainly possible for a country to be on an import basis initially and to switch to exporting as a result of the tariff and export subsidy combination. Of course, if either of the two sample trade measures were to be removed, so that prices declined, outputs would be adjusted downward and resources freed up to return to other uses. Welfare would increase.

3.2.2 Gains from trade, winners and losers, adjustment costs and vested interests

Some trade is, under almost any circumstances, better than no trade (autarky) for an economy as a whole. Even on a piecemeal or market-by-market basis, opening up trade is typically beneficial. This is true whether a country ends up importing or exporting the product in question. Consider a simplified world prune juice market where there are two countries, the Klingon Empire and the Federation. While there are, in reality, many importing and exporting countries that are aggregated to make up the world market, Figure 3.5 shows the essentials of how the world price is determined. In the absence of trade, the equilibrium in the Klingon Empire would be at a quantity of Qa litres of prune juice and a price of Pa dollars per litre where demand and supply in the Klingon Empire are in balance. Similarly, in the Federation the autarky quantity is Qa^* litres of prune juice, and the autarky price is Pa^* dollars per litre.

In practice, producers and consumers in both countries may have access to international markets. The supply curves are drawn such that the Federation is a lower-cost producer of prune juice than the Klingon Empire and therefore has a lower autarky price. As a result, the Klingon Empire will tend to import prune juice and the Federation will tend to export prune juice. We refer to the price in international markets as the world price. To clarify the essential issues, we assume that there are neither transport nor transactions costs, and we are ignoring the wide array of policy measures that cause differences between domestic and world prices.

At world prices below Pa, there is excess demand for prune juice in the Klingon Empire, representing desired imports. This excess demand or desired imports is graphed in the centre panel of Figure 3.5 as a demand for imports curve, Dm. Notice that the distance between the demand and the supply curve in the left panel of the figure is exactly equal to the distance from the vertical axis to the import demand curve in the centre panel. Thus, at lower prices more is imported. While there would be excess supply of prune juice and the Klingon Empire would choose to export at prices higher than Pa, we will see that the Klingon Empire will import in the trading equilibrium. If the world price is above Pa^*, there will be excess supply of prune juice in the Federation, which represents desired exports. These desired

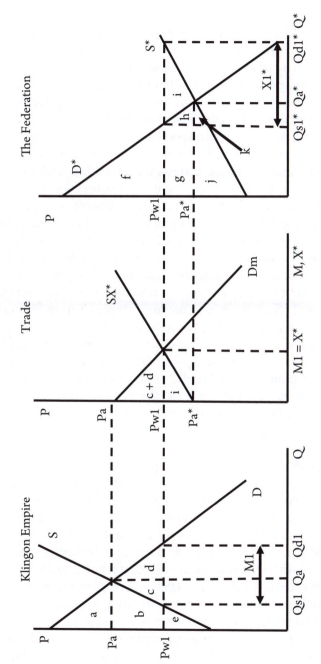

Figure 3.5 Mutual gains from trade

exports of the Federation give rise to the export supply curve, Sx^*, in the centre panel of Figure 3.5.

In Figure 3.5, there is a trading equilibrium at the world price of $Pw1$ dollars per litre of prune juice where the Klingon Empire's desired imports of $M1$ litres exactly balance with the Federation's desired exports of $X1^*$ litres. At this world price, the Klingon Empire consumes $Qd1$ litres of prune juice and produces $Qs1$ litres, with the difference being the $M1$ litres that are imported. Meanwhile, the Federation produces $Qs1^*$ litres, consumes $Qd1^*$ litres and, as we have seen, exports the difference of $X1^*$ litres. Let us consider how the opening of trade affects overall welfare in the Federation and the Klingon Empire. The move to free trade leads to overall gains for the exporting country, the Federation, but it also creates clear winners and losers. In the absence of trade in prune juice, the consumer surplus is equal to $f + g + h$ dollars, and the producer surplus is equal to $j + k$ dollars. Opening trade at the world price of $Pw1$ leads to a decline in consumer surplus of $g + h$ dollars and an increase in producer surplus of $g + h + i$ dollars. Allowing exports of prune juice therefore generates a gain in total surplus of area i dollars. Since the Federation becomes an exporter, the impact on producers is decisive in overall effect; the gain in producer surplus is unambiguously larger than the loss in consumer surplus. In a similar fashion, equivalent overall gains from trade arise for South Africa in the beef market depicted in Figure 3.4. Under free trade at a world price of Pw, $Qs0 - Qd0$ gives exports. The price increase from Pa to Pw benefits producers by generating an increase in producer surplus equal to areas $z1 + z2 + z3 + z4$. Consumers are harmed by the loss of consumer surplus equal to area $z1 + z2 + z3$. While producers win and consumers lose, there is an overall gain to South Africa of $z4$.

When only one market is being opened, there may be beneficial or harmful indirect effects on other markets from the price change on the liberalized market. For example, higher prune juice prices will generate indirect benefits (i.e. more consumer surplus) from the consumption of substitute products such as carrot juice and prune cola, and indirect costs (i.e. less consumer surplus) from the consumption of any complementary products. In the rare instance where the harmful indirect effects not only dominate the beneficial indirect effects but also outweigh the direct gains that we have just examined, the Federation could lose from liberalizing trade on a single market. If the entire economy were to move from autarky to free trade, there is a very strong presumption of overall gains from trade. Such gains would be a certainty if the economy consisted entirely of competitive markets of the type being considered here. In such a situation, there would be direct benefits on each market that would in aggregate more than offset any adverse indirect benefits.

While it seems broadly sensible that there are direct gains from trade generated on an export market, perhaps it is more surprising to find that there are also net gains for the country that imports. In the market of the Klingon Empire that is being opened to imports, the consumers are the winners and the producers are the losers. Prior to trade, the consumer surplus is equal to a dollars and the producer surplus is equal to $b + e$ dollars. When trade commences, producers are hurt by the price reduction and experience a loss of producer surplus equal to area b dollars. Meanwhile, lower prune juice prices yield a benefit to consumers or a gain in consumer surplus given by $b + c + d$ dollars. Thus there is an unambiguous gain in total surplus to the Klingon Empire from introducing free trade equal to $c + d$ dollars. Since the Klingon Empire imports, the impact on consumers dominates; the consumers gain more than producers lose. An equivalent analysis applies to South African maize imports in Figure 3.3. The reduction in price from Pa to Pw leads to imports of $Qd0 - Qs0$. Producer surplus declines by areas $z1 + a1$, but consumer surplus rises by areas $z1 + z2 + z3 + a1 + \ldots + a5$. Thus, there is an unambiguous gain in total surplus to South Africa from introducing free trade equal to $z2 + z3 + a2 + \ldots + a5$.

Overtrading cannot be as beneficial as free trade when markets are competitive. As we saw in subsection 3.2.1, the imposition of an export subsidy starting from a position of free trade resulted in a loss in total surplus of area $a2 + a4$ in Figure 3.4. The losses of the consumers (i.e. area $a1$) and the government (i.e. area $a2 + a3 + a4$) exceed the gain to the producers (i.e. area $a1 + a2 + a3$). Even if the country is small, so that its export subsidy has no adverse effect on world prices, it loses from overtrading relative to free trade.

If the country is small and has no effective market power over world price, it will also lose from restricting trade starting from free trade. In subsection 3.2.1 (Figure 3.3), we saw that South Africa would lose areas $a2 + a5$ relative to free trade if it imposed a tariff on the maize market. The loss to consumers (i.e. areas $a1 + \ldots + a5$) exceeded the gains to producers (i.e. area $a1$) and the government (i.e. areas $a3 + a4$). Since neither overtrading nor undertrading pays, free trade is a national-welfare-maximizing policy for a small country. In the current case of a large player, such as the Klingon Empire, limited trade restrictions can be better than free trade, because of the induced decline in the world price that would arise from moving down and to the left along the Federation's export supply curve, Sx^*, in Figure 3.5.

In agriculture, as in other sectors of the economy, national interests rarely drive trade-related policy exclusively, or even predominantly. Rather, policy tends to be driven by the interests of producers, input suppliers and owners (factor groups). They represent 'vested interests'. While governments tend to be relatively immune to proactive 'rent seeking' by factor and industry lobby groups, disadvantaged factor and producer groups that are already under stress and reacting to forces such as technological change tend to receive a more sympathetic hearing from governments. In practice, such pressures have been felt most acutely in sectors such as agriculture where there has been a long-term secular decline in employment. Within developed countries, similar pressures have also affected industries such as textiles, footwear and steel.

In reality, the producers within any industry are typically heterogeneous. At any point in time there are many vintages of technology in use. Further, since technologies tend to be embodied in physical, human and biological capital, it is often extremely costly for existing producers to adopt new technologies. In the absence of government intervention, therefore, the least technologically efficient producers often face bankruptcy. When technological change is rapid and demand responses to increasing consumer incomes are low, as is often the case in agriculture, there may be large numbers of such inefficient producers. The percentage response in quantity demanded to a small percentage increase in income is formally known as the product's income elasticity of demand. For most food products and other necessities, income elasticities are low.

Bankruptcy and exit from an industry entail substantial adjustment costs. Labour must undergo retraining and search for alternative employment, while individuals experience capital losses on other productive assets. Moving location to find new employment opportunities often involves particularly traumatic lifestyle changes that constitute a further adjustment cost. Factors of production do not move freely from one sector to another, as is often assumed in the models that were examined in Chapter 2.

Faced with financial ruin, inefficient producers often react by lobbying governments for support. Even when increased foreign competition is more of a side effect than root cause of long-term sectoral decline, it is often a convenient scapegoat. For instance, when a technological advance such as better pesticides or more disease-resistant seed leads to falling world grain prices, it is natural for farmers to lobby for protectionist measures that raise the domestic price above the world price. Since we take domestic price support as the criterion for protectionism, we include export-enhancing measures such as export subsidies as well as import-restricting measures such as tariffs.

Care must be exercised in identifying all producers as winners from this type of reactive protectionism. Protectionism reduces or removes the incentives for the least technologically efficient producers to move to alternative activities. As a result, producers who would otherwise have been forced to exit the industry will be able to remain in business. Such producers maintain a tenuous foothold in the industry, but they can hardly be classified as winners in an absolute sense. The real winners, therefore, are the technologically efficient producers who obtain windfall benefits from protection as well as technological advance.

Of course, the big losers from protectionism are consumers. Since consumer interests are widely distributed, individual consumers – especially those who are threatened by a single tariff – tend to invest little in lobbying against tariffs. A tariff on, for example, ice cream, which most consumers purchase only intermittently and which in any case does not represent a significant portion of a consumer's food budget, is simply not worth the consumer's time and effort to lobby against. Producer interests, however, are much more focused, and so producers invest much more in lobbying for protection when their economic position becomes tenuous. As a result, domestic and trade policy tends to be driven largely by producer interests, especially the interests of inefficient producers, at the expense of consumers. While obtaining protection from politicians on the basis of one losing out to more efficient foreign producers is certainly possible, it is unlikely to be easy given that it is well understood that granting protection to vested interests is welfare reducing. As a result, protectionists often seek legitimacy by attempting to cloak their requests for protectionism in arguments suggesting it would be in the general interests of the broader society to grant it. Protectionists tend to be persistent, well organized, inventive and persuasive in their arguments. After all they usually have a lot to lose. They have also been relatively successful, as protectionist measures exist, to a greater or lesser degree, in the policies of all economies.

3.3 The political economy of protection and trade liberalization

Given the analysis in section 3.2 it seems inconceivable that arguments against free trade would be advanced, but they are, and politicians are seen to legislate for protection and governments argue strongly against the reduction of trade barriers at international negotiations. Again we may ask ourselves why are trade restrictions so prevalent? To answer this question, a discussion of the political economy of protection is required. (A number of references for further reading suggest themselves, some of the best being Pincus, 1975; Baldwin, 1979; Finger, 1979; Becker, 1983; and Hillman, 1989.) One potential way to overcome the resistance of those who resist the removal of trade barriers would be for the potential winners from such a change to compensate the potential losers. After all, if trade liberalization is welfare enhancing, the benefits from trade liberalization must be bigger than the losses. Thus, compensation could theoretically be paid by the winners and they would still be better off. To generalize, in order to generate benefits for the country as a whole, moving to a free trade system requires the gainers to compensate the losers. Unless the gainers are altruistic (or have an acquaintance with economic theory so they can see the need to compensate the losers), a third agency in the shape of the government will have to intervene and secure the benefits on behalf of the nation as a whole.

Whether the government will act in this foresighted way is, of course, questionable. Governments are made up of the members of political parties whose prime function is to represent the interests of their supporters (Frey, 1984). If the government relies on the votes of the gainers to keep it in power then it might not wish to alienate this support by taxing some of their gains in order to give the proceeds to the losers. Even if both the government and its supporters wished to compensate the losers there might be practical difficulties in identifying the losers and compensating them for their losses.

It is with these possibilities in mind that potential losers may form groups to lobby governments for the imposition of trade barriers. The strength of this **protectionist** lobby can be substantial for a number of reasons. Firstly, the pressure to organize is greater amongst the losers because they are a well-defined group, while the gainers – the rest of society – are a more diverse body. For the winners, the benefits of barrier reductions and free trade accrue over time and are spread thinly over individuals. Hence, those who gain may not be as willing, or as likely, to organize to prevent trade restrictions from being put in place or to lobby for them to be removed as those who are likely to lose out.

Secondly, the losers may well be better represented in parliaments and legislatures than the prospective gainers. This is particularly the case where the losers are favourably distributed regionally. For example, if the losers have a majority of 51 per cent in two out of three constituencies, then they need only 34 per cent of the total vote to command a majority in parliament. If they have the same majority in say 13 out of 25 constituencies, then they can command a majority in parliament with only 27 per cent of the total vote.

Thirdly, this position can be strengthened further, or a majority can be cobbled together, if the political group supporting protection in the legislature is willing to trade its votes with another group in order to achieve mutually beneficial legislation. This process is called **log rolling** and works as follows: say there are two groups of voters engaged in industries threatened by competitive imports. Group I is strongly in favour of import barriers to protect its industry – proposition A – but weakly in favour of reducing the levels of protection afforded to group II's industry – proposition B. Group II takes the opposite line. If groups I and II are minorities in parliament then their proposals will be voted down and free trade will be the result. If, however, they can combine and agree to support one another then they may be able to form a majority and get their respective proposals through parliament and into law.

The result can be a political market for protection. The composition of the demand and supply side of this market will now be examined in greater detail. Demand will come from groups that can identify a reduction in trade barriers that will lead to a loss of sales, lower output and unemployment. In practice, this means domestic firms in competition with foreign firms supplying the home market, trade unions and worker organizations representing the workers employed in the domestic firms, and component suppliers to the domestic firms. Of course, demand for the imposition of barriers when trade is free will come from those who perceive a threat from a new source of competition.

The pressure of demand for protection will be reduced by opposition from groups that will lose out from protection, for example companies that rely on an open trading system to sell their goods (e.g. those that sell imported Japanese cars in the British market) and domestic companies sending a higher proportion of their output geared to export. Other interest groups that will support this anti-protectionist stance include the component suppliers to these export-oriented companies and workers who rely on them for their employment, as well as consumer groups who may fear that barriers will lead to higher prices.

On the supply side, those willing to grant protection are politicians and bureaucrats/civil servants. Politicians wanting to remain in power may be willing to make concessions to the pro-protectionist lobby if it is stronger and has more political clout than the anti-protectionist lobby. This sort of pressure has been brought to bear on politicians in many countries. It is said, for example, that the over-representation of rural areas, in terms of seats, in the parliaments of France and Japan has coloured their governments' views towards the liberalization of agricultural trade. In countries where the governments are not democratic, potential losers may have preferred access to politicians owing to their being cronies of the political elite (Kimbugwe et al., 2012).

Although supposedly neutral, civil servants can also have an important role to play in the granting of protection. Their **utility** function – or what makes them happy – can be expressed as being made up of the prestige, power and influence that they enjoy relative to the economic group they serve, for example the positions of the civil servants in ministries of agriculture vis-à-vis the farmers and the agribusiness sector in general. The main constraint that a civil service faces is the power of parliament and the government, but, since both these institutions may rely on the civil service for advice, its discretionary power in policy making can be great.

In the political marketplace, therefore, a strong homogeneous group in favour of protectionism, faced by a weaker more heterogeneous opposition and a weak government seeking to stay in power advised by a sympathetic civil service, may well achieve its protectionist aims despite the economic arguments against such a policy.

3.3.1 Full employment and the balance of payments

It is often argued that unemployment can be alleviated by the imposition of tariffs and restrictions on foreign goods entering the home market. The logic behind this argument often runs like this. Restricting imports and, hence, making them more expensive will force domestic purchasers of these goods to switch their expenditure from foreign-produced goods to home-produced goods. This increase in demand for home-produced goods will lead to an expansion of the sectors involved and an increase in the demand for labour. The beauty of this policy, or so the argument runs, is that the domestic economy can be expanded without a deterioration in the **balance of trade**. The balance of trade is the net result of subtracting the sum of the value of imports and financial outflows from the sum of the value of exports and financial inflows. The importance of the balance of trade can be explained through an example. Suppose imports and financial inflows exceed exports and financial outflows for a sustained period at the current exchange rate. This would mean that more of a nation's currency would be flowing into international exchange markets than foreigners would need to buy exports or make investments. A surplus of the country's currency would exist. This would put downward pressure on the exchange rate. The value of the currency relative to its trading partners would eventually have to fall. Certainly the influential economist John Maynard Keynes advocated the adoption of such a policy to boost employment in Britain in the 1930s (Keynes, 1972).

For this analysis to be applied, rigidities in the labour market must exist. Traditional trade theory assumes that factor markets are perfect, so unemployment will be eliminated by declines in wages and, hence, no sustained unemployment can exist. Of course, in the real world unemployment can persist and become a major social problem. The question again arises: is it better to impose a tariff or to tackle the seat of the problem and encourage the market to work more efficiently? It may be the case that as, for example, wheat workers are made redundant they will not be able to find employment in, for example, the automobile industry, which may be expanding, because they lack the necessary skills. In this situation, it might make more sense to subsidize the retraining of these workers and, hence, provide the labour required to further the expansion of the automobile industry in which the country has a long-term comparative advantage. For example, if the balance of payments was the main constraint, then would it not be better to devalue the currency, thereby increasing not only domestic demand, as people switched from the now more expensive imports to domestic products, but also foreign demand for the country's goods, as they would now be less expensive in the eyes of foreigners and thereby mop up unemployment? Keynes's advocacy for tariffs was based on the premise that Britain could not devalue its currency. Once it did, he withdrew his suggestion for an employment-stimulating tariff.

A slightly more subtle argument concerning the balance of payments has been put forward by a group of economists known as the New **Cambridge School**. Their view is clearly expressed in the *Cambridge Economics Policy Review*, especially that for 1978. They point out that devaluation no longer works because the reduction in workers' real incomes as a consequence of the increase in foreign prices leads them to demand, and be granted, higher wages. This stimulates inflation and domestic costs rise until the original impact of the devaluation is neutralized. The Cambridge School suggests that a tariff will not have the same inflationary impact if the revenue raised by the tariff is paid to workers to offset the price rises it creates. The redistribution of this tariff revenue thus keeps real wages constant and helps maintain the stimulus on the economy. A tariff on final goods will not, furthermore, affect input prices and so, in turn, will not adversely affect home industries' costs as would a devaluation.

While balance of payments arguments are accepted by multilateral organizations as a legitimate reason for imposing tariffs, and both the US (1971) and the UK (1964) have resorted to them, albeit temporarily, once again counter-arguments suggest that this may not be the best policy to follow (Hindley, 1983). For instance, the protection of real wages is at the expense of profits that could have an adverse effect on investment in the long run. The dampening of foreign competition could also lead to the long-run deterioration of the home industry's productivity. It is also questionable that wage pressure would be less under a tariff policy than under devaluation for two reasons. Firstly, since the reduction in the choice of goods is equivalent to reduction in the average wage, workers may attempt to offset the decline through demands for higher wages. Secondly, it is quite likely that the reduction of foreign competition affected by tariffs would encourage home producers to raise their own domestic prices. It thus seems unlikely that a policy of tariff protection is preferable to that of devaluation, and again it seems that it should only be undertaken when alternative policies are not available, and then only in the short run. In the longer term, it is probably better for the country to attempt to overcome the problems its industries face by tackling them head on rather than to protect them indefinitely (Leger et al., 1999).

3.3.2 Reasons of national security

Nations may feel that if they follow the free trade path then they will become totally dependent – or at least greatly dependent – on another country for imports of sensitive goods. If something should happen to disrupt the flow of these goods then the country might find itself in major difficulties. It is for this reason that countries have often protected their agricultural and primary products sectors. The argument is made that if a war occurred and a country's food imports were disrupted then a major disruption would arise and hardship would be caused. Hence, it is important to protect the sector in question so that it provides enough products to cover basic needs, or at least a core that can be expanded in times of trouble. The agricultural policies of Britain, Japan and the EU have, to some extent, been based on this premise. Whether trade barriers are the best way to provide the desired security is once more a moot point. A sceptical view of this protectionist argument is found in Winters (1990). It could well be the case that stockpiling might be a cheaper policy. There are few industries that could not be brought into production while stockpiles are being run down. Subsidizing important sectors directly rather than using tariffs can also lead to higher benefits to society. Which of these should be adopted depends on the cost and benefits of each and the probabilities that the worst-case scenarios would result.

3.3.3 The optimum tariff

If a country is a major purchaser of a particular commodity then it might, if it uses this power, move the terms of trade in its favour by imposing tariffs on the import in question (Metzler, 1949). How would this work? When a country places a tariff on an import, it pushes up its price in the domestic market and, as a result, demand falls. As sales to this country are very important to the exporting country, it will be forced to reduce its prices to recapture the lost market. As prices fall, the **terms of trade** – the rate at which it can exchange domestic products for imports – of the tariff-imposing country will improve, and this will allow it to be better off than when it did not impose the tariff. While this argument is valid and recognized by many economists, it was also noted that both countries can play the tariff game, and the country on whose goods the tariff has been placed can retaliate with one of its own on imports from the imposing country (Johnson, 1965). The result of this retaliation would be a reduction in the volume of trade taking place between the two countries. Neither country, nor the firms involved in trade, would benefit.

3.3.4 The revenue-raising tariff

Many countries, especially those with low incomes and ineffective governments, have difficulties in raising adequate revenues via the usual routes of taxing incomes and/or the sale of goods. By taxing imports they are able to supplement these sources of tax revenue, and for many lower-income developing countries this can be a prime source of funding (Greenaway and Sadsford, 1987). The wisdom of carrying out this practice has been questioned (IBRD, 1987). Tariffs distort the economy by protecting home industries and thereby hinder the competitive process. Further, they mask the true cost of government expenditure.

3.4 The strategic or dynamic reasons for protection

The strategic and dynamic reasons for protection differ from the previous static arguments in that they do not envisage the permanent maintenance of barriers to trade. Barriers are to be adopted only to achieve a specific objective. Once this has been assured, then the barriers to trade can be removed and the home economy exposed to the full rigours of international competition. Barriers are, therefore, justified on the basis of countering the strategic use of market advantage by foreign companies or acquiring a comparative advantage for an industry – the infant industry or infant economy cases.

3.4.1 Countering strategic behaviour

Foreign firms may attempt to capitalize on weaknesses of domestic firms to increase their market share. They may be able to deny domestic firms the technology required to become competitive through the manipulation of other firms that own the technology. If the foreign firm is a large user of the technology, it may be able to pressure the supplier not to sell the technology to firms in the importing country. Imposing trade restrictions on the foreign firm's products can eliminate the incentive for the exporter to limit access to the technology. Sophisticated marketing programmes, which are beyond the capability of domestic firms, may be used to increase or protect the market share of foreign firms. Trade restrictions can limit market shares. One possible use of strategic advantage is the international version of predatory pricing whereby a foreign firm attempts to drive domestic firms in the importing country out of business by selling below cost in the short run. These short-run losses can be covered by profitable sales in the firm's home market. Once the competing firms are driven out of the market, the foreign firm can monopolize the import market and reap large profits. Predatory pricing is not legal if practised in most modern market economies and is controlled by competition policy. International predatory pricing is known as **dumping**. The issue of dumping has gained more prominence recently both among business people and among academic economists (Yarrow, 1987). Unfortunately, the definition of dumping used in international trade law, while it can be used to prevent predatory activities, can also be used to limit market access for firms following normal business practices that are legal in domestic competition law. As a result, anti-dumping measures are open to protectionist abuse and have become a major international trade irritant (Kerr, 2001, 2006; Kerr and Loppacher, 2004). Dumping is dealt with in greater detail in Chapter 10.

One aspect of international predatory pricing is the selling of goods in a foreign market at prices below the cost of production in the home market. In the static sense, a country able to purchase goods at prices below cost can only benefit at the expense of the country producing the good. Why should a country complain if a foreign firm wishes to beneficially price imports for consumers? The static approach, however, ignores the longer-term implications, which can be damaging. If the strategy of international predatory pricing is successful, once competitors in the importing market are out of business the foreign firm can then exploit a new-found **monopoly** position and raise prices, possibly above original levels. In order to prevent this from happening and for the country to avoid the start-up costs required to re-establish a domestic industry, anti-dumping duties in the form of tariffs may be levied on the foreign firm's exports. These duties would continue until the foreign firm ceased its predatory activities. As we will see in Chapter 10, few anti-dumping cases deal with the practice of international predatory pricing.

3.4.2 The case for infant industries

New businesses facing competition from well-established industries in exporting countries may find it difficult to establish themselves because of high initial start-up costs (Myint, 1963). In order that economies of scale can be reaped and competitiveness vis-à-vis foreign producers established, the home market needs to be protected for domestic producers. High initial costs need not arise only from high **fixed costs**; they can also arise from the inexperience of the managers and workers in producing and selling the good in question. As output expands and familiarity with production and sales increases, then costs fall and competitiveness is established. Again, protecting the home market for the domestic firm would encourage it to achieve lower costs.

There are many problems with this argument (Baldwin, 1969). The first is in trying to identify **infant industries** – how does the government separate those new industries that have the potential to become internationally competitive from those that do not? Secondly, even if one can pick potential 'winners', it is possible that, behind the protective barrier, the domestic industry may not grow up, preferring rather to continue special pleading that allows it to continue to enjoy little or no foreign competition. This may well become the case if the industry achieves the role of an important employer and investor in the domestic economy and, hence, garners political influence.

Finally, we have to consider whether protection via tariffs is the best policy, or would an alternative such as a subsidy be just as effective and less of a distortion for the economy? Tariffs will raise the price of goods to the consumer, whereas subsidizing the high initial costs will keep prices at world levels and, thereby, not harm the consumer. This, however, shifts the burden from the consumer to the taxpayer. For the infant industry argument to be valid requires that the costs of fostering the industry's development, whether imposed on consumers or taxpayers, are outweighed by the future benefits. While some industries in some countries have been successfully established in this way, it is not totally clear that one can predict the benefits streams at the outset. There are, in fact, many industries in a variety of countries where adopting this sort of policy has led to the establishment of industries that never became competitive internationally and proved to be a burden rather than a benefit on their home economies. This leads us to the 'infant economy' arguments, which we discuss in subsection 3.4.3.

Before we do this, let us examine a variant of the infant industry argument – the '**senile industry**' argument. This theory suggests that an industry that has lost its comparative advantage may regain it if it receives protection so that it can re-equip its factories and retrain its work force and managers. These costs could then be recouped if it acquires a greater share of the home market. Whether one can distinguish between a loss of competitiveness due to bad management or some other reason and a genuine change in the country's comparative advantage is questionable. Both the infant and the senile industry arguments depend on entrepreneurs not being able to see the future benefits of making the investments needed to improve international competitiveness themselves, thus requiring a third agency in the form of the government to step in. Again, governments' ability to pick winners is patchy at best (Davies and Kerr, 1997).

3.4.3 The infant economy and import substitution

In the mid-1800s, the German economist List, seeing that the British economy had developed into the world's major industrial power, argued that the only way that other countries could catch up was to erect barriers to trade and industrialize behind these barriers (List, 1841). Many colonies, on gaining their independence in the 1950s and 1960s, took up this theme in their development plans. A number of Latin American countries also adopted this development strategy. The basic argument ran like this. Traditional agricultural and raw materials exports could not be relied upon to underpin economic development (Lewis, 1969; Prebisch, 1969). As supply increased, prices would fall and revenues would decrease. Further, as incomes in developed countries grew, the demand for developing countries' products would not increase in line with incomes – they have relatively low **income elasticities**. Developing countries would be condemned to a position always behind that of developed countries. To overcome this problem, developing countries would have to pursue industrialization policies in order to produce goods with better market potential. Industrialization had to be carried out behind high barriers so that economies of scale could be achieved. In the development stage, domestic products would be substituted for products previously imported – this strategy became formally known as **import substitution** (Clement et al., 1999).

As with the infant industry argument, many inefficient industries might arise that would be unable to compete internationally (Gerber, 2007a). They would then act as a brake on economic development rather than a spur (Morgan, 1959; Flanders, 1964). Studies have shown that the more successful countries were those that adopted open policies and promoted exports (Gerber, 2007b).

Barriers have also been used not to protect the home market for a domestic company but rather to encourage a foreign firm to come and set up its plant and supply the domestic economy from within its own borders. The main benefit that can flow from this policy is that it may encourage industrialization, as firms such as component suppliers are set up to supply the new firm. The major disadvantage is that barriers may encourage suboptimal-size plants to be established. Much of Canada's manufacturing industry suffered from this problem in the era before the North American Free Trade Agreement removed most tariffs on US imports (Clement et al., 1999). Having higher costs than foreign firms can be potentially detrimental to the long-run development of the economy, as it becomes trapped having a small-scale, high-cost industrial structure that ultimately inhibits growth and allows living standards to languish relative to other countries.

3.5 Lessons for business

It is said that the free traders win all the arguments but the protectionists get the votes (Knight, 1951). Firms threatened by foreign competition can always find arguments for protection. It is natural to make those arguments. There is a lot to lose. We have not even presented some of these arguments, such as the inability to compete with 'cheap foreign labour', because for an individual firm they may be true. Raising trade barriers for these reasons simply protects a particular vested interest. The cost to the society is the gains to trade forgone. Sometimes these simple arguments win public support. It is important, however, for the long-run consequences of protectionism to be well understood by business people. They will mean slower growth and less national income. In the short run, protectionism may even appear to provide general benefits, but only if there is no retaliation by other countries. Protectionism can lead to a downward spiral of reduced trade and the loss of its benefits.

The more sophisticated arguments for protection have been explored in this chapter. It is important that businesses understand these arguments and their flaws. Each must be judged within the context in which they are proposed. Alternatives to trade restrictions are almost always available to address problems with competitiveness. Governments will often consult with the business community before proceeding with trade measures or other policies aimed at improving the ability of its firms to compete with foreign firms. Trade restrictions often appear to be 'cheap policies' when compared with subsidies or retraining schemes. This is because the costs of trade restrictions, often spread over a large number of consumers, are not as obvious as budgetary expenditures. The theory, however, suggests that protection will almost always be more expensive. This is particularly true over time if a country becomes saddled with an uncompetitive industrial base. Currently, protectionism's acceptability as a government objective is on the wane. It is clearly identified with particular vested interests rather than the national good. This is an important outcome of the work of trade theorists. As a result, firms relying on the protection provided by trade restrictions may be vulnerable and should consider alternative long-term company strategies and/or alternative avenues of government support.

REFERENCES

Baldwin, R.E. (1969) The case against infant industry protection. *Journal of Political Economy*, 77, 295–305.

Baldwin, R.E. (1979) *The Political Economy of US Import Trade Policy*, MIT Press, Cambridge, MA.

Becker, G.S. (1983) A theory of competition among pressure groups. *Quarterly Journal of Economics*, 98(3), 371–400.

Bhagwati, J. and Ramaswami, V.K. (1963) Domestic distortions, tariffs and the optimum subsidy. *Journal of Political Economy*, 71, 44–50.

Clement, N.C., Castillo Vera, G. del, Gerber, J., Kerr, W.A., MacFadyen, A.J., Shedd, S., Zepeda, E. and Alarcon, D. (1999) *North American Economic Integration: Theory and Practice*, Edward Elgar Publishing, Cheltenham, UK and Northampton, MA, USA.

Corden, W.M. (1957) Tariffs, subsidies and the terms of trade. *Economica*, 24, 235–42.

Culbertson, J.M. (1986) The folly of free trade. *Harvard Business Review*, 86(5), 122–8.

Davies, A.S. and Kerr, W.A. (1997) Picking winners: Agricultural research and the allocation of public funds. *Review of Policy Issues*, 3(3), 39–50.

Finger, J.M. (1979) Trade liberalisation and public choice perspective, in *Challenges to a Liberal Economic Order*, ed. R.C. Amacher, G. Haberler and T.D. Willet, American Enterprise Institute, Washington, DC, pp. 421–53.

Flanders, M.J. (1964) Prebisch on protectionism: An evaluation. *Economic Journal*, 71, 305–26.

Frey, B. (1984) *International Political Economics*, Blackwell, Oxford.

Gaisford, J.D. and Kerr, W.A. (2001) *Economic Analysis for International Trade Negotiations*, Edward Elgar Publishing, Cheltenham, UK and Northampton, MA, USA.

Gerber, J.B. (2007a) Import substitution industrialization, in *Handbook on International Trade Policy*, ed. W.A. Kerr and J.D. Gaisford, Edward Elgar Publishing, Cheltenham, UK and Northampton, MA, USA, pp. 441–9.

Gerber, J.B. (2007b) Export promotion policies, in *Handbook on International Trade Policy*, ed. W.A. Kerr and J.D. Gaisford, Edward Elgar Publishing, Cheltenham, UK and Northampton, MA, USA, pp. 450–56.

Greenaway, D. and Sadsford, D. (1987) Further econometric analysis of the relationship between fiscal dependence on trade taxes and economic development. *Public Finance*, 42(2), 309–19.

Heckscher, E. (1935) *Mercantilism*, George Allen & Unwin, London.

Hillman, A.L. (1989) *The Political Economy of Protection*, Harwood Academic Publishers, Chur.

Hindley, B. (1983) Trade policy, economic performance and Britain's economic problem, in *Policy* and *Performance in International Trade*, ed. J. Black and A. Winters, Macmillan, London, pp. 25–42.

IBRD (1987) *World Bank Development Report*, International Bank for Reconstruction and Development, Washington, DC.

Johnson, H.G. (1965) Optimal trade intervention in the presence of domestic distortions, in *Trade Growth and the Balance of Payments*, ed. R.E. Caves, P. Kenen and H.G. Johnson, North Holland, Amsterdam, pp. 3–34.

Kerr, W.A. (2001) Dumping – one of those economic myths. *Journal of International Law and Trade Policy*, 2(2), 1–10, www.esteyjournal.com.

Kerr, W.A. (2006) Dumping: Trade policy in need of a theoretical make over. *Canadian Journal of Agricultural Economics*, 54(1), 11–31.

Kerr, W.A. (2007) Introduction to trade policy, in *Handbook on International Trade Policy*, ed. W.A. Kerr and J.D. Gaisford, Edward Elgar Publishing, Cheltenham, UK and Northampton, MA, USA, pp. 1–8.

Kerr, W.A. and Loppacher, L.J. (2004) Antidumping in the Doha negotiations: Fairy tales at the World Trade Organization. *Journal of World Trade*, 38(2), 211–44.

Keynes, J.M. (1972) Mitigation by tariff, in *Collected Writings*, Vol. 9: *Essays in Persuasion*, Macmillan, Houndmills, pp. 231–44.

Kimbugwe, K., Perdikis, N., Yeung, M.T. and Kerr, W.A. (2012) *Economic Development through Regional Trade*, Palgrave Macmillan, London.

Knight, F.H. (1951) The role of principles in economics and politics. *American Economic Review*, 41(1), 1–29.

Leger, L.A., Gaisford, J.D. and Kerr, W.A. (1999) Labour market adjustments to international trade shocks, in *The Current State of Economic Science*, Vol. 4, ed. S. Bhagwan Dahiya, Spellbound Publications, Rohtak, pp. 2011–34.

Leontief, W. (1993) The use of indifference curves in international trade. *Quarterly Journal of Economics*, 47, 493–503.

Lewis, W.A. (1969) *Aspects of Tropical Trade 1883–1965*, Almquist & Wicksell, Stockholm.

List, F. (1841) *Das Nationale System der Politischen Oekonomie*, Der internationale Handel, die Handelspolitik und der deutsche zollverein, J.G. Colta, Scher Verlag, Stuttgart.

Metzler, L.A. (1949) Tariffs, the terms of trade, and the distribution of national income. *Journal of Political Economy*, 57, 1–29.

Morgan, T. (1959) The long run terms of trade between agriculture and manufacturing. *Economic Development and Cultural Change*, 8(1), 1–23.

Myint, H. (1963) Infant industry arguments for assistance to industries in the setting of dynamic trade theory, in *International Theory in a Developing World*, ed. R.F. Harrod and T.D.C. Hague, Macmillan, London, pp. 173–93.

Pincus, J.J. (1975) Pressure groups and the pattern of tariffs. *Journal of Political Economy*, 83(4), 757–78.

Prebisch, R. (1950) *The Economic Development of Latin America and Its Principal Problems*, UN Department of Economic Affairs, New York.

Ricardo, D. (1951) On the principles of political economy and taxation, in *The Works and Correspondence of David Ricardo*, ed. P. Sraffa, Cambridge University Press, Cambridge.

Smith, A. (1961) *An Inquiry into the Nature and Causes of the Wealth of Nations*, ed. E. Cannan, reprint, Methuen, London.

Winters, A. (1990) The national security argument for protection. *World Economy*, 13(2), 170–90.

Yarrow, Y. (1987) Economic aspects of anti-dumping. *Oxford Review of Economic Policy*, 3(1), 66–79.

Appendix

3A.1 Protectionism in general equilibrium analysis

Mercantilism was the earliest major theory advocating protectionism. Mercantilist writers in the eighteenth and nineteenth centuries proposed that nations limit their imports as much as possible in order to run a trade surplus – more exports than imports (Heckscher, 1935). In the mercantilist era, international accounts were settled in gold and silver. A surplus would lead to the accumulation of precious metals that could be used to finance government expenditure. By spending these surpluses in the home economy and restricting the purchases of foreign goods the flow of precious metals abroad was minimized. Domestic business activity would be stimulated, as consumers were forced to purchase domestically produced goods. Restricting foreign purchases might reduce consumers' choice but it maximized the revenue accruing to the state. In the mercantilists' scheme of things, maximizing the state's revenue was akin to maximizing a country's welfare. This premise was totally opposite to that of the **classical** economists such as Adam Smith (1961) and Ricardo (1951), who equated the nation's welfare with the sum of each individual's welfare. In other words, what benefited the individual benefited the country. How did they reach this conclusion?

The conclusion can be derived by using some basic economic theory. Figure 3A.1 shows the **production possibility frontier** (PP) of a country producing two goods, wheat and cars. The production possibility frontier shows the maximum combinations of outputs it is possible for a country to produce if it uses all of its available resources. As one moves along the frontier from right to left more cars are obtained at the cost of producing less wheat. At any point on the frontier the quantity of wheat given up for an additional car is known as a car's **opportunity cost**. The concavity of the curve illustrates that as one moves along the curve the opportunity cost of giving up wheat in order to obtain cars increases. The reason for this is that some factors of production may be more suited to the production of one commodity rather than another and so more of a factor must be used to obtain one more unit of the chosen good. Although the production possibility frontier shows us how much of each good a country can produce, it does not tell us how much of each is produced. This can be derived, in turn, by imposing the country's or community's indifference map on to the diagram.

Community indifference curves are constructed, in theory, by aggregating the **indifference curves** of all the individual consumers residing in the country (Leontief, 1993). An individual's indifference curve shows his or her

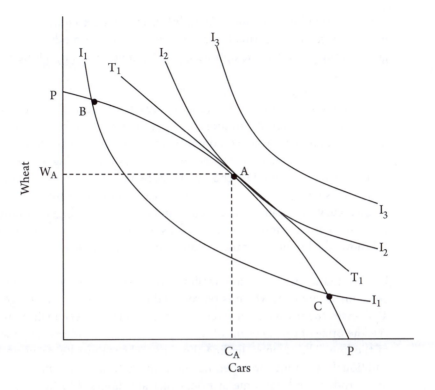

Figure 3A.1   Consumption and production under autarky

willingness to trade off possible combinations of consumption goods. Each curve shows the individual's trade-offs at a fixed level of satisfaction, in other words the combinations among which he or she is indifferent. For example, a person may be equally satisfied to have two beers and six pieces of pizza or three beers and four pieces of pizza. Of course, each individual will value beer and pizza in his or her own way. Combinations that give greater satisfaction put the individual on a higher curve.

Rational individuals are assumed to want to consume combinations of products that give them the highest level of satisfaction. As with the individual, it is assumed that the nation attempts to achieve the greatest satisfaction, which means that it tries to carry out consumption somewhere on the highest possible community indifference curve. What constrains the nation in achieving this is the productive capacity of the domestic economy as shown by the production possibility frontier. In Figure 3A.1, this is illustrated by point A, where the community indifference curve I_2I_2 is tangential to the production possibility frontier PP. To put it more technically, at point A the nation's **marginal** (meaning one more) **rate of substitution** between wheat and cars, as shown by the community indifference curve, is equal to the nation's marginal rate of transformation or opportunity cost of producing these two goods. Why point A is the optimum point can be shown by a little counterfactual logic.

For example, community indifference curve I_1I_1 intersects PP at points B and C and these points could be chosen – because they could be produced – but the community or nation would not be maximizing its satisfaction since, by changing the combination of wheat and cars, a point on a higher community indifference curve could be chosen. Thus, by reducing the amount of wheat and increasing the quantity of cars purchased, point A on community indifference curve I_2I_2 can be achieved. Points on an even higher indifference curve such as I_3I_3 cannot be achieved, as the production possibility frontier PP shows the boundary of the nation's productive potential.

Under autarky, the situation without trade, the nation will produce and consume at point A, which is reproduced in Figure 3A.2. The tangent line T_1T_1 gives the price line or internal terms of trade between wheat and cars (i.e. the price of cars in terms of wheat or vice versa is indicated by the slope of the line. The steeper the line the more wheat must be given up for an additional car). Once we open up the country to international trade it can now produce and consume at prices that are different to those prevailing under autarky. This is illustrated by the price line, now the international terms of trade line T_2T_2. This indicates that cars are now more expensive – in terms of wheat – in the international market than they were in the home market. Domestic producers will now take advantage of these higher prices by moving out of wheat production and into car production. This will continue until point D is reached, where the international terms of trade line is tangential to the production possibility frontier. We can also see in Figure 3A.2 that T_2T_2 is not tangential to community indifference curve I_2I_2, but it is tangential to I_4I_4 at point E. As I_4I_4 is to the right of I_2I_2, if the nation could consume the bundle of goods illustrated by point E it would be better off. It can in fact achieve this through international trade. The country could exchange DF cars for FE wheat.

Despite there having been a change in the composition of its consumption pattern – more wheat, fewer cars – as it has moved from autarky to free trade, the nation has been able to achieve a higher level of satisfaction and is in material terms better off. Even if it could not change its pattern of production, opening up its economy to world prices will still lead to an improvement for the country. This is again illustrated in Figure 3A.2. In contrast to the free trade situation, the international terms of trade line $T'_2T'_2$ (which is

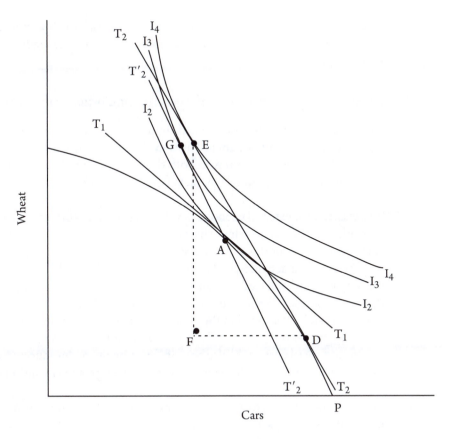

Figure 3A.2   Consumption and production under free trade

parallel to T_2T_2, indicating the same international prices) passes through the original autarkic production point A. Although indifference curve I_4I_4 cannot be reached, $T'_2T'_2$ is now tangential to I_3I_3 at point G, which is to the right of I_2I_2 and therefore an improvement on the original autarkic consumption point A. Again cars – although fewer of them – could be traded for wheat. By having opened up its economy to the forces of international competition the country's citizens are able to rejig their consumption and achieve greater satisfaction.

This illustration shows us that the overall gain from adopting an open trading system falls into two parts:

1. that which comes from exchange, that is, moving from position A to G;
2. that from adjusting production to international competitive pressures, that is, moving from position G to E.

The results of this general equilibrium analysis lead to the same conclusion reached in section 3.2 – that opening an economy to trade is welfare enhancing.

3A.1.1 An argument for protection in the general equilibrium framework

The static case for protection, which implies trade-restricting intervention against imports on a permanent basis, evolves from the existence of distortions in the domestic economy in both the consumer markets and the factor (raw material, labour, capital) markets (Corden, 1957).

The existence of external economies will bring about distortions in commodity markets. (This section draws heavily on Bhagwati and Ramaswami, 1963.) A classic example of this type of distortion is the possibility that farmers, in carrying out their activities, will employ techniques that lead to soil erosion. In the long run, this will lead to reduced farm output. This loss of output means that society as a whole will lose – there is a social cost. These consequences may not, however, be perceived in the short run. Hence, the private costs of these farming activities do not reflect their true social costs. The divergence between private and social cost could also arise if, for some reason, producers were not using techniques that lead to economies of scale being reaped in the long run.

To illustrate, let us return to our example of a wheat- and car-producing economy, now represented by Figure 3A.3.

Again PP is the country's production possibility frontier, but, because of the existence of external diseconomies in the wheat-producing sector, the internal terms of trade line T_1T_1 is not tangential to it. The slope of T_1T_1 represents the private cost trade-off rather than the true social cost trade-off. Instead, T_1T_1 cuts through PP at point A, with the country's community indifference I_1I_1 curve tangential to T_1T_1 at this point. Hence, consumption and production take place at A. If the economy is opened up to trade and T_2T_2 represents the new international terms of trade, production will take place at B and consumption at C on the lower indifference curve I_2I_2. As a result of the distortion in its commodity markets, the country is now worse off with trade, because its comparative advantage in wheat at distorted prices has moved it into increased wheat production. Reimposition of trade restrictions will change the price line back to T_1T_1 and allow the country to achieve higher levels of satisfaction.

Is this, however, the best policy to be followed? The answer is no. A preferred policy would be one of taxing wheat production, which is prone to external

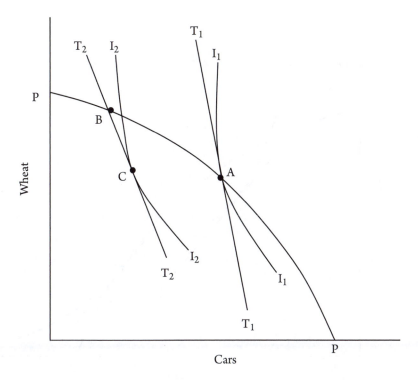

Figure 3A.3   Consumption, production and commodity market distortions

diseconomies, and subsidizing car production, in which the country's true comparative advantage lies. By examining Figure 3A.4 we will see why this is the case. As in Figure 3A.3, point B is the free trade production point.

If we impose taxes on wheat production and **subsidies** on car production, then production will be shifted in favour of the latter, which is illustrated by point D. At this point the international terms of trade line $T'_2 T'_2$ becomes tangential to the production possibility curve PP ($T'_2 T'_2$ being parallel to $T_2 T_2$). This terms of trade line is tangential to the community indifference curve $I_3 I_3$, and as a result the marginal rate of substitution is equal to the opportunity cost of production and, moreover, the nation achieves a higher level of satisfaction than hitherto, as $I_3 I_3$ is to the right of $I_2 I_2$.

Distortions in factor markets arise when a particular factor is paid more than the value it contributes to production – its **marginal product**. It has been asserted that the abundance of labour concentrated in the agricultural sectors of some developing countries means that labour's marginal product is close to zero. For a number of reasons, however, such as tradition, or on humanitarian grounds, labour is paid a wage that is above this level. Trade unions may also be

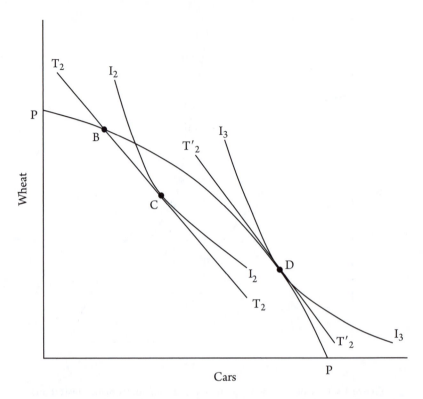

Figure 3A.4   Consumption and production after the removal of commodity market
distortions

successful in raising workers' wages above their marginal product by exerting
their collective bargaining power in a particular labour market. For whatever
reasons, these distortions have implications for the consumption and production patterns in an economy, in that they bias production against the product.
Figure 3A.5 illustrates the effect of factor market distortion on an economy.

As in our previous examples, the economy produces wheat and cars, and its
production possibility frontier is shown by the curve PAP. If distortions did
not exist, then the productive potential would be greater, as illustrated by
the curve PBP. In a free trade situation, let us assume that production takes
place at point E (through which the international price line passes) and consumption takes place at F. If a **tariff** is placed on car imports to redress the
distortion existing in that industry, the slope of the price line changes and
production moves in favour of car production from E to G. The new price
line T^2T^2 will now become tangential to a higher indifference curve, say at
point H, and the nation's consumers will now be better off than they were at
point F.

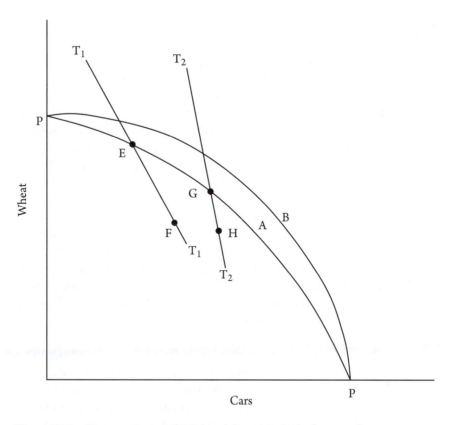

Figure 3A.5 Consumption, production and distortions in the factor markets

Is this the best outcome for the nation? The optimum would be to rid the economy of its distortions and capture the potential shown by the production possibility curve PBP and then allow free trade. How can this potential be realized? The simplest way is by subsidizing, or taxing, the use of the factor in question. For example, if trade union power has raised wages above labour's marginal product in the car industry, then subsidizing this factor will equalize the marginal product of labour in both industries. Taxing the use of labour in the wheat sector would have the same effect. Without distortions existing in the labour market the production possibility curve facing the economy would move out from PAP to PBP.

Distortions in both the commodity and the factor markets can be overcome by the imposition of trade barriers in the form of tariffs. Tariffs are taxes collected as goods enter a country and, hence, raise their price. As we have seen, though, this may not be the best policy. A system of subsidies and/or taxation will lead to a greater level of welfare. It is for these reasons that economists often call the imposition of tariffs a **second-best** policy.

Summary of Section II

The economic analysis carried out in Section II showed that, by adopting a policy of free trade, countries, and hence the world economy in general, can maximize their welfare. Our analysis also showed that any opening up from complete autarky will lead to an improvement. This improvement, however, will not be costless. Some room is therefore left for political forces to influence the extent to which an economy exposes itself to the rigours of world trade. The openness or closeness of the world economy thus depends on the political power of protectionist forces in all countries. This power can be considerable, because competition, while it will mean some will gain, also creates losers, who given the rigidities that exist in all economies may not be absorbed quickly into the expanding industries. The losers, therefore, have a greater incentive to mobilize opposition to changes that they see as potentially detrimental to their interests. If the losers are producers, being a more homogeneous group than the gainers, they will find it easier to organize and press for the reversal of any opening up of the economy or to seek protection from foreign competition.

The arguments for protection are numerous and varied but can usually be split into those that demand continuous protection – the static variety – and those that involve temporary measures – the dynamic set. In examining the static group, such as rigidities in the commodity and factor markets, balance of payments problems and employment reasons, protection via the imposition of tariffs and quotas may not be the best policy. Subsidies and improvements in the workings of the market mechanisms are better policies to follow. The use of revenue-raising tariffs is also questionable, and improving the basis on which public finance is raised is again a better policy. The only justifiable argument for the imposition of tariffs is the optimal tariff argument, but this can be counterproductive and lead to a general decline in world trade if other countries retaliate.

The dynamic reasons for protection are more subtle in that they are proposed for only a limited period until some improvement has been gained. Hence, arguments for protection against predatory pricing or help for infant and senile firms and economies can be very appealing. Again, it may be questioned whether protectionist policies of a traditional type are the most appropriate, with perhaps the exception of predatory pricing. The possibility that temporary measures may become permanent is a strong one. More appropriate policies might be those that attack root causes, which in turn might be deeply imbedded in the country's economy and society. The factors affecting competitiveness identified in Chapter 2 tend to be long-run forces. Trade restrictions may bring short-run relief from the adverse effects of changes in these factors. Improving competitiveness has no quick fix. It is the key to long-term prosperity. The conflict between the interests of those who seek a more open and a more closed trading system is very powerful, and politicians have tried to channel these forces by setting up institutions to defuse potential conflicts. These institutions are examined in detail in Section III.

Section III

The international trading system

Introduction to Section III

Section II described why trade takes place between countries and why an open trading system is preferable to one that is closed. We also outlined the reasons why vested interests might well pursue governments to modify free trade policies. In Section III we examine the institutional framework within which trade takes place. We will examine in greater depth the role of the nation state in establishing international trade institutions and their role in determining the nature of international economic relations. In particular we will look at the development of bilateral and multilateral agreements, and the reasons behind the growth of regional trade associations. The types of measures that countries can use to restrict trade are examined, as well as the international controls which attempt to limit their use.

4

The search for an orderly system for trade

4.1 The nation state and economic sovereignty

Firms which engage in international commerce desire a degree of order for their international undertakings. Without order, planning becomes impossible. The risks associated with conducting business in distant markets with different business ethics and cultures are difficult enough to overcome without having to worry about the unpredictable actions by individual countries' governments. Governments, on the other hand, do not wish to give up the right to act swiftly to protect their national interests – including business interests. They may, however, want other countries to agree to limit their powers. The evolution of the international trading system is a manifestation of a compromise between these two forces.

Despite the growth of international institutions, regional trade associations and transnational companies, the nation state is still the primary actor on the world economic stage. In the domestic arena it is the nation state, or rather its government, which has to arbitrate between the demands of interest groups, put forward compromises and formulate policies accordingly. On the international front, the nation state is faced with similar responsibilities. It has to promote the interests of its stakeholders while not upsetting its trading partners in such a way as to incur adverse reactions. As the international economy has become more integrated, the role of the nation state in intergovernmental bargaining or economic diplomacy has remained strong. With greater economic integration come domestic rules, regulations and health and safety standards that affect not only domestic producers but also, increasingly, foreign producers.

The nation state is not, however, just a trumpeter of domestic economic interests. It has a wider and more direct role in seeing that both domestic and international economic policies aimed at expanding economic growth do not upset their country's internal stability or challenge its national security.

In many ways, the continued importance of the nation state is contrary to what one would expect. The rapid growth in world economic integration and the consequent transfer of economic decision making to supranational bodies have led to some limits on the economic and political sovereignty of nation states – albeit ones that can always be removed if the country chooses to reassert its sovereignty. Where, however, this economic and political sovereignty has been conceded, particularly in the area of trade relations, the nation state still represents and expounds domestic national interests. Examples of this are clearly illustrated by the approach taken in multilateral trade negotiations by the US government in its pursuit of the interests of US farmers and also that of the European Union for their farmers (Gaisford and Kerr, 2001).

4.2   The state and the structure of international trade

The role of the nation state, as it is portrayed by neo-classical economic theory, is confined to the maximization of its economic well-being. In its approach to international trade the state should then stand against protectionism and join with other states in promoting an **open economic system** based on the principles of free trade. To do otherwise would not be rational and would reflect, at best, that governments and their advisers did not understand the most basic of economic principles or, at worst, were in league with those having a vested interest in protection from foreign competition.

The reality, of course, is somewhat different. The pursuit of maximizing economic welfare may be only one of several goals the nation state may wish to pursue (Gaisford and Hester, 2007). It has been said that the state tries to achieve four goals, namely enhance its political power, maximize aggregate national income, enhance economic growth and maintain social stability (Krasner, 1976). Sometimes these goals are in harmony, while at other times they may conflict. They are affected, furthermore, by the degree of openness of the economy in question, the relative size of the economy and its level of development.

How are these four goals related to trade structures? Conventional economic theory suggests that the greater the degree of openness, the greater the level of aggregate income and that this applies equally to small and large states and to developed or underdeveloped countries. The static benefits of openness are, however, inversely related to size. For example, small states lacking the diversity in economic resources or the potential for economies of scale that are generally possessed by large states are able to gain more by specializing and trading than are large states.

The effect of openness on social stability may, however, be adverse. For example, as an economy is opened up to world competition some sectors will expand while others will contract, implying factor movements from declining to growing industries. As we saw in Chapter 3, those in the contracting sectors will oppose openness and change. Their opposition will lead to friction and social tensions. There is evidence to suggest that the adverse impact on social stability will be greater the smaller the state and the lower its level of economic development. Larger states have proportionately less of their resources tied up in the international marketplace, while the higher levels of skills found in developed countries enable workers to move fairly easily between one sector and another. Social stability is thus inversely related to openness, although economic size and the level of development reduce the worst consequences.

A country can also enhance its political power vis-à-vis other states by supporting an open trading structure, if it knows that the adoption of a closed structure would have a significant adverse effect on its trading partners. In other words, the higher the relative cost of closure the weaker the position of the partner states. As larger developed countries have lower direct income losses and lower adjustment costs than smaller countries when closed trading structures are adopted, their economic power is enhanced vis-à-vis smaller or less developed countries. Large countries will, therefore, prefer open trading systems, since they can use their political power to achieve economic and non-economic goals.

As discussed in Chapter 3, there is some controversy as to whether an open or closed trading system promotes economic growth. Openness allows small states to produce for a world market that allows their industries to achieve the economies of scale that would be denied to them under a closed system. Openness is also deemed to be in the interests of large, rich countries whose comparative advantage is in technologically advanced goods, which also require large, growing markets to enhance their commercial success. Openness, however, may have adverse consequences for economic growth if a country begins to lose its competitive edge and lag significantly behind its rivals in the production of new and advanced products. With capital and technology free to move, these resources will leave declining economies in search of higher rewards in the relatively more expansive economies. It has been suggested that the US and Britain have experienced periods of capital outflows and that their economic growth suffered as a result. Economists who study developing economies have also identified a similar phenomenon for poor countries. Which view is correct has not been finally decided. As noted in Chapter 3, those countries that tend to have open trading regimes seem to have higher levels of economic growth (Little et al., 1993).

Given that states have more than one goal and that these are influenced by the degree to which the trading regime is open or closed, what is the likelihood that a more open or closed trading structure or system will be adopted by the international community? Section 4.3 attempts to answer this question.

4.3 The nature of the international trading system

As states have a variety of goals, whose compatibility may well vary according to their size and stage of economic development, it is understandable that they will vary in their attitudes towards the degree of openness of the international trading system (Krasner, 1976).

If the world is composed of a large number of small highly developed states, the probability is that they will adopt an open trading system. The reason for this is that this system will increase these countries' aggregate income and encourage their economic growth, while the social instability envisaged from restructuring will be mitigated by the ease of factor mobility, which is made possible by their high level of economic development. As the costs of closure fall symmetrically on all countries, there is no loss of political power to any state supporting this open system.

In a situation where a few large, unequally developed states make up the world economy a **closed economic system** is likely to follow. Why? True, each state could enhance its income by adopting an open system, but the gains would be very small and would not appear worthwhile when compared to the social instability that would result. This is particularly true in developing economies. Given their rigid factor mobility that makes it difficult, for example, for labour to move to take advantage of new opportunities, the relative costs of openness would be greater for them. It would not, therefore, make sense to adopt or encourage the development of an open international trading system. The more advanced states might prefer an open system, but short of enforcing their will by military means they would have to accept the position of the large less developed countries. One option available to them is that they could open up trade between themselves by forming regional trade associations, an issue that will be discussed in Chapter 5.

In a system that is dominated by one large relatively more advanced country – the hegemonic state – an open economic system is again likely to result. This is the so-called **hegemonic system**, and the reason for its openness is easy to see. An open system will give the hegemonic state higher aggregate income and increase its economic growth. This will be especially so when its industrial structure and technological base are in advance of those of the other countries. An open system will enhance its political power, since the opportunity cost of closure is less for it than for those that trade with it. The advanced nature of this state will mean that reallocation costs and social instability will be kept to manageable proportions given its low overall exposure to international trade.

The reaction towards this sort of system by other countries in the world would depend on their size relative to the hegemonic state. Small states are likely to adopt an open system, since the economic gains that will accrue to them are likely to be large relative to the costs. Their political power is unlikely to be adversely affected, since given their size they are unlikely to have much anyway.

It is harder to predict the reaction of medium-sized states. It will depend on how the dominant state chooses to use its economic resources. In the extreme, the hegemonic state could coerce them into adopting an open system by military means, although this is unlikely, since other more positive incentives can be offered.

The hegemonic state, for example, can offer medium-sized states and their industries, in particular, access to its large domestic market and to its relatively cheap exports. Instead of these positive incentives, it can put in place negative ones that can damage the medium-sized countries' economic potential. The large state, with its greater political power, can persuade smaller countries to discriminate in favour of its firms' products and against those of the medium-sized states. It can also withhold aid and support from less developed medium-sized states and political and economic support from the more advanced. In this way, the hegemonic state can ensure that the world trading system is an open one.

The hegemony of one state, or its absence, means that international commerce is conducted at the whim of national states. The politicians in those states will have to balance the demands of the various parties with an interest in trade. Restrictions can be added (or removed) at will. Even if there is a hegemonic state, to ensure that other states acknowledge its position the hegemonic state will periodically have to demonstrate its power. The use of economic power will likely mean that the rules of trade are changed. International commerce will be disrupted and the expectations of management dampened. Losses will arise and trade opportunities will be forgone. As a result, there has been a long search for a more orderly system for trade relations.

The scenarios developed in this chapter suggest that open trading systems are more likely to occur when there is a hegemonic state and one that is, more particularly, in the ascendancy. An open trading system is also likely to be the case when the world is made up of a large number of small advanced states. The opposite is likely to occur when the world economy is characterized by a few but relatively large unequally developed states. Evidence for these views can be seen in the development of the international trading system since the last century.

4.4 The international trading system through history

Before discussing the historical development of the international trading system it is important to define what is meant by an open trading system. Economists associate openness with three factors. Firstly, the height of trade barriers such as tariffs, the restrictive nature of non-tariff barriers, such as quantitative limits on imports, and the degree to which an exchange rate is undervalued must be assessed. The latter gives a country a competitive trade advantage.

The second measure of openness is the ratio of a country's trade to its national income. A period in which this ratio is increasing would suggest that the world trading system is open and rising.

The third indicator is the extent to which international trade is concentrated within regions that are made up of countries at different levels of economic development. If trade is concentrated within regional groupings of countries – often called **trading blocs** – and trade outside the bloc is limited to a few states selected largely for political rather than economic reasons, then the conclusion one can draw is that the international trading system is tending towards the closed end of the spectrum.

An open economic system can be defined as one in which trade barriers are falling, the ratios of trade to national income are rising and regional trade is becoming less concentrated. Using these criteria, six relatively distinct periods in world trade history can be identified. These periods have alternated between relatively more and relatively less open phases for the international trading system.

Excluding the times when major wars occurred, the period from the 1820s to the late 1870s was characterized by openness, as tariff levels were reduced and trade ratios increased, although there were some exceptions to this, for example the United States, which increased its tariffs in the 1860s.

This was a period of British hegemony in both commerce and international politics. The international trading system was largely open. A major boost to openness came with the signing of the Anglo-French Treaty of 1860 and led to a large number of other trade agreements. By 1866, France had signed commercial treaties with Belgium, Italy, Switzerland, Sweden, Norway, Spain, the Netherlands, Austria and a trade association of German states known as the Zollverein. The principal European trading partners were thus linked by a whole series of trade agreements. Britain, in the meantime, adopted a unilateral free trade policy towards its trade partners. The nations with overseas empires brought their colonies into this trading system by ensuring they adopted the mother country's tariff structures or at least lowered their tariff levels.

The period from the late 1870s to the end of the century contrasts with this relatively open era, as Britain faced challenges to its economic supremacy and its influence began to wane. The assumption that free trade was best also faced a serious intellectual challenge from the infant economy theorists, whose major proponent was the German economist Friedrich List (1904). Economists, both in Europe and in the United States, put forward theories that proposed protectionism as an aid to economic development. This period was characterized by increases in tariff levels and a decline in trade ratios.

One of the major factors that led to this decline in openness was the competition that the agricultural sectors of Western Europe experienced from the emerging economies such as the US, South America and Russia. The deterioration of the open trading system should not, however, be over-exaggerated, as real tariff rates remained relatively low up to the end of the century (Capie, 1983).

From the beginning of the twentieth century up to the First World War, openness began to reassert itself. This was due more to the increase in trade as a proportion of countries' national incomes, and the decline in the concentration of regional trade, than to a reduction in tariffs. Tariffs remained near their original levels.

During the period between the First World War and the Second World War, the international trading system entered a downward spiral of increasing trade restrictions on a massive scale. The onset of the world **depression** after 1929 led governments to attempt to isolate their economies from its effects by raising trade barriers. In a system without rules, when one country raised barriers other countries retaliated. This led to second- and third-round retaliations. Economists call these rounds of retaliation **beggar-thy-neighbour** policies. Beggar-thy-neighbour retaliations made matters worse, and trade ratios fell dramatically. As countries traded only with those who provided them with essentials, or with which they had political links, trade became highly concentrated (Madsen, 2001).

The growing openness of the world trading system from 1945 can be attributed to the hegemony of the United States and the acceptance of this by other advanced states, particularly those in Western Europe. In the immediate period after the Second World War, Western European countries needed to trade with the US in order to accumulate dollars to finance the reconstruction of their devastated economies. Later, these European countries viewed an open system as being beneficial. Their comparative advantage lay in sophisticated manufactures that required large markets if economies of scale were to be gained.

While the period was one of exceptional growth it was also characterized by the growth of economic blocs – principally in Europe with the development of the predecessor of the EU (and the European Community), the European Economic Community (EEC), as well as the European Free Trade Area (EFTA). Although these economic institutions led to trade being concentrated more heavily between their member states, the rapid growth in world trade did not damage the prospects of the industrial countries that lay outside these blocs. The US, for political reasons, wanted to see an economically strong Western Europe acting as a bulwark against the perceived communist threat coming from the east. As a result, the US openly encouraged the closer integration of the Western European economies.

There was a period in the 1970s and 1980s when the openness of the world economy looked under threat. The deep recessions brought about by severe oil price increases that arose from the creation of an effective production-restricting cartel among major oil-producing countries, OPEC, and the deflationary policy responses of the oil-importing countries led to a rise in protectionist activity. During this period, however, no one country had the power or authority to dissuade others from imposing trade barriers. It was during this period that the US began to lose its hegemonic role in the world and began to have conflicts with its trade partners. These conflicts were particularly acrimonious with Japan over cars, electronic goods and agriculture. There have also been conflicts with the EU, principally over agricultural products.

This trend to a more closed system was somewhat reversed in the 1990s and into the early years of the twenty-first century. This increase in openness arose from two sources. First came the fall of the Russian-led Soviet empire and the demise of communism with its emphasis on economic self-sufficiency. At the same time, while the Communist Party retained power in China, its pragmatic leaders determined that trade and foreign investment were the best way for their country to acquire the technology it needed to develop (Hobbs and Kerr, 2000; Coase and Wang, 2012). As a result, Russia, former communist Eastern Europe and China had to be integrated into the international trading system, boosting openness. The second source of increased openness was the realization by most modern market economies that part of the reason for their economic malaise arose because the multilateral trading system set up in 1947 with the establishment of the GATT was no longer adequate for a world where services had become much more important and the proportion of the value of goods that is made up of intellectual property was increasing rapidly. Further the GATT did not have an effective dispute settlement mechanism, something that was required to fight increasing protectionism. The result of this realization was, after years of difficult negotiations, the reformulation of the GATT into a new multilateral trade organization, the World Trade Organization (WTO). The WTO also incorporated a new phase of trade barrier reduction that spurred the growth in international trade (Kerr, 2010). The world experienced another major economic downturn in the wake of a major banking crisis in 2008. For the most part, governments have resisted pressure to impose or strengthen barriers to trade, although economic performance in developed countries remained anaemic up to 2013. Thus, the inverse relationship between declining economic activity and increases in trade barriers may have finally been broken (Viju and Kerr, 2011).

4.5 Bilateral and multilateral trading relationships

Trade and trade negotiations can be carried out on either a **bilateral** or a **multilateral** basis. Either two countries can negotiate and agree on a framework within which trade can be carried out between them, or a number of countries can negotiate collectively and apply equally to one another any agreements that are reached. The technical term used for the equal treatment of all the signatories of an agreement is the **most favoured nation (MFN)** principle. All this means is that no signatory will be treated any worse, or any better, than any other. It is a principle that became enshrined in the articles of the World Trade Organization.

What is the purpose of agreements? Their most important function is to provide rules for trade relationships so that firms have a basis upon which to plan their international commercial transactions. Principally, they provide mechanisms which help to increase trade by removing restrictions and to reduce the risks involved in trading across frontiers. Bilateral trade agreements usually have clauses incorporated in them which outline the procedures that should be used when difficulties arise. In this way, the risks become more transparent and enable business people to cover them through, for example, insurance markets. Bilateral agreements may, furthermore, outline the dispute settlement procedures that must be followed, how this process is to function and which country's laws are to apply.

A problem with bilateral agreements is that they are subject to political erosion. Over time, the central tenets of the agreement may become eroded as domestic legislation in one or both countries supersedes them. Bilateral agreements are also prone to obsolescence in that they often apply for only a specified period and then have to be renegotiated. This makes them subject to attack from protectionist vested interests.

Further, although dispute settlement procedures may be agreed, it is possible that governments might be reluctant to allow them to operate fully if they perceive that their economic and political sovereignty is being challenged. As there is no objective measure of sovereignty, its interpretation depends very much on the political outlook of the government. It is to be expected that the more 'nationalistic' its credentials, the more likely it will be to resist restitution via the mechanisms laid down in the agreement.

Business people may well turn to their home governments for support when the other country's government does not live up to its commitments, but short of using military force it is difficult for home governments to do very much about broken agreements. They may attempt to retaliate using economic sanctions such as trade embargoes or the suspension of aid, but the impact of such measures may have little effect. There are also other issues to consider, such as the adverse effect a policy may have on the foreign country's population. A government may consider it best not to damage long-term relationships with a foreign country in order to support its business people in the short run. There have been, nevertheless, some examples of military action taken on behalf of home nationals. Usually the process is, however, more covert and involves diplomatic channels and negotiations.

Until recently, the heyday of bilateral trading arrangements existed from the latter half of the nineteenth century up until the beginning of the First World War. The already mentioned Anglo-French treaty of 1860 and those that France concluded with Belgium, the German Zollverein, Italy, Switzerland,

Sweden, Norway, Spain, the Netherlands and Austria were all conducted on a bilateral basis.

After the First World War, bilateralism re-established itself, albeit in a more restricted form. While it could not be said that the bilateral system was to blame for the collapse of world trade, the deficiencies inherent in it contributed to its decline. For example, the limited duration of bilateral treaties made them vulnerable to attack from interest groups adversely affected by the depression of the 1930s. Many were simply not renewed. Further, bilateral treaties were broken, as there was no real international control over states taking this course of action. It was not surprising, then, that policy makers proposed that trade in the post-Second World War period should be based on multilateralism.

The multilateral system, as we shall see in Chapter 6, largely removed the tariffs and other discriminating devices that were imposed in the interwar years. It also drew up rules that restricted the use of quantitative restrictions, established procedures to settle trade disputes between countries and encouraged a series of trade negotiations, known as rounds, that progressively liberalized world trade. There were deficiencies in the multilateral system, principally with regard to the dispute settlement system and newer trade restrictions that fell outside its purview such as voluntary export restraints (VERs). Nevertheless, it was a stronger system than the one that was based on bilateral treaties. Some of these deficiencies were removed or lessened in the negotiations that led to the formation of the WTO in 1994.

While the international trading system since the Second World War has been, and is, shaped by multilateralism, there is still a place for bilateral deals and negotiations. Trade relations with countries that are not members of the WTO are largely carried out in this way. The trade deals between the EU and the former communist countries were negotiated bilaterally. Bilateral agreements are not confined to non-WTO member states, however, as they also exist between WTO members. Issues or instruments that fall outside WTO rules provide the *raison d'être* for such agreements. By conducting discussions and drawing up bilateral agreements, countries can further reduce and minimize potential areas of conflict between them. In the first decade of the twenty-first century, bilateral agreements again came into vogue, in part because the multilateral WTO negotiations pertaining to further liberalization of the global economy did not reach a successful conclusion, and as a result countries have sought liberalization in a plethora of preferential trade agreements (Khorana et al., 2010; Kerr, 2011).

There are many examples of these types of agreements. Only a few will be presented here to illustrate the points made. The first is the US–Canadian Automobile Agreement of 1965. The background to this agreement was that in the 1950s Canada was experiencing a balance of trade deficit with the US. The deficit was largely due to the latter country's successful exportation of cars, accessories and parts. The Canadian government responded by offering subsidies to its domestic car industry, which also included US **subsidiaries**, in order to increase its competitiveness and switch consumption away from imported automobiles from the US. The policy was so successful that the deficit in cars, accessories and parts was not only eliminated but reversed. The US threatened to impose a counter-duty to protect its industry. Before matters came to a head, both governments sat down and resolved the dispute. The experience gained by both parties in settling this dispute contributed to the establishment of the 1988 Canada–US Trade Agreement (CUSTA).

Our second example relates to the conflict in the 1980s between the US and Japan relating to a whole range of goods but principally agricultural commodities and electronics. Once again, the conflict is one centred on the balance of trade, with the US running a deficit with Japan.

In the area of agriculture, the US felt that Japanese protectionist policies prevented it from successfully exporting to that market. The US believed that it had a comparative advantage when it came to agricultural production and its producers were being barred from entering the market. There were also cultural or culinary factors inhibiting the ease of some agricultural exports to Japan, but trade barriers were important too in explaining the poor export performance of the US. Direct negotiation between the two countries led to the partial opening up of the agricultural sector, in particular the beef and citrus markets (Kerr et al., 1994).

A similar story applies to the trade in electronics. Here the US, feeling that its conductor industry was under threat, reached an agreement with the Japanese government whereby the Japanese electronics industry would guarantee to purchase a proportion of its components from US firms. While none of these discussions were without acrimony, face-to-face negotiations prevented the situation from deteriorating into a trade war.

Bilateral agreements also form the framework within which economic frontiers between countries are defined. For example, in the North Sea, the border between the British and Norwegian oil fields is determined by a bilateral agreement.

In some cases neither bilateral nor multilateral agreements are optimal, and groups of countries may perceive it to be in their interest to organize themselves into a trading bloc. These regional trade associations are discussed in detail in Chapter 5.

 REFERENCES

Capie, J. (1983) Tariff protection and economic performance in the nineteenth century, in *Policy and Performance in International Trade*, ed. J. Black and L.A. Winters, Macmillan, London, pp. 17–47.

Coase, R. and Wang, W. (2012) *How China Became Capitalist*, Palgrave Macmillan, London.

Gaisford, J.D. and Hester, A. (2007) Why are there trade agreements?, in *Handbook on International Trade Policy*, ed. W.A. Kerr and J.D. Gaisford, Edward Elgar Publishing, Cheltenham, UK and Northampton, MA, USA, pp. 57–70.

Gaisford, J.D. and Kerr, W.A. (2001) *Economic Analysis for International Trade Negotiations*, Edward Elgar Publishing, Cheltenham, UK and Northampton, MA, USA.

Hobbs, A.L. and Kerr, W.A. (2000) Is the WTO ready for China? *Current Politics and Economics of Asia*, 9(4), 262–78.

Kerr, W.A. (2010) GATT-1947: A living legacy fostering the liberalization of international trade. *Journal of International Law and Trade Policy*, 11(1), 1–11.

Kerr, W.A. (2011) The preference for new preferential trade agreements: Does it lead to a good use of scarce resources? *Journal of International Law and Trade Policy*, 12(1), 1–11.

Kerr, W.A., Klein, K.K., Hobbs, J.E. and Kagatsume, M. (1994) *Marketing Beef in Japan*, Haworth Press, New York.

Khorana, S., Perdikis, N., Yeung, M.T. and Kerr, W.A. (2010) *Bilateral Trade Agreements in the Era of Globalization*, Edward Elgar Publishing, Cheltenham, UK and Northampton, MA, USA.

Krasner, S.D. (1976) State power and the structure of international trade. *World Politics*, 28, 317–47.

List, F. (1904) *The Natural System of Political Economy*, Longmans, Green, New York.

Little, I.M.D., Cooper, R.N., Corden, W.M. and Sarath, R. (1993) *Boom, Crisis, and Adjustment: The Macroeconomic Experience of Developing Countries*, Oxford University Press, New York.

Madsen, J.B. (2001) Trade barriers and the collapse of world trade during the Great Depression. *Southern Economic Journal*, 67(4), 848–68.

Viju, C. and Kerr, W.A. (2011) Protectionism and global recession: Has the link been broken? *Journal of World Trade*, 45(3), 605–28.

5

Regional trade associations

5.1 Economic blocs and regional economic integration

The formation of economic blocs is allowed under the broad umbrella of multilateral trade arrangements. The question still remains as to why a group of countries will eliminate trade barriers between themselves instead of pursuing liberalization through multilateral negotiations. There are several answers to this question. Firstly, the participants may feel that opening up their economies to a limited group of countries will bring some of the benefits of free trade but not all the adjustment costs. Secondly, while global free trade may be the economist's ideal, integrating an economy with its principal trading partners may be politically more desirable and feasible (Brada and Méndez, 1993; Phillips, 2007). It will always be easier to negotiate agreements to liberalize when legal systems, business practices and cultures are similar. Negotiations among small groups of countries can often be accomplished more quickly than among large numbers of countries (Yeung et al., 1999; Pugel, 2007). What forms can economic blocs take?

5.2 Definitions and levels of economic integration

An economic bloc can be defined as a grouping of countries that mutually grant trading preferences to one another. Economists have identified four major types of economic blocs (Perdikis, 2007; Pugel, 2007). They are now described, moving from the loosest to the tightest form of economic integration.

5.2.1 Free trade areas

In a **free trade area**, trade restrictions between the member states are reduced to zero for either all or a set of goods agreed on by the member states. Each country is allowed to maintain its own trade or commercial policy towards countries that are not part of the free trade area. As a result, the level of trade barriers toward non-members will differ among members.

To prevent non-members from shipping their goods into the member state with the lowest restrictions and then transporting them tariff free to countries where restrictions are higher, the members of the bloc usually establish a common set of rules to prevent this form of behaviour. Within free trade areas, although the individual countries monitor their own trade policies, procedures exist for defusing potential conflicts between the member states. A central secretariat is usually created to deal with conflicts.

5.2.2 Customs unions

As a form of economic integration, **customs unions** are one step up from free trade areas. All members trade freely with one another but adopt a common external tariff against non-member countries. In trade negotiations they are, therefore, required to act as one and coordinate their policies, again usually via a central body.

5.2.3 Common markets

A **common market** is everything a customs union is plus the free movement of capital and labour. To work effectively, a common market requires that taxes are harmonized between the member states. If taxes are not harmonized then similar goods will vary in price across frontiers, giving rise to 'false' trade flows. A further requirement is the coordination of health and safety regulations. Otherwise, the price of goods will vary and business people will complain that the commercial environment is not equal between countries – the 'playing field' is not level. The difficulties involved in coordinating this type of legislation lead very often to differences in interpretation between countries. The role of a central body to arbitrate and negotiate on such issues becomes even more important than in a customs union or free trade area.

5.2.4 Full economic union

The last form of economic bloc in our taxonomy is the **economic union,** which incorporates all the aspects of a customs union but also includes the total **harmonization** of fiscal and monetary policies. It does not, however, require the adoption of a single currency. Another requirement of an economic union is elimination of national preference in the purchasing – or procurement – policies of member governments, as this acts as a distortion to free trade amongst the participants.

As countries progress through the forms of economic integration outlined above, they give up some of their economic sovereignty. It is sometimes argued that the eventual outcome of economic union is political union, because governments have ceded most of their powers to a central authority or supranational body. This issue has led to major difficulties and conflicts for some governments in the European Union (EU). Despite the decline in national economic sovereignty, the economic power or sovereignty of the economic union will increase. In the economist's language, therefore, there is a trade-off between national sovereignty and the economic benefits that arise from the union.

Before we proceed to examine some real-world examples of regional economic integration we must first consider in more detail the attraction of economic integration to the participating nations. For firms, economic blocs mean increased opportunities for exporting within the bloc (and also increased competition). Trade opportunities with firms in non-member countries may, however, have to be forgone.

5.3   The theory of regional economic integration

Economists have approached the study of economic integration from both the static and the dynamic perspective. Static models will be dealt with first.

5.3.1   The static approach to trade blocs

The best way to evaluate the potential of an economic bloc is to examine the benefits and the costs that will arise from the mutual reduction of trade barriers between the participating countries (Viner, 1950). Benefits will result from the reduction in barriers as opportunities for new trade amongst the participants are created. Costs, however, will arise as more competitive producers remaining outside the bloc are discriminated against and consumption is diverted towards goods produced within the bloc. A numerical example will illustrate this point (see Table 5.1).

Let us assume that Europa imports goods from two countries, Americana and Iberia, and that the goods produced by these countries can be sold at a price equal to their cost of production. If it could enter Europa tariff free, Americana could sell its goods for 300 euros (the currency adopted by Europa), while Iberia would charge 320 euros. Suppose, however, that Europa charged a 20 per cent tax. The price of these goods would increase subsequently to 360 euros and 384 euros respectively. Under a situation of free trade, and one where a tariff existed, Americana's goods would be cheaper than Iberia's and it would capture the market. Assume now that Europa and Iberia agree to form an economic bloc within which tariffs on member states' goods are

Table 5.1 Trade creation and trade diversion

Exporters	Tariff rates	
	0%	20%
Americana	300 euros	360 euros
Iberia	320 euros	384 euros

abolished. Tariffs on non-members remain in place. The result of this is to reduce the price of Iberia's good to 320 euros, which will now mean that it can undercut Americana's price and capture its market. In this example, trade has been created, as Europa's consumers can now buy more goods at 320 euros than at the original price of 360 euros, but trade has been diverted, because consumers now buy from Iberia rather than from Americana. Hence, whereas trade creation is a positive move towards free trade since it lowers prices to consumers, trade diversion is negative as it moves consumption away from the low-cost country with the comparative advantage and towards the higher-cost producer.

This argument can also be illustrated by examining Figure 5.1. Europa's domestic demand and supply curves are denoted D_E and S_E for the good in question. Americana and Iberia's supply curves are S_A and S_I. Their horizontal nature implies that they are both constant cost producers, while the S_A supply curve, being below S_I, shows that Americana is the lower-cost producer.

At price level PE and above, Europa's demand is satisfied by home supply (i.e. Q). Applying a tariff of 't+' to both Americana's good and Iberia's good ensures that the latter's goods are priced out of Europa's market. Americana's supply curve would now become S_A + 't+', while Iberia's would be above this (although it is not shown in Figure 5.1). Let us assume, however, that the tariff rate 't' is in operation and it is not prohibitive, so that Americana's supply curve is denoted by S_A + 't'. This implies that demand in Europa's market is N, of which M is supplied domestically while M – N is supplied by Americana. Why is this the case? The reason is that, up to M, Europa's costs are lower than Americana's (as shown by the supply curves), so it can undercut the competition, but beyond quantity M the reverse is the case.

If Europa and Iberia now form an economic bloc that abolishes tariffs, Iberia's supply curve will re-establish itself at its original position S_I. Hence, S_I is between the tariff-free and with-tariff position of Americana's supply curve. The result of the removal of the tariff is to lower the price of the good in Europa's domestic market to P_I, thus expanding demand to K and

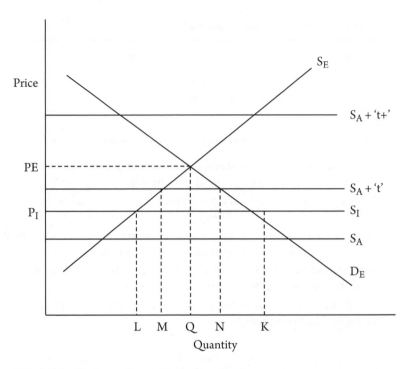

Figure 5.1 Trade creation and trade diversion

reducing domestic supply to L. By reducing tariffs the formation of the economic bloc has created extra trade of the magnitude LM + NK. This is the '**trade creation**' effect. With the removal of the tariffs on Iberia's good, it is able to undercut Americana's good and capture its market. Americana's original supply of MN is now superseded by that of Iberia. In other words, '**trade diversion**' has taken place. The economic bloc has thus increased the level of trade, but it has transferred trade towards the higher-cost producer.

The formation of the economic bloc can only be considered beneficial if the gains from trade creation outweigh the losses incurred from trade diversion. How can these gains and losses be measured? In Figure 5.2 (which is essentially the same as Figure 5.1), the reduction in price from P_A + t to P_I brought about by the formation of the economic bloc has increased the **consumer surplus**. Remember, from Chapter 3, that the consumer surplus is the area between the demand curve and the price. It is considered a surplus owing to the unique character of market prices whereby all consumers pay the same price. The demand curve indicates willingness to pay. As some consumers are willing to pay more than the market price they get a bonus or 'surplus' from the existence of a market price system. The surplus could be captured

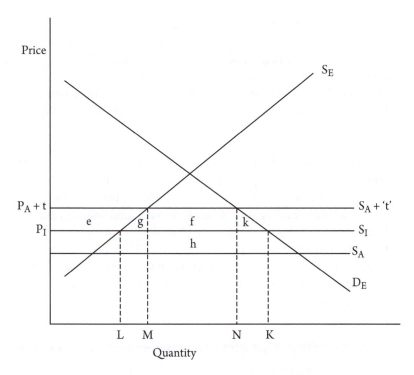

Figure 5.2 Costs and benefits of trade creation and trade diversion

by sellers in a non-market price system like haggling or bargaining where the price is the subject of negotiation.

A smart seller would be able to get the consumer to pay closer to what he or she is willing to pay and, hence, capture part of the surplus. In this case the consumer surplus increases by area e + g + f + k. Again, as defined in Chapter 3, the **producer surplus** is the area between the supply curve and the price. It is considered a surplus owing to the unique character of market prices whereby all sellers receive the same price. The supply curve indicates willingness to sell. As some producers would be willing to sell at a price less than the going market price they get a bonus or 'surplus' from the existence of a market price system. The surplus could be captured by buyers in a non-market price system like haggling or bargaining where the price is the subject of negotiation. A smart buyer would be able to get the producer to charge closer to its supply price and, hence, capture part of the surplus. In this case the producer surplus accruing to domestic suppliers is reduced by area e, as their sales are reduced to L. The tariff revenue that Europa used to extract on the volume of trade with Americana (f + h) is now lost, as trade is diverted to tariff-free Iberia.

As long as the benefits (e + g + f + k) brought about from trade creation exceed the losses of e + f + h from trade diversion, the formation of the economic bloc will be beneficial to the parties involved. There are exceptions to these conclusions (Cooper and Massell, 1965), but in general they tend to hold. It is, furthermore, possible to identify the conditions that will maximize trade creation and minimize trade diversion, ultimately leading to a successful economic bloc.

The first set of conditions is the degree of overlap in the economies of the countries contemplating the formation of an economic bloc. The greater the overlap between the economies, the greater the likelihood that the bloc will be a trade-creating one in terms of both inter-industry trade and intra-industry trade. It has been suggested that the growth in trade is likely to be of the intra-industry variety (Verdoorn, 1960). If economies do not overlap, as in the case when an agricultural producing country joins a mainly manufacturing country, then there is little scope for trade creation but a great deal for trade diversion.

The second group of conditions relates to the differences in production costs between the potential members in their overlapping industries. The greater the difference in these costs, the greater the potential for trade creation. Conversely, if the differences in costs are small, so too will be the gains.

The third set of conditions concerns the height of tariff rates prior to the amalgamation of the economies. The higher they are, the greater the gains from the associated tariff reductions. Hence, the greatest gains from the formation of an economic bloc can be achieved if:

1. the economic structure of the economies overlaps;
2. the industries that are common to both have a wide variation in their costs;
3. the tariffs placed on imports by these countries on one another's goods are high prior to the formation of the bloc.

5.3.2 Dynamic factors and economic integration

Dynamic models relating to the process of regional economic integration do not give rise to one-off benefits but rather accumulate them through time, thus adding to the static benefits. Some economists have argued that these dynamic factors are more important than those discussed in static models (Yeung et al., 1999).

The first dynamic effect to consider is the increased competition that emanates from the formation of an economic bloc. This is often seen as acting as a spur to greater efficiency by the participant industries. Stripped of their protection, to survive domestic firms have to find more efficient production methods, which will in turn have the effect of lowering costs (Jacquemin, 1982).

The second dynamic factor is the impact that a larger market may have on the investment and output decisions of firms. The abolition of trade barriers means that the 'domestic' market has been expanded. As each firm expands its output to meet the new demand, it is able to reap the benefits of economies of scale. If the bloc allows not only the free movement of goods and services, but also the free movement of capital and labour, then these factors will gravitate to where their returns are highest, thus increasing overall productivity.

5.3.3 The enhancement of economic and political power and credibility

While it is true to say that the economic integration of one economy with another, along with the adoption of common trade or economic policies, sharply reduces the individual economic sovereignty of the member states, it is also true to say that collective economic sovereignty is increased. As a result, small or medium-sized states may find it beneficial to join or form economic blocs. For example, the combined power of the bloc might enable the member countries to achieve objectives, say in trade negotiations, which would have been impossible had they tried to do so individually (Mundell, 1964).

A phenomenon that has emerged recently is the attempt by some countries to join a regional grouping when it would seem that their economies are not compatible (i.e. do not overlap) with those of existing member states. Usually this has been justified by the dynamic benefits to be gained from closer integration. It can also represent an attempt to gain credibility for domestic economic policies or political reforms recently undertaken. While the importance of the potential trade gains should not be overlooked, this was a major motivation for Mexico's willingness to enter into the North American Free Trade Agreement (Gerber and Kerr, 1995; Pugel, 2007).

In the European context the application and subsequent entry of Greece, Portugal and Spain to the European Union were as much an attempt to secure democracy in those countries as they were to gain the benefits of economic integration. The more recent application of Turkey can also be viewed as one to gain credibility for its political structures and its new 'liberal' economic policies. In a similar fashion, the desire of some of the former communist states in Central Europe to join the EU was, in part, driven by fears that their economic moves toward becoming market economies may have been eroded and that their democratic institutions were not secure.

5.4 Regional economic blocs

To understand the operation and the problems associated with the development of economic blocs it is essential to examine some of those that currently exist. We begin by examining the development of economic integration in Europe. We then look at the situation in the Western Hemisphere and the Pacific Rim. Finally we can make some general comments on economic blocs in the rest of the world.

5.4.1 Europe

In Europe there has been a long evolutionary process since the Second World War, which first saw the establishment of competing economic groupings, followed by a long process whereby one of those groupings, the European Union, expanded and grew until it included almost the entire continent. At the start of the twenty-first century, there were 15 countries in the EU. Twelve new countries joined in the new century's first decade, leaving only Norway and Switzerland that voted not to join. Other than Slovenia, the countries in the Balkans that were part of the former Yugoslavia, plus Albania, have not yet qualified for membership. Turkey has applied to join. The original competing economic groupings, the European Free Trade Area (EFTA) and the former Council for Mutual Economic Assistance (CMEA), which was also known as COMECON, have had the majority of their members join the EU. Norway and Switzerland enjoy most of the trade benefits provided by the EU even though as non-members they are not party to the EU's decision-making process.

In Western Europe, post-Second World War economic cooperation began with the establishment of the Organisation for European Economic Co-operation (OEEC) in 1948. It was a body designed to administer US **Marshall Plan** aid on a Europe-wide basis and to ensure that scarce resources were not squandered. This body eventually evolved into the present-day Organisation for Economic Co-operation and Development (OECD).

Another aspect of the integration process began with the attempt by Belgium, France, West Germany, Italy, the Netherlands and Luxembourg to revitalize the European coal and steel industries so as to become internationally competitive. In 1952 these countries decided to establish the European Coal and Steel Community. Essentially, its aim was to create a free trade area in coal and steel. The success of this institution led these six countries to propose extending the community to cover other goods, principally manufactures and agricultural products, and to deepen their relationship by forming a customs union.

Economic matters were not the only determinant of integration. Political issues also played their part. There was a general consensus that European countries should not go to war again. The devastation of two world wars had caused enough economic and political turmoil, and it was felt that it should not happen again. This was particularly keenly felt in France, which had fought three wars with Germany since the 1870s. It was believed that, by integrating the European economies closely, the possibility of a future war would be greatly diminished. While this argument galvanized much of the thinking behind the formation of the European Economic Community (EEC), political factors also contributed to the formation of separate economic blocs, namely EFTA and CMEA. The countries that made up EFTA either did not like the political implications of close economic ties or were debarred from joining on political grounds, while those that made up the latter grouping were suspicious and ideologically opposed to the EEC.

The EEC was established with the signing of the Treaty of Rome in 1957 and was originally composed of West Germany, France, Italy, the Netherlands, Belgium and Luxembourg – sometimes called 'the six'. The principal trade provisions of the treaty were as follows:

1. to establish a free trade area with the elimination of tariffs and quantitative restrictions, such as quotas, on goods;
2. to form a customs union by adopting a common external tariff that would be imposed on non-member countries with some exceptions such as former colonies;
3. to engender a common market by removing barriers to the free movement of capital and labour;
4. to devise a common agricultural policy that would coordinate farm policies among the member states and regulate agricultural trade with non-member states.

The history of what was to become of the EU up to the mid-1980s is really one of the implementation and consolidation of these provisions. In the 1970s 'the six' were expanded by the accession of the United Kingdom,

Denmark and Ireland. The so-called southern enlargement began in 1981 with Greece, a former associate member, achieving full status and was completed in 1986 with the entry of Spain and Portugal. As a result of these additions, 'the six' became 12.

Meanwhile, the European Free Trade Area was established in 1960 from the Western European countries that either did not want or could not join the then EEC. Austria, Finland, Sweden and Switzerland believed that to join the EEC, which was made up of NATO countries, would compromise their neutral status. The UK was also in a dilemma. Since the 1930s, British trade policy had been based on Imperial Preference – relatively open access to products from its former colonies – and these ties and guaranteed markets would be threatened if it jointed the EEC. It was also suspicious of the closer political links and loss of sovereignty that membership implied. Denmark too had reservations on this point. It also feared losing the British markets for its goods if it joined the EEC and the UK failed to join. Spain and Portugal could not join, as they had totalitarian governments. A country has to have a democratic government before it can join the EU. Forming a free trade area was, therefore, a way by which the benefits of closer economic integration could be achieved but without the closer political ties, which would compromise neutrality and existing commercial policies.

Seeing the success of the EEC, however, the UK joined in 1972, followed by Denmark. The remaining EFTA countries realized that they had to come to some agreement with the EEC or suffer the consequences of trade diversion. A number of bilateral arrangements were negotiated which were aimed at abolishing tariffs on industrial goods by 1977. The process of tariff removal was not, however, completed until 1983.

With better access to a much larger market, EFTA gained more than the EEC from these agreements. While on the surface trade seemed free between the two groups, many barriers to trade remained (Herin, 1986).

The close trading links between the EU and EFTA made it inevitable that an even greater degree of economic integration would be sought by the participants. Discussions began in 1984 concerning the difficulties that had arisen between the two blocs regarding rules of origin and the closer coordination of policies that affected trade. Areas covered included road and rail links, customs documentation, and state aid to industries, to name but a few.

In the EU there was, however, considerable dissatisfaction with low growth rates, which were blamed on internal factors. As a result, the member countries decided to embark on a further attempt to eliminate internal trade barriers and form a true common market (Commission of the European Communities, 1985). While it is likely that external factors, such as the lower rate of growth of the world economy, played their part, the continued existence of hundreds of restrictions on the free movement of goods, services, capital and labour was largely held responsible for the bloc's economic performance. For example, the continued border restrictions requiring the presentation of customs documentation at frontiers caused delays, which increased the cost of transportation and raised the price of goods. Other examples that hindered the functioning of the common market were the mutual non-recognition of employees' qualifications, which impeded the movement of labour, and various restrictions on the movement of capital – the latter were particularly relevant in France, Italy, Greece, Portugal and Spain. The activities of service industries such as banking and insurance were impeded by a whole host of national regulations. Differing health and safety standards and practices also played their part in raising costs and impeding trade (Cecchini, 1988).

Spurred on by estimates that the abolition of the remaining barriers to trade would lead to an increase in growth of between 4 and 7 per cent, the member states agreed to set a timetable for their elimination starting in 1987. This became known as the 1992 programme, which was to be completed by 31 December of that year.

The main trade impediments were dealt with by opening up government procurement to competitive tendering, and mutually recognizing one another's health and safety standards, as well as employee qualifications. New customs documentation and practices were also enforced, which cut out waiting time at the borders. Regulations covering service industries were harmonized. More problematical was the harmonization of taxation. The continued existence of variations in sales taxes and excise duties has led to some **false border trade**. This is particularly true in the area of alcoholic beverages between the UK and France and petrol between Belgium, the Netherlands, Germany and France, where national taxes vary. Despite these discrepancies, their adverse impact is considered to be small.

The 1992 programme was looked upon by some of the EU's trading partners, in particular the US and Japan, with some suspicion. The process is sometimes characterized as a move towards developing a 'Fortress Europe'. The main concern was that as the EU reduced its internal barriers it would increase its external barriers (Brainard and Perry, 1989). What led to such a view? The principal evidence put forward was:

1. The EU's insistence that foreign producers should 'monitor' their exports in some sensitive industries for an undefined limited period after 1992 (e.g. US television programmes, Japanese cars, etc.).
2. The requirement that foreign companies setting up plants in the EU should guarantee a local input content of 60–80 per cent.
3. The adoption of the so-called 'new trade policy instrument', which allowed individual firms to appeal directly to the EU for the imposition of measures to counter unfair trade. Prior to this, firms had to appeal to their governments, which were considered to be less willing than the EU to take up their case.
4. The tightening of the EU's anti-dumping measures.

This evidence, coupled with the general thrust of EU industrial policy which supported the electronic, aircraft and computer sectors and its resistance to liberalization in cinematic products and agricultural commodities, confirmed many of the misgivings held by its trading partners.

There was another view of the 1992 programme that ran contrary to the protectionist interpretation. This suggested that the boost to economic growth, particularly in the long run, would benefit foreign companies just as much as those of the EU. The uniformity in EU regulations would give all companies, not just domestic firms, cost advantages. Ease of transportation would allow firms, whether they were foreign or from the EU, to establish optimum-sized plants in the most cost-effective locations.

This contrary view also suggested that becoming protectionist would not be in the EU's interests, as it relied very heavily on exports and inward investment. The EU as a whole provided 25 per cent of the world's exports. These exports accounted for 15 per cent of its GDP. The EU also received 40 per cent of all the direct investment carried out by the developed countries.

Which view is correct is, of course, a moot point and depends on the position from which one views the process. The 1992 process encouraged further internal growth – trade creation – and inevitably led to some further trade diversion. This had an adverse effect on some companies that exported directly to the EU but little on those that had subsidiaries operating within it. Certainly, a number of the EU's trading partners' companies viewed the 1992 programme with suspicion and began to form joint ventures with EU companies, for example Saab–Renault.

The onset of the 1992 single market programme in the EU was also a spur to the EFTA countries to seek a further accommodation with the EU (Norman,

1989). The EU agreed to extend the programme to include the EFTA countries, and the European Economic Area (EEA) came into being on 1 January 1994. The EEA stretches from the Arctic to the Mediterranean and was, at the time, the largest economic bloc in the world. Not all the EFTA members are participants. Austria, Finland, Iceland, Norway and Sweden decided to join, while Liechtenstein and Switzerland remained outside.

While the EEA was a major move towards European integration, Austria, Finland, Norway and Sweden saw it as a step on the road to becoming full members of the EU. The political changes in Europe since the collapse of communism rendered their neutral position unnecessary, while not being able to participate fully in the decision-making bodies of its principal market placed them at a disadvantage. Norway's citizens, in the end, chose not to have their country join. Austria, Finland and Sweden joined the EU as full members in 1995, and the EU-12 became the EU-15.

The former Council for Mutual Economic Assistance was composed of all those European states that made up the former Soviet bloc (and included in later years Cuba, Mongolia and Vietnam). It was principally established to coordinate trade amongst these countries and to reap the benefits from harmonizing its member states' national central plans (Considine and Kerr, 2002).

The concentration on heavy industry by **command economies** and the pricing of goods with very little regard to their cost of production led to a pattern of trade that did not adhere to the principles of comparative advantage. By the mid-1980s, it became evident to the majority of participants that something was wrong with the workings of the CMEA (Smith, 1992). Certainly, the hegemonic Soviet Union believed that it was subsidizing the other members and demanded payment for its products in convertible currencies, principally US dollars.

The collapse of the Soviet Union at the end of the 1980s led to the collapse of the CMEA and the emergence of free Central and Eastern European states that wished to participate in the world economy. In particular, they wanted closer trade relations with the EU. As many of their industries were based on obsolete technology, it was unlikely that they would have been able to compete with those of the EU if they were opened up to full competition. The EU suggested that the former command economies first join an institution like EEA as a halfway house before applying for full EU membership. After a decade and a half spent making the difficult transition from economies based on central planning and command to ones based largely on market incentives

(Hobbs et al., 1997), Poland, Hungary, the Czech Republic, Slovakia, Slovenia, Estonia, Lithuania, Latvia, Bulgaria and Romania have acceded to the EU. Malta and Cyprus also joined the EU, bringing its membership up to 27 countries. Negotiating the terms of accession was a difficult process (Gaisford et al., 2003).

In addition to expanding, the EU has also continued the deepening of economic integration so that it becomes a true economic union – the **Maastricht** process. The next major step along the road to economic integration was the establishment of a common currency for EU members and along with it a European central bank. This was accomplished in early 1999 with the launch of the *euro*. The loss of economic sovereignty associated with abandoning a national currency and, more important, the ability to control domestic interest rates through a national central bank was considered unacceptable by the UK and Sweden, which decided not to adopt the euro and so remain outside the *euro area*. For a number of other EU countries, the transition from national currencies to the euro has been relatively painless, and firms in the euro area have reaped considerable benefits from reduced currency conversion fees and the removal of the risks associated with fluctuating exchange rates. A number of the more recent countries acceding to the EU have yet to qualify for membership in the euro. In the wake of the 2008 financial crisis, the euro has been under considerable pressure, as countries in difficult fiscal positions are denied to option of devaluing a national currency (Kerr, 2012). This pressure has led to the establishment of new institutions among euro zone members and an expanded role and powers for the European Central Bank.

The elaborate legal structures that bind the EU together give plenty of scope for conflicts to arise between the member states regarding the interpretation of EU legislation. To provide a framework for defusing conflicts, the European Court was established. Countries, individuals, firms and institutions can apply to this court for a ruling regarding the actions of other countries or individuals and companies. Most disputes of a trade nature are resolved between the states before the Court is brought into the picture.

5.4.2 The Western Hemisphere

As previously mentioned, the original catalyst for economic integration in North America was the series of discussions between the US and Canada regarding trade in automobile parts and components. The experience gained in those negotiations led to the eventual signing of a free trade agreement between these two countries that came into effect on 1 January 1989.

The Canada–US Trade Agreement

The Canada–US Trade Agreement (CUSTA) brought into existence a market of approximately 272 million people. These two countries were already the world's largest trading partners and enjoyed zero or low tariffs on most goods. Sectoral trade agreements governed some other sectors. The agreement nevertheless envisaged the elimination, over a period of ten years, of the remaining restrictions and the opening up of Canada to US direct investment (Schott, 1988). To iron out difficulties that might arise in the operation of the agreement, very elaborate dispute settlement procedures were established (Apuzzo and Kerr, 1988).

The North American Free Trade Agreement

In 1991 negotiations on a North American Free Trade Agreement (NAFTA) began, which were aimed at creating a market of 364 million people. NAFTA is a series of bilateral agreements between Canada, the US and Mexico building upon the CUSTA framework. The Mexican government believed that by integrating its economy with that of its northern neighbour it would gain not only economically but also politically. The mutual reduction in trade barriers would lead, given Mexico's comparative advantage, to an inflow of direct investment. The products that would be produced by these factories could then be exported duty free back into the US and Canada. This process would promote Mexican economic growth.

The benefits that were assumed to accrue to Mexico have, however, created problems for labour-intensive industries in the US. Over time, a number of industries have taken advantage of Mexican 'free trade zones' or '**maquiladoras**' and have moved some of their operations south of the border. The potential losers are expected to be those working in the auto parts, furniture, glass and seafood industries, as well as producers of agricultural produce, particularly citrus fruits and vegetables. As in the CUSTA, in order to settle the inevitable conflicts that are likely to arise, elaborate trade dispute procedures have been created.

Despite the inevitable losers that arise from trade liberalization on a regional basis, the NAFTA has been a significant success. All three countries have seen considerable economic integration and a realigning of trade flows on a north–south axis. While trade irritants remain, particularly relating to US anti-dumping and 'unfair' subsidy procedures, NAFTA has removed most of the barriers to trade among the three countries (Clement et al., 1999). Unlike the EU, however, the NAFTA has no mechanism whereby the economic bloc can be reformulated to facilitate the process of deepening economic integration. As a result, the NAFTA looks increasingly like a 'one-shot deal' which lacks dynamism. Wider hemispheric initiatives may provide the institutional structure for deepening economic integration of the NAFTA countries (Kerr, 2002a).

Other countries in the Western Hemisphere

The creation of NAFTA has had a dynamic effect on the area's trading partners in both the rest of Latin America and the Caribbean. There were a number of initiatives in the past to promote integration and free trade in Latin America, but they have usually not been very successful. The reasons are many but very broadly are concerned with conflicting economic ideologies and disagreements regarding the distribution of the benefits among participating countries. In particular, the course of import substitution industrialization – high tariffs to foster domestic industries – followed by many of the countries in the region was the antithesis of regional cooperation (Clement et al., 1999)

In South America, the Latin American Free Trade Area formed in 1961 largely foundered because the member states continued to pursue import substitution policies. Its replacement, the Latin American Integration Association established in 1980, also suffered from this problem. Realizing that they needed to revitalize their economies by opening them up to greater international competition, two new regional groupings were formed to encourage, as a first step, regional free trade. These are the Andean Common Market (ANCOM), comprising Bolivia, Colombia, Ecuador, Peru and Venezuela, and MERCOSUR, which is made up of Argentina, Brazil, Paraguay and Uruguay. In 2012, Venezuela became a member of MERCOSUR. The latter organization, in particular, initially had considerable success and began to look like the nucleus of a regional economic powerhouse similar to that of the EU in Europe. This momentum could not be sustained, however, because the economies of individual member states suffered considerable setbacks, Argentina in particular at the end of the twentieth century. Changes in governments of MERCOSUR members have also weakened support for free trade among the bloc members.

Initiatives attempting to foster integration have also taken place in Central America with the establishment of the Central American Common Market (CACM) and the Caribbean Community and Common Market (CARICO). The former, while successful in reducing trade restrictions amongst its members, has suffered from not only political conflicts in the area but disagreements between the states regarding the distribution of the benefits from trade liberalization. The latter grouping has had difficulties in trying to integrate the diverse and dispersed set of island economies that make up its membership.

The emergence of NAFTA led to some fears in Latin America regarding their future growth of exports to the US, because their competitor Mexico had preferential access to the US market. The Central American nations and the Caribbean economies in particular have been affected by the loss of preferential status for exports that existed prior to NAFTA under the US Caribbean Basin Initiative. The US Enterprise for the Americas Initiative (EAI) was designed to alleviate some of these effects by extending incentives to those countries that encouraged capitalist development and trade liberalization.

In a major initiative, all of the countries in the Western Hemisphere except Cuba agreed to negotiate the establishment of a hemispheric-wide Free Trade Area of the Americas (FTAA). Negotiations had a target date of 2005 for their conclusion, but most countries see that this was unrealistically optimistic. It was certainly a bold vision that could capture the imagination of political leaders in region. Looking past its political vision, the FTAA was the most ambitious regional trade undertaking ever attempted. It encompassed 34 countries – the multilateral GATT negotiations in 1947 had only 23 signatories. When the GATT came into being on 1 January 1948, there were only ten countries that had ratified the agreement (Kerr, 2002b). The EU started with only six countries and over its long life has grown to encompass only 27 countries. The NAFTA has grown from two to only three members.

The potential membership of the FTAA also encompassed an extremely wide range of economies. Arguably, it includes the world's best long-run economic performer, the United States, and one of its worst (if not the worst), Haiti. It includes only two members of the G10 and three members of the OECD. It included countries whose economic performance has been sluggish for decades and countries whose performance plots like the plan for a roller coaster. It included economic giants like Brazil and the United States and a large group of what are classed as 'small island economies' in the Caribbean. While the benefits of preferred access to the US market were obvious, a number of countries, particularly Brazil, worried about US domination of the FTAA. As a result, the negotiation of a meaningful hemispheric agreement has not progressed, and it is no longer taken seriously as a potential trade bloc.

5.4.3 Economic regionalism and the Pacific Rim

The rapid growth of trade between the countries bordering the Pacific Ocean has led to growing interest in the formalization of economic relationships. These ideas are not new, with Japan having suggested a **Greater East Asia Co-Prosperity Sphere** before the Second World War. In the late 1960s, the Association of Southeast Asian Nations (ASEAN) was formed largely to counter a perceived communist threat. Its initial members were Malaysia, Thailand, Indonesia, the Philippines, Singapore and Brunei. By the late 1970s an economic dimension to this organization was developed largely based on cooperative activities amongst the states and preferential trading arrangements (Suriyamongkol, 1988). ASEAN began to attract additional members near the end of the twentieth century – Vietnam, Laos and Cambodia.

By the late 1980s or early 1990s it had become evident to the majority of Pacific Rim states that the growth of the EU and the development of NAFTA required a more formal response. This took place in 1989 with the formation of the Asia-Pacific Economic Cooperation forum (APEC), which was made up of the six ASEAN nations plus Australia, Canada, Japan, New Zealand, South Korea and the US. The group was enlarged in 1991 to include China, Hong Kong and Taiwan. The new ASEAN members along with Mexico and Chile joined in subsequent years.

The main principle of APEC is the stimulation of the area's economic growth through the promotion of regional trade. Currently, it has concentrated on the removal of trade barriers and the establishment of dispute settlement mechanisms. In other words, it has concentrated on areas which do not necessarily damage the interest of nations or blocs outside the area (Kirkpatrick, 1994). A permanent secretariat has been established in Singapore to coordinate the activities of the several working parties established to examine areas of mutual interest.

Worries over Japanese and latterly Chinese hegemony in the region have prevented a true regional bloc from arising (Yeung et al., 1999). While many countries of the region exhibited stellar economic performance in the 1970s, 1980s and first half of the 1990s, there was a major Asian economic crisis in 1997. As suggested above, it becomes much more difficult to find enthusiasm for liberalization initiatives in times of economic hardship. The Asian economic crisis set back further serious regional initiatives for a decade. Further, China joined the WTO in 2001, which set in motion a sea of changes whereby China's economy had to be absorbed into the global economy. This put the entire region into considerable disequilibrium, as existing trade relations between Asian economies and the US and the EU were altered. This made the negotiation of regional trade agreements difficult, because future patterns of trade could not be easily discerned. The other major change in Asia has been India's movement from being a largely closed economy to one which is much more open (Perdikis, 2000). India has negotiated limited trade agreements with regional trade partners since it has begun its transformation into a more open economy. Long-standing political problems between India and Pakistan will probably prevent further economic integration in the region.

5.4.4 Economic blocs in the rest of the world

Having covered Europe, the Americas and the Asian–Pacific area we are left with Africa and the Middle East. In Africa there have been some limited successes such as the Economic Community of West African States (ECOWAS) and the East African Common Market. Low incomes and disputes once again concerning the distribution of the benefits, coupled with largely protectionist national policies, have not led to much success in trade expansion. There was also an initiative in the first decade of the twenty-first century to revitalize the regional trade agreement in East Africa – Kenya, Uganda and Tanzania – with mixed results (Kimbugwe et al., 2012). As with Africa, in the Middle East many of the original initiatives to foster greater regional economic cooperation have not been fruitful (Fischer, 1992). In the twenty-first century thus far, the major military conflicts in the region have inhibited trade and potential attempts at regional agreements. One exception has been the Gulf Cooperation Council (GCC), which was established largely for political and strategic reasons but has achieved with some success a measure of economic integration amongst the member states of Kuwait, Oman, Qatar, Saudi Arabia and the United Arab Emirates. Even here, however, with their limited economic base the benefits of trade creation must be regarded as small.

5.4.5 A major policy change in the United States and EU initiatives

From 1947 and the formation of the GATT until the close of the twentieth century near the end of the Clinton administration, the US had largely eschewed regional trade agreements in favour of multilateralism (Kerr, 2005). The basic US position was: 'If you want better access to the US market, join the GATT and work through its trade liberalization negotiations.' The NAFTA was a clear exception, but virtually the only one – the US did also have a trade agreement with Israel. The US position was a great boost for the multilateral GATT process. With the change of policy, the US moved to a three-tracked policy based on bilateral, regional and multilateral initiatives. As a result, there was a flurry of bilateral and regional activity as countries sought better than GATT access to the US market (Kerr, 2005). The US negotiated agreements with Australia, the Dominican Republic and a group of Central American countries, Chile, Singapore, Morocco, Jordan and Bahrain among others. In 2012 a major agreement with South Korea came into being. A major new US initiative, the Trans-Pacific Partnership, was under way in 2012, with Australia, Brunei, Canada, Chile, Malaysia, Mexico, New Zealand, Peru, Singapore and Vietnam being part of the negotiations. The US move to bilateral and regional initiatives has allowed the US to take advantage of its relative economic power in the negotiations, something that was somewhat muted in multilateral venues (Kerr and Hobbs, 2006).

In part as a response to the US seeking bilateral and regional trade agreements, the EU's interest in preferential trade arrangements was revitalized. In 2012 the EU reached an agreement with South Korea. It began negotiations with Canada in 2009 over a Comprehensive Economic and Trade Agreement – negotiations were still ongoing in 2014 (Viju and Kerr, 2011). In the wake of India's unilateral decision to begin the process of integrating its economy into the global market (Kerr et al., 2000), the EU has opened negotiations with India. The proposed EU–India agreement has the potential to reap global-scale benefits from the exploitation of economies of scale (Khorana et al., 2010). In 2013, in what could be the most important preferential agreement yet, the EU and the US began negotiations on the Transatlantic Trade and Investment Partnership (TTIP).

5.5 Economic blocs and the nation state

Despite the growth of regional institutions, international economic relations are still very much in the purview of the nation state. The degree of openness of the international economic system depends very much on how the nation state perceives its interests. Nation states juggling a number of possibly conflicting goals may not wish to pursue a policy of unilateral free trade (Gaisford and Hester, 2007). Nation states, furthermore, exist in a world of nation states where power is not distributed equally amongst them and where freedom of action may well be constrained in the area of trade policy. The openness, or otherwise, of the world trading system has depended very much on how the leading trading nations view their interests.

In conducting international economic relations, a state can select either a bilateral or a multilateral basis on which to pursue its aims. Most choose to use a combination of the two. The fragility of the set of alliances and treaties that formed the basis of trade before the Second World War was fully exposed during the depression of the 1930s. As a result, the architects of the post-Second World War economic order set the basis for trade on a multilateral footing.

One area where bilateral negotiations and agreements have dominated is in the formation of regional trade associations. As a result of the long-term success of the EU there has been a rapid expansion in the number of regional trade associations. Whether they will lead to the further expansion of world trade or whether they will begin to actively compete and lead to its contraction is not yet clear (de Melo and Panagariya, 1992; Pugel, 2007). Currently, all the groupings that have taken place have been trade creating in that they have not sought to impose tariffs that are higher than those that applied prior to their formation. Time will tell.

 REFERENCES

Apuzzo, A.M. and Kerr, W.A. (1988) International arbitration – the dispute settlement procedures chosen for the Canada–U.S. Free Trade Agreement. *Journal of International Arbitration*, 5(4), 7–15.

Brada, J.C. and Méndez, J.A. (1993) Political and economic factors in regional economic integration. *Kyklos*, 46, 183–201.

Brainard, W.C. and Perry, G.L. (eds) (1989) *Brookings Papers on Economic Activity*, No. 2, Brookings Institution, Washington, DC.

Cecchini, P. (1988) *The Costs of Non-Europe*, Wildwood House, London.

Clement, N.C., Castillo Vera, G. del, Gerber, J., Kerr, W.A., MacFadyen, A.J., Shedd, S., Zepeda, E. and Alarcon, D. (1999) *North American Economic Integration: Theory and Practice*, Edward Elgar Publishing, Cheltenham, UK and Northampton, MA, USA.

Commission of the European Communities (1985) *Completing the Internal Market: White Paper*, Office for Official Publications of the European Communities, Luxembourg.

Considine, J.I. and Kerr, W.A. (2002) *The Russian Oil Economy*, Edward Elgar Publishing, Cheltenham, UK and Northampton, MA, USA.

Cooper, R.N. and Massell, B.F. (1965) A new look at customs union theory. *Economic Journal*, 75, 742–7.

Fischer, S. (1992) Prospects for integration in the Middle East, paper presented to the World Bank and CEPR conference on New Dimensions in Regional Integration, Washington, DC.

Gaisford, J.D. and Hester, A. (2007) Why are there trade agreements?, in *Handbook on International Trade Policy*, ed. W.A. Kerr and J.D. Gaisford, Edward Elgar Publishing, Cheltenham, UK and Northampton, MA, USA, pp. 57–70.

Gaisford, J.D., Kerr, W.A. and Perdikis, N. (2003) *Economic Analysis for EU Accession Negotiations*, Edward Elgar Publishing, Cheltenham, UK and Northampton, MA, USA.

Gerber, J. and Kerr, W.A. (1995) Trade as an agency of social policy: NAFTA's schizophrenic role in agriculture, in *NAFTA in Transition*, ed. S.J. Randal and H.W. Konrad, University of Calgary Press, Calgary, pp. 93–111.

Herin, J. (1986) *Rules of Origin and Differences between Tariff Levels in EFTA and the EEC*, EFTA Occasional Paper No. 3, EFTA, Geneva.

Hobbs, J.E., Kerr, W.A. and Gaisford, J.D. (1997) *Transformation of the Agrifood System in Central and Eastern Europe and the New Independent States*, CAB International, Wallingford.

Jacquemin, A. (1982) Imperfect market structure and international trade – some recent research. *Kyklos*, 35, 75–93.

Kerr, W.A. (2002a) NAFTA and beyond: Challenges for extending free trade in the hemisphere. *Journal of International Law and Trade Policy*, 3(2), 224–38, www.esteyjournal.com.

Kerr, W.A. (2002b) A club no more – the WTO after Doha. *Journal of International Law and Trade Policy*, 3(1), 1–9, www.esteyjournal.com.

Kerr, W.A. (2005) Vested interests in queuing and the loss of the WTO's club good: The long-run costs of US bilateralism. *Journal of International Law and Trade Policy*, 6(1), 1–10.

Kerr, W.A. (2012) Strategic devaluation, trade and political convenience. *Journal of International Law and Trade Policy*, 13(1), 1–13.

Kerr, W.A. and Hobbs, J.E. (2006) Bilateralism – a radical shift in US trade policy: What will it mean for agricultural trade? *Journal of World Trade*, 40(6), 1049–58.

Kerr, W.A., Perdikis, N. and Hobbs, J.E. (2000) NAFTA and the 'New India', in *The Indian Economy: Contemporary Issues*, ed. N. Perdikis, Ashgate, Aldershot, pp. 37–57.

Khorana, S., Perdikis, N., Yeung, M.T. and Kerr, W.A. (2010) *Bilateral Trade Agreements in the Era of Globalization*, Edward Elgar Publishing, Cheltenham, UK and Northampton, MA, USA.

Kimbugwe, K., Perdikis, N., Yeung, M.T. and Kerr, W.A. (2012) *Economic Development through Regional Trade*, Palgrave Macmillan, London.

Kirkpatrick, C. (1994) Regionalisation, regionalism and East Asian economic co-operation. *World Economy*, 17, 191–202.

Melo, J. de and Panagariya, A. (1992) *The New Regionalism in Trade Policy*, World Bank/CEPR, Washington, DC.

Mundell, R.A. (1964) Tariff preferences and the terms of trade. *Manchester School of Economic and Social Studies*, 32, 1–13.

Norman, V. (1989) *EFTA and the Internal European Market Economic Policy: A European Forum*, EFTA Occasional Paper No.20, EFTA, Geneva.

Perdikis, N. (ed.) (2000) *The Indian Economy: Contemporary Issues*, Ashgate, Aldershot.

Perdikis, N. (2007) Trade agreements: Depth of integration, in *Handbook on International Trade Policy*, ed. W.A. Kerr and J.D. Gaisford, Edward Elgar Publishing, Cheltenham, UK and Northampton, MA, USA, pp. 106–19.

Phillips, P.W.B. (2007) The breadth of integration arising from trade agreements, in *Handbook on International Trade Policy*, ed. W.A. Kerr and J.D. Gaisford, Edward Elgar Publishing, Cheltenham, UK and Northampton, MA, USA, pp. 94–105.

Pugel, T.A. (2007) *International Economics*, 13th edn, McGraw-Hill, Boston, MA.

Schott, J. (1988) *United States–Canada Free Trade: An Evaluation of the Agreement*, Institute for International Economics, Washington, DC.

Smith, A.H. (1992) Integration under communism and economic relations after communism in Eastern Europe, in *The European Economy*, ed. D. Dyker, Longman, London.

Suriyamongkol, M.L. (1988) *The Politics of ASEAN Economic Co-operation*, Oxford University Press, Oxford.

Verdoorn, P. (1960) The intra-block trade of Benelux, in *Economic Consequences of the Size of Nations*, ed. E.A.G. Robinson, Macmillan, London.

Viju, C. and Kerr, W.A. (2011) Agriculture in the Canada–EU Economic and Trade Agreement. *International Journal*, 76(3), 677–94.

Viner, J. (1950) *The Customs Union Issue*, Carnegie Endowment for International Peace, New York.

Yeung, M.T., Perdikis, N. and Kerr, W.A. (1999) *Regional Trading Blocs in the Global Economy: The EU and ASEAN*, Edward Elgar Publishing, Cheltenham, UK and Northampton, MA, USA.

6

Institutions of the multilateral trading system

6.1 The basis of the multilateral system

Unfortunately, the world of international commerce is not governed by one set of rules by which the movement of goods between countries is to be conducted. Irrespective of the country in which it operates, a business that is involved in international commerce will deal with a wide variety of regulatory regimes. These sets of rules will vary both with the individual countries with which business is being conducted and with the commodity traded. Making the investment in acquiring a good working knowledge of this myriad of rules and regulations can be very important for the development of business strategies. If they are understood and used strategically, they can enhance a firm's competitive advantage and, under the right conditions, simultaneously reduce the competitive position of one's rivals. Firms operating in the international sphere may also find it to their advantage to provide input into the process by which their government formulates both the domestic legislation governing the conduct of international business and the strategies to be used in trade negotiations with other countries. Hence, it is important for business people to understand both how the institutions operate and the array of trade regulations which one is likely to be faced with when undertaking commercial relations across international boundaries.

No multinational organization exists which is comprehensive in its coverage of international trade matters or to which all countries belong. An attempt to negotiate a comprehensive International Trade Organization was made at the end of the Second World War. No agreement could be reached except on a limited subset of trade matters that had been negotiated in the *General Agreement on Tariffs and Trade* (GATT), and a comprehensive organization was stillborn (Kerr, 2000; Josling, 2007). The GATT, by default, subsequently became the principal multilateral organization regulating trade. A number of countries, for the most part current or former communist countries, chose to remain outside its structure. The GATT, however, had been negotiated in a period when much of the world was still colonized. While nations could join when they gained independence, there has been an ongoing general concern that the GATT has not adequately addressed the needs of these new, largely third world, nations. In 1965, the **United Nations Conference on Trade and Development (UNCTAD)** was organized to address problems of trade between developing and developed countries.

The GATT's original mandate was limited to trade in goods. In the absence of a more comprehensive international trade organization, nations attempted to extend the activities of the GATT to cover other areas of international commerce. International rules covering trade in services, protection of intellectual property, investment, and so on were required. As the GATT's organizational structure was not designed for this wider role, negotiations undertaken under the auspices of the GATT resulted in an agreement to establish a *World Trade Organization* (WTO) being reached in 1993. In 1995, the WTO came into being. It is the most comprehensive international trade organization to date, as it is responsible not only for trade in goods but also for trade in services and for the international protection of intellectual property rights. The GATT continues to operate under the wider WTO umbrella. The WTO and UNCTAD are the main multilateral trade organizations. Certainly, as discussed in Chapter 5, a large number of bilateral and regional trade organizations exist. Most of these, at least in theory, conform to the conventions of the WTO and/or UNCTAD.

6.2   The World Trade Organization

The agreement to establish the World Trade Organization was reached at the Uruguay Round (so called because the decision to undertake the negotiations was made in Uruguay) of GATT negotiations. Members of the GATT automatically became WTO members. The WTO is responsible for administering all of the agreements arising from the Uruguay Round.

Unlike the GATT, the WTO is a permanent organization. It is guided by a regularly scheduled conference of ministers from all WTO members. The day-to-day administration of the WTO is the responsibility of the General Council. The WTO's General Council acts as the body which both settles disputes between members and reviews, on a regular basis, the trade policies of members. At the conclusion of the Uruguay Round, as well as a new GATT agreement covering trade in goods, new agreements on trade in services – the General Agreement on Trade in Services (GATS) – and on the international protection of intellectual property – the Agreement on Trade-Related Aspects of Intellectual Property (TRIPS) – were reached.

The WTO is responsible for implementing these agreements. It coordinates the work of three institutions, the Goods Council, the Services Council and the Intellectual Property Council, which are charged with administering the three central agreements of the WTO.

The Goods Council oversees the functioning of the GATT – which deals with tariffs – and 12 other sub-agreements negotiated at the Uruguay Round which relate to specialized aspects of trade in goods. The Services Council oversees the GATS, and the Intellectual Property Council oversees the TRIPS agreement.

The WTO's trade policy review mechanism, whereby the trade regimes of individual countries are reviewed on a regular basis, keeps members informed of changes in each other's trade policies. It can also require governments to explain their trade policies. The dispute settlement procedures given to the WTO are much more effective than those that were administered previously by the GATT. Further, a common set of dispute procedures are used for trade in goods, for trade in services and for the protection of intellectual property.

The WTO is often a frustrating institution for business people, because it is seldom what one might expect it to be. This frustration and confusion arises primarily because one's normal frame of reference is national institutions whose regulations are backed by the force of law. Those who break domestic laws of commerce similar to those that the WTO oversees internationally are punished by the courts and compensation is often provided to the injured party. On the surface, the WTO appears to act as both the regulator and, through its dispute resolution mechanisms, the adjudicator of international commercial relations between nations. There is, however, no supranational legal authority, and the WTO must rely on the voluntary compliance of its members, encouraged by the weight of international moral pressure. It is probably most useful to think of the WTO as an additional 'special interest' which must be considered by domestic politicians when they weigh trade issues. When a WTO member's domestic economy is showing solid growth and when trade tensions are low, the WTO's influence will grow. On the other hand, when a domestic economy falters and when trade tensions are high, WTO concerns will receive less weight.

The WTO is the only truly multilateral body which lays down agreed rules for the international trade in goods. Approximately 160 countries currently subscribe to it, and together they account for nearly 90 per cent of world trade. Russia was the last major economy to remain outside the WTO. After nearly 20 years of negotiation, Russia was able to accede to the WTO in 2012

(Kerr, 2012). The WTO's principal objective is to liberalize the international trade in goods and services and provide international protection for intellectual property. A secure environment under which international commercial activities can be conducted is its underlying mission. It provides a set of rules by which contracting countries agree to conduct their trade relations.

Both the liberalization of international commerce and the ongoing development of rules for its regulation by governments have been accomplished through successive rounds of negotiations, first under the GATT and subsequently the WTO, which have become the buzz words of international trade – Annecy Round (1948), Torquay (1950–51), Dillon (1956, 1960–62), Kennedy (1964–67), Tokyo (1973–79) and Uruguay Round (1986–94). As the number of countries has expanded and the breadth of issues the negotiations have attempted to resolve increased, so have the lengths of the various rounds. Part of the problem arose because the GATT, as originally conceived, was only part of a package that was to have become a comprehensive international trade organization – that portion concerned with the reduction of tariffs. Until the agreement to establish the World Trade Organization, the GATT was forced to act in a much wider context than originally intended. In 2001 the WTO members agreed to a new Doha (sometimes Development) Round, which was optimistically scheduled for completion in 2005. The Doha Round has proved to be particularly acrimonious, with developing countries for the first time forcefully putting forth their agenda. As in the Uruguay Round, agriculture has proved an area where reaching an agreement is difficult, but there are a number of areas where significant differences among the members remain. An agreement requires consensus among WTO members. Negotiations were suspended in 2008 and were not formally reconvened until 2013. The global economic recession in the wake of the banking crisis in 2008 diverted the attention of countries and private sector stakeholders in the smooth functioning of international trade away from the pursuit of trade liberalization (Viju and Kerr, 2011). While the apparent failure of the Doha Round is seen as a crisis for the organization by some, the Uruguay Round negotiations were also characterized by 'fits and starts' and took seven years to complete. As a result, the Doha Round cannot be written off yet (Kerr, 2010; Brink, 2011). In any case, the WTO remains in place and the Uruguay Round agreements remain in force and constitute the multilateral rules of trade – it is business as usual. The failure to reach an agreement in the Doha Round is, however, probably damaging to the reputation of the organization and may reduce its efficacy.

The framers of the 'new world order' that arose in the wake of the Second World War believed in trade liberalization both philosophically and by observation. They could remember the relatively smooth-functioning system prior to the Great Depression and had observed first-hand the disastrous effects of the tariff wars of the 1930s. They set up the GATT with the single objective of removing trade barriers. At the time, there was considerable discussion of the so-called 'spirit of the GATT', whereby any disputes that did arise could be handled by rational diplomats according to economic principles (Kerr, 2000). Underlying the spirit of the GATT was a fundamental disdain for lawyers and a distrust of legalistic approaches to international rules of trade. In essence, the GATT was conceived as a club of around 25 diplomats from countries with similar philosophical-cultural backgrounds where 'things could be worked out'. Life for 'club members' was made easy, however, because they did not have to deal with countries having alternative economic systems. The communist countries were not interested in joining, and most of the developing world was still under colonial administration. Further, it was an era when governments played a much smaller role in their national economies than is common today (Kerr, 2002).

High tariffs had been erected in the beggar-thy-neighbour period of the 1930s, and these were still in place at the end of the Second World War. These high tariffs acted to obscure a plethora of potential trade problems that would become visible as tariffs declined over time. When tariffs are the major barrier to trade, countries can put a large number of policies and regulations in place that would be considered trade inhibiting in the absence of the tariffs. In other words, behind high-tariff walls countries can pursue domestically desirable policies without worrying about their trade effects.

Tariff reduction combined with **tariffication** is the major liberalizing mechanism for trade in goods used in the WTO. Tariffication is a process whereby alternative trade-restricting practices are converted into tariffs that provide an equivalent degree of protection. When trade restrictions are in the form of tariffs they can be directly compared because their relative values can be formally calculated. As they can be compared, negotiating their removal is simplified. A major WTO principle is that once a country agrees to lower its tariff rates they become 'bound' – cannot be raised – at that new level. The early rounds of GATT negotiations were very successful in reducing the high tariffs of the 1930s.

A second major principle of the WTO is non-discrimination. This means that tariff concessions given to any member must be extended to all members – the previously mentioned 'most favoured nation' rate. Non-members can be charged any rate and, hence, an incentive is provided for non-members to join. Non-discrimination is also one of the major principles which enables the WTO system to function as it was intended. For example, a country might be faced with protectionist pressures to restrict the product of one country – say low-cost electronics from South Korea. If the importing country was allowed to discriminate, it could impose tariffs only on South Korean electronics and suffer the retaliation of only the South Korean government. The next example of domestic protectionist pressure might be for the reduction of fish imports from Iceland. In this situation, trade problems must be addressed one by one, and the protectionist country would suffer only mild economic and political fallout each time. Hence, non-discrimination makes acquiescence to domestic protectionist pressure more difficult for politicians by greatly increasing both the political and the economic cost.

A third major principle of the WTO is transparency. Transparency means that any trade action taken by a country must be reported to all of the members of the WTO. Further, once informed, other countries can bring forward their concerns at the WTO. Basically, there can be no secret deals and, hence, transparency acts to strengthen non-discrimination.

Accepted retaliation is the WTO's fourth principle. As individual countries can ignore the trade rules established by the WTO in ways which could injure other countries, the injured countries have the right to retaliate up to an amount of equivalent value without fear of second-round retaliation. There is fundamental acceptance of the fact that there may be overwhelming domestic priorities which require countries to renege on their WTO commitments and that those instances should not lead to beggar-thy-neighbour retaliations.

As the original GATT was not conceived as a legal entity, its formal mechanisms for settling disputes were weak. The dispute mechanisms agreed to at the Uruguay Round and administered by the WTO are much stronger. Adjudication by former GATT 'panels' centred on legal interpretations of GATT articles. This is because GATT panels were only initiated when the 'club of reasonable people' approach failed. The process was cumbersome. Having a GATT panel hear a dispute depended on the agreement of all participants, including the contending parties. The new rules administered by the WTO allow a panel to be struck when only one party requests it. The results of WTO panels are binding, unlike those of the previous GATT panels, which could only come into force if the country that lost the dispute would agree to its implementation. Of course, WTO countries can still choose to use the 'out' built into the agreement by agreeing to accept retaliation rather than to comply.

As the organization grew to include a large number of countries with a variety of economic systems at various stages of development, the 'club' became too big and philosophically diverse. As a result, the consensus on what is reasonable was eroded, leading to a greater reliance on legal approaches to trade disputes. This weakened the organization's effectiveness (Wolf, 1986; Josling, 2007). With the erosion of the principles associated with a 'club of reasonable people', the stronger dispute mechanisms of the WTO are needed to help enforce increasingly legal interpretations.

Further, as tariffs came down with successive GATT rounds, many domestic economic policies have been exposed as being considerable barriers to trade. As a result, nations wishing to maintain their domestic systems have found other means to limit trade. The rapid pace of technological change and the rising proportion which services constitute of national economic activity have meant that the basis of international commerce has broadened beyond trade in goods. As a result, starting with the Tokyo Round, there was an attempt to extend the GATT into new areas – non-tariff barriers, trade in services, protection of intellectual property, rules of international investment and a number of other topics. The attempt to expand the scope of the GATT was only partially successful, and it became clear that the organization was not sufficiently robust to deal with the changes expected of it (Jackson, 1978). The WTO was established to provide a more comprehensive organization. The GATT remains the organization responsible for trade in goods, while the new GATS and TRIPS agreements are responsible for other areas of international economic activity. The GATT rules regarding trade in goods are dealt with in greater detail later in Section III.

6.3   The United Nations Conference on Trade and Development

The United Nations Conference on Trade and Development is more geographically encompassing than the WTO. It deals with issues concerning trade relations between developing and developed countries and, hence, is narrower in focus. Its scope is very wide ranging, however, covering almost all topics of concern in international trade. The mandate of UNCTAD is to attempt to enhance developing countries' economic prospects by improving their trade opportunities. Its effectiveness is limited, and it remains primarily a forum for the presentation of ideas and the exchange of information on trade problems. It attempts to reform trade through the use of persuasive arguments based on ideas of obligation and responsibility – *moral suasion*. The major policy-making forum of UNCTAD is international conferences convened every four years. These conferences are commonly referred to by their chronological orderings, for example UNCTAD VI. The major topics of concern at UNCTAD have been attempts to find mechanisms to stabilize and/or raise the prices of commodities exported from developing countries to developed countries, to improve market access for developing countries' manufactured goods in developed countries, to increase and improve the use of aid transfers, to facilitate the resolution of developing-country debt problems and to enhance technology transfer (UNCTAD, 1985).

The organization has been active in attempts to bring 'orderly marketing' to the volatile markets of economically important commodities exported from developing countries. Largely through the ability of UNCTAD to keep problems in the public eye and the moral suasion applied, a number of international commodity agreements were negotiated – rubber, sugar, tin, coffee and cocoa. The success of the agreements in operation has varied considerably, and most are now moribund. The fact that these agreements existed at all, and that solutions to market volatility are sought through international cooperation, can largely be attributed to the work at UNCTAD.

Businesses conducting international trade in products covered by UNCTAD initiatives should take care to follow UNCTAD initiatives. Further, the deliberations of UNCTAD bear watching, because they often provide a barometer for new issues that may become important for the conduct of international commerce. Firms should also be aware that UNCTAD investigates the industrial organization of supply chains engaged in the international trade in commodities that are important components of developing countries' economies. Attempts are made to identify when opportunities exist to use market power in ways that are detrimental to developing countries. Being exposed as an 'exploiter of poor countries' can be damaging to firms' reputations and can lead to public policy measures or actions, such as boycotts by non-government organizations (NGOs), aimed at compelling or inducing firms to change their international commercial practices. Finally, UNCTAD's extensive list of publications provides an excellent, sometimes the only, source of information on product movements, international market structures and trade problems.

REFERENCES

Brink, L. (2011) The WTO disciplines on domestic support, in *Disciplines on Agricultural Support*, ed. D. Orden, D. Blandford and T. Josling, Cambridge University Press, Cambridge, pp. 23–58.

Jackson, J.H. (1978) The crumbling institutions of the liberal trade system. *Journal of World Trade Law*, 12(2), 93–106.

Josling, T. (2007) Overview of trade agreements: The multilateral system, in *Handbook on*

International Trade Policy, ed. W.A. Kerr and J.D. Gaisford, Edward Elgar Publishing, Cheltenham, UK and Northampton, MA, USA, pp. 71–81.

Kerr, W.A. (2000) A new world chaos? International institutions in the information age. *Journal of International Law and Trade Policy*, 1(1), 1–10, www.esteycentre.com.

Kerr, W.A. (2002) A club no more – the WTO after Doha. *Journal of International Law and Trade Policy*, 3(1), 1–9.

Kerr, W.A. (2010) *Conflict, Chaos and Confusion: The Crisis in the International Trading System*, Edward Elgar Publishing, Cheltenham, UK and Northampton, MA, USA.

Kerr, W.A. (2012) Taming the bear: The WTO after the accession of Russia. *Journal of International Law and Trade Policy*, 13(2), 150–59.

UNCTAD (1985) *The History of UNCTAD 1964–1984*, United Nations, New York.

Viju, C. and Kerr, W.A. (2011) Protectionism and global recession: Has the link been broken? *Journal of World Trade*, 45(3), 605–28.

Wolf, M. (1986) Fiddling while the GATT burns. *World Economy*, 9(1), 1–18.

7

Orderly markets

7.1 Why orderly markets are desired

Many international trade problems can be attributed to rapidly changing markets. Rapidly changing markets arise primarily from volatile supply conditions or rapid rates of technological change that cannot be used to equal effect in all countries. Instability may cause economic hardship for some market participants. Further, in some nations the economic 'outcome' which some or all markets provide may be considered politically unacceptable and alternative non-market allocation mechanisms put in place. Under these conditions, nations may wish to cooperate to regulate the international movement of goods through non-market means. The stated rationale is bringing 'order' to the international trading system. Three mechanisms that attempt to provide 'orderly markets' are examined in this chapter – international commodity agreements, voluntary export restraints and countertrade.

7.2 International commodity agreements

A number of international commodity and product agreements currently exist or have existed in the recent past. Some have been initiated under WTO auspices – the Multifibre Agreement (textiles and clothing), the Arrangement Regarding Bovine Meat (beef) and the International Dairy Arrangement. Other agreements have been fostered by UNCTAD – for tin, natural rubber, sugar, cocoa, jute and tropical timber. The agreements are commodity specific, and the provisions negotiated are tailored to the particular problems associated with the commodity. The range of powers agreed to in the negotiations vary greatly, from the Arrangement Regarding Bovine Meat, which attempts to help nations anticipate problems by providing better information on a multilateral basis, to the Multifibre Agreement, which had, until its removal as part of the Uruguay Round agreements, explicit and complicated restrictions on product movements. All, however, were put in place to prevent or limit the effect of rapid changes in international market prices. There is a perception that by fostering orderly markets both importers and exporters will benefit from the resulting stability. Many of the benefits are expected to arise from being better able to plan business investments, whether they be in tin mines in developing countries or in textile plants in developed countries.

In some cases, instability arises from rapid technological change taking place at different times in different countries. Technological change lowers costs and, as a result, the nation undergoing the most rapid technological change will become more competitive. A country unable to effectively use the new technology may find that the rates of adjustment imposed on its domestic suppliers by competitively priced imports are unacceptable. It may wish to slow the process of adjustment to an acceptable rate by imposing some form of import restriction. Exporters, faced with the spectre of decreased import markets and, as a result, fiercer competition from other exporters for remaining markets, may opt to cooperate with importing nations in return for a guarantee of market share. This was the essence of the Multifibre Agreement prior to it being phased out (Das, 1985). Once an exporting firm receives its share of the total imports that were negotiated by its government, it has a relatively secure market. This type of arrangement often specifies rates of growth for imports so that firms can better plan their investments. Firms in importing countries are assured that they will not have to compete with imports for a portion of the domestic market, and the future rate of growth in imports is known. Investments can then be made in technology to improve efficiency without the fear of volatile and/or falling prices arising from uncontrolled imports. These agreements may, however, become 'too successful'. They can create a vested interest in perpetuating the agreement in both importing and exporting countries.

It is vitally important for firms that wish to begin exporting to know whether such an arrangement exists for their product. Unless the firm has secured a portion of its nation's share of the importing country's market, exports will not be possible. The WTO is, however, likely to discourage these types of agreements in the future.

In markets where there can be large changes in supply, due either to the vicissitudes of the weather – a reduction of the Brazilian coffee harvest as a result of frost – or to rapid entry and exit of producers in response to price changes, attempts are often made to stabilize prices. Prices will be particularly volatile if the demand curve has a steep slope. This is the type of demand curve many tropical products face.

The usual mechanism used to stabilize prices is the strategic use of storage. Price bands are established in the agreement, and storage is used to keep prices between the maximum and minimum prices specified for the band.

When prices are low, the commodity is removed from the international market by storing it. On the other hand, when prices approach the top of the band, stocks are released into the market to slow the price rise.

A number of issues must be settled before the agreement can come into force. Who will pay the cost of storage – exporters, importers – or will the costs be shared? The width of the price band must be negotiated. The wider the band the less will have to be stored; the narrower the band the larger the proportion of the crop which must be stored. Hence, who pays the storage cost becomes vitally important. Some long-term mechanism must also be included to adjust the price bands over time. If the minimum price is set too high, then stocks will simply grow over time, making the scheme unviable. In an attempt to increase their incomes, exporters have sometimes negotiated a minimum price that is set too high and an agreement has become unviable. This certainly was the major contributing factor to the collapse of the sixth International Tin Agreement in 1985. While all agreements have provisions for lowering the price, they are not automatic. Lowering price requires the agreement of most, if not all, of the sellers. In practice, a price reduction has proved difficult to secure. Further, any agreement must include the major players in the market or those excluded will be able to act opportunistically, making the scheme unviable over time (Gilbert, 1987). While such agreements are largely in abeyance currently (Gilbert, 2007), increasingly volatile food prices in the latter part of the first decade of the twenty-first century led to renewed calls for measures such as the strategic use of storage and other means of coordinating food markets internationally to enhance food security (Kerr, 2011a).

It is important for firms that deal in commodities covered by such agreements to take an interest in the agreement's long-term viability. If an agreement is not structured on a sound basis it will eventually collapse and the markets will return to their previous volatility. Investments made on the basis of the stable prices when the agreement was in operation may not yield the expected returns if prices change.

7.3 Voluntary export restraints

Voluntary export restraints (VERs) are bilateral arrangements whereby a country voluntarily agrees to restrict its exports at the suggestion of an importer. The question immediately arises as to why a country would 'voluntarily' agree to such a suggestion. Of course it wouldn't. The agreement is only 'voluntary' in the sense that a country chooses this course of action in the face of a threat by the importing country to impose a more costly trade restriction.

It should always be remembered that, given sufficient domestic pressure for protection, any country can slip outside the WTO rules and impose restrictions on imports. The country may suffer economically from retaliation up to a level of equivalent value on a mix of its exports, but the benefits to the protected importers may be perceived politically as exceeding the costs imposed on the country's exporters. Of course, the importer will not wish to suffer the retaliation of all its trading partners and may request that they agree to restrict their exports.

An exporter, faced with this choice, may wish to exercise the option to voluntarily restrict its exports. First, retaliation to the level of equivalent value may impose considerable additional costs on the exporter's economy. To retaliate, it will have to restrict imports from the other country. This will increase the cost of the trading partner's goods. If few alternative suppliers are available, detrimental increases in input costs and consumer prices will result.

Second, if the protectionist country imposes a tariff, it collects a duty when the product crosses the border and increases government revenue. The exporting country sells less at the same or lower price. If, on the other hand, the country restricts its own exports, the effect is to reduce the supply to the protectionist country, driving up the market price. The exporter's firms could ship the same quantity of goods as would be the case with the tariff in place but receive the higher price. Hence, while there may be a loss in the volume of trade, at least firms in the exporting country benefit from high prices on their remaining sales to the importing country. Alternatively, a reduction in exports can be achieved by the imposition of an export tax so that the government of the exporting country receives the revenue rather than the importing country. Third, by 'voluntarily' agreeing to cooperate with the importing country's request, an exporting country may be able to secure a better deal than if tariffs are unilaterally imposed. This might come in the form of a less severe restriction on the commodity in question or trade concessions on other commodities.

When a country agrees to restrict its exports to a specified quantity, it must then allocate the agreed amount among its exporting firms. If it wants firms to receive the benefit, it will use some non-price allocation mechanism. It is extremely important that these opportunities be watched closely by firms producing the commodity. Even if a firm has not previously been exporting to the protectionist country, the new higher price expected for the commodity may justify the effort required to obtain an allocation. As the remaining exports are more valuable, existing exporting firms will have to work hard to ensure that they garner as large a portion of the allocation as possible. Competition among current and potential exporters is likely to be fierce.

If the government in the exporting country wishes to capture the revenue arising from the difference between the cost at which firms in the exporting country are willing to supply the commodity and the price in the importing country, then it can auction the rights to export. It becomes very important that exporting firms estimate the long-term value of these rights so that they do not pay more for them than they are worth. Of course, once an allocation is secured by a firm, it will have an incentive to attempt to ensure that the VER continues.

In the 1980s, voluntary export restraints became the preferred method for circumventing the 'spirit of the GATT'. While often seen as a means for more powerful countries to discriminate against weaker trading partners, VERs were also used by major trading powers to defuse politically sensitive trade issues among themselves. Japan 'voluntarily' restricted its automobile exports to the US and video recorder exports to the EU. Canada continues to negotiate VERs with the US for exports of its softwood lumber.

The proliferation of VERs led to a considerable degree of concern, especially among the middle-sized trading nations, and the issue of VERs was included in the Uruguay Round negotiations. Under the terms of the Uruguay Round agreement, WTO members are not supposed to initiate any new VERs, and existing ones were to be removed. Hence, the importance of VERs as trade instruments may decrease over time. It is still possible for countries to negotiate VERs with nations that are not members of the WTO. Further, while VERs may not be sanctioned by the WTO, if two member states negotiate this type of arrangement it will only come under scrutiny at the WTO if a third country launches a formal complaint. Given that a VER usually means an increase in price in the importing country, firms in other countries that export into that market are likely to benefit from the higher prices and not lobby their governments to launch a complaint. Thus, while the use of VERs has been reduced since the end of the Uruguay Round, they will not disappear, as the case of Canada's restricted exports of softwood lumber to the US illustrates, and exporting firms should monitor import markets closely for the conditions whereby the likely negotiation of a VER exists. They should position themselves to take advantage of the opportunities it may provide or the loss of access to the import market it may impose.

Voluntary export restraint agreements between countries should not be confused with unilateral export bans or restrictions imposed by individual exporting countries. Such export restrictions are imposed to keep domestic prices of commodities low in times of rising international prices. A number of countries, for example, put in place export bans during the global spike in food prices in 2008 and 2011 to lower domestic food prices (Kerr, 2011b). Such export restrictions add to international price spikes and lower incentives to increase production in countries imposing the ban. WTO disciplines on the use of unilaterally imposed export restraints are weak.

7.4   Countertrade

Countertrade is international trade conducted on a barter basis – goods for goods. As much as 20 per cent of world trade was once conducted on a countertrade basis. Thus, countertrade can be an important aspect of international commerce and particularly important to individual firms in market economies because of the size of individual countertrade deals. Countertrade transactions take place in the absence of transparent market prices, although there may be non-comparable (and hence useless) accounting prices available. The absence of market prices significantly increases the costs associated with conducting international commerce – costs economists generally refer to as transactions costs.

Why would a country wish to undertake international trade without the use of money? Countertrade arises when a country has a currency that is not freely convertible into other nations' currencies or when access to foreign exchange is rationed. In the past, the countries that initiated countertrade programmes were often command – or centrally planned – economies. Developing countries which are maintaining their currency at an overvalued and fixed international exchange rate remain users of countertrade arrangements.

For a variety of reasons, countries do not allow the relative value of their currencies to be determined on international money markets. Typically, the 'official' exchange rate overvalues the domestic currency. In some cases the currency is overvalued to keep down the prices of vital imports. Whatever the reason for following this practice, the effect is to make foreign goods appear cheap to prospective importers. As the currency is overvalued, more foreign goods can be purchased for each unit of domestic currency. Given that foreign goods appear inexpensive, there will be an excess demand for them at the official rate of exchange. The government then must find some means of prioritizing access to the foreign exchange needed to pay for imports. This means that the government decides which imports have priority and allocates the available foreign exchange to those imports. Further, it makes the country's exports appear expensive and, hence, unattractive to foreign buyers. To get around this dual problem, value-for-value exchanges of goods are promoted. In this case, countertrade is an attempt to obtain non-priority imports in exchange for what otherwise would be unattractively priced exports.

Why do the transactions costs increase for firms that may wish to export to or import from countries with countertrade programmes? Freely convertible currencies, combined with domestic prices determined by market forces, provide an extremely low-cost method for importing firms to determine the value of the goods they are purchasing. All of this inexpensive information disappears with countertrade. All contracts become goods-for-goods swaps. This means that the value of the commodity received in trade in the import- er's market must be determined in the absence of meaningful price informa- tion. Unless the market is already well developed, the price consumers will be willing to pay for an unknown product may be extremely hard to determine. Before a deal is struck, experts may have to be hired to assess the value of the products offered in payment.

Costs will also increase, because each transaction will require a one-on- one matching of buyer and seller. A counterpart must be searched out, meaning a larger number of sales staff. In the case of a firm wishing to import, a bundle of commodities which is acceptable to the agency with export goods on offer will have to be identified and acquired. As every transaction becomes a one-on-one negotiation regarding the exchangeabil- ity of two different goods, the negotiations are often protracted and costly in terms of staff time and expenses. Finally, it is often difficult for person- nel who are used to prices as a measure of value to deal in situations where prices are meaningless, and any referral to 'official' prices can be dangerous. Personnel involved in countertrade will need special training and extensive briefings (Kosticki, 1987). Profitable deals are available from countertrade, but the cost of identifying those deals can be considerable. The problems which firms face in countertrade transactions are discussed in greater detail in Chapter 12.

The WTO, with its orientation towards market-based trade, has never been able to deal adequately with countertrade activities. Most former communist countries did not belong to the GATT, and those that did belong were toler- ated because the amounts traded were small (Jackson, 1992). The WTO more or less turns a blind eye to bilateral countertrade arrangements between countries.

 **REFERENCES**

Das, D.K. (1985) Dismantling the Multifibre Arrangement. *Journal of World Trade Law*, 19, 67–80.

Gilbert, C.L. (1987) International commodity agreements: Design and performance. *World Development*, 15(5), 519–616.

Gilbert, C.L. (2007) International commodity agreements, in *Handbook on International Trade Policy*, ed. W.A. Kerr and J.D. Gaisford, Edward Elgar Publishing, Cheltenham, UK and Northampton, MA, USA, pp. 470–81.

Jackson, J.H. (1992) *The World Trading System*, MIT Press, Cambridge, MA.

Kerr, W.A. (2011a) Food sovereignty – old protectionism in somewhat recycled bottles. *African Technology Development Forum Journal*, 8(1 and 2), 4–9.

Kerr, W.A. (2011b) The role of international trade in achieving food security. *Journal of International Law and Trade Policy*, 12(2), 44–53.

Kosticki, M. (1987) Should one countertrade? *Journal of World Trade Law*, 21(2), 7–9.

8

How countries restrict trade

8.1 Unilateral action by countries

When countries can find no means to cooperate with other countries to mitigate the effects of adverse external market forces on their economy or on a particular industry, they may wish to resort to unilaterally imposed trade measures. If the unilateral action affects a country that is also a member of WTO, then the country imposing the trade restriction should expect to face trade measure retaliation up to a level of equivalent value. However, the WTO rules on many trade-restricting practices other than tariffs and **import quotas** are sometimes weak and easily circumvented. While the WTO discourages any attempts to initiate unilateral trade-restricting actions, it also recognizes that there may be situations where domestic political pressure requires a country to take such action. Countries that belong to the WTO have made commitments regarding their level of tariffs and some other trade barriers in the Uruguay Round that are laid out in 'schedules' appended to the GATT agreement. New members that accede to the WTO agree to the tariff levels they will charge during the accession negotiations with existing members of the WTO.

8.2 Trade-restricting measures

In theory, tariffs are the only trade-restricting measure that should be used by WTO members to restrict the movement of goods from other WTO countries. Of course, any trade-restricting measure can be used against a non-member. Trade barriers can affect international commerce in a multitude of ways, and it is important for firms to identify the measures that are in place and anticipate their ramifications.

8.2.1 Tariffs

A tariff is a tax on goods collected when they pass through an importing country's customs. Tariffs are pre-announced at a fixed level and may be either in a set monetary amount per unit of import – flat rate – or calculated as a percentage of the imported good's value. The latter are known by the Latin term **_ad valorem_**. Hence, tariffs are narrowly defined and should not be confused with other border taxes that can be varied at the discretion of the importer. It is the fixed and pre-announced nature of tariffs that makes them the WTO's preferred trade measure. Tariffs are the least distortionary trade measure for a given level of protection because, when tariffs are applied to exporting countries in a non-discriminatory fashion, it is relative prices which determine the choice of foreign suppliers. In other words, while a tariff provides protection to an importer's industry, as the price at which the commodity becomes available in the importer's country is determined on the basis of the exporter's price plus a fixed tax, the lowest-cost foreign supplier will be the most competitive. As relative competitiveness among exporters changes, the source of imports will automatically shift to the lowest-cost supplier.

Ad valorem tariffs tend to discriminate in favour of trade in raw materials and against trade in goods with a high degree of processing or manufacturing. As the value of processing is included in the price, the absolute size of the tariff increases given that its calculation is based on a percentage of the price. Hence, _ad valorem_ tariffs encourage a greater proportion of the economic activity associated with processing to be undertaken in the importing country. On the other hand, _ad valorem_ tariffs are open to manipulation by importers and exporters, as the real price (as opposed to the price reported on the manifest) may be difficult for customs officials to determine. Flat-rate tariffs based on the quantity of imports are, hence, less costly to monitor.

It is important that importing firms add in the cost of tariffs when determining their expected selling price. _Ad valorem_ tariffs can be calculated on different base prices. For example, they can be calculated on a price that includes the 'cost, insurance and freight' (**c.i.f.**) associated with moving the good to the importer's port of entry. They can also be based on the 'free on board' (**f.o.b.**) price, which is the price of the good once it is loaded on to the ship, plane, train or truck in the exporter's country. When tariffs are calculated on an _ad valorem_ basis and an expensive transportation mode such as air freight is used, the cost of the tariff will be considerably higher when it is calculated on a c.i.f. basis.

8.2.2 Import quotas

While strictly a non-tariff barrier, import quotas probably deserve to be in a category all of their own. This is because, historically, they have been the major trade-restricting policy alternative to tariffs. They are, however, a more distortionary measure than tariffs and can be easily administered in a fashion that violates the major WTO principle of non-discrimination. The official WTO position on import quotas is that they should be transformed into tariffs which give the importing country an equivalent degree of protection. Once tariffication takes place then tariff reductions can be negotiated under the auspices of the WTO.

An import quota is a pre-announced numerical limit on the number of units of a product that can be imported over a specified period of time – normally one year. The effect of a quota is to limit the total supply in the importer's market to the sum of the quantity which domestic firms wish to supply plus the quantity of imports equal to that specified in the quota. The reduction in total supply available in the domestic market increases the price of the good.

Import quotas have a major advantage over tariffs when international prices are volatile. A tariff, with its fixed rate, simply adds a constant to the exporter's price. If the international market price fluctuates, that volatility is passed through to the domestic market. An import quota, on the other hand, simply fixes the total supply in the domestic economy regardless of the international price.

Quotas are bureaucratic in nature. Once the importing country determines the total quantity that is to be allowed into the country, this quota must be apportioned among the countries wishing to export. This apportioning often becomes a political process involving bilateral negotiations and is virtually impossible to administer in a fashion that appears non-discriminatory. Further, even if some simple rule is used to apportion import quotas such as each exporting nation receiving a share of the total quota equal to its previous market share, over time distortions will increase. If the relative costs in supplying nations change, then, to minimize the trade distortion, their proportion of the quota should also be altered to reflect this change. In practice, both identifying cost changes and renegotiating the quotas will be very difficult. Further, new countries that wish to export must be given a portion of the quota, raising the issues of what size this allocation should be and whose allocation should be reduced to accommodate the new exporter. These questions can be resolved only through political negotiations. It is very important for exporting firms to monitor such developments and ensure that their government negotiators are informed of the benefits from acquiring a share of the import quota.

An import quota system can be very lucrative for importing firms. The imported product can be acquired at the low international price and sold at the higher domestic price. Governments must monitor the rate at which imports enter the country to ensure that the quota is not exceeded. Often, to facilitate this monitoring, the government issues domestic firms with import licences. Without an import licence it is impossible for a firm to import. This creates a vested interest in the quota system for firms having import licences. New firms that wish to import must get the 'ear of government' to ensure that they acquire a licence, while those that have licences will attempt to have them extended. Firms which have licences will lobby hard to keep the import quota system in place and against tariffication, where the government instead of the firm collects the difference between the international and domestic price.

While many import quotas have been changed to tariffs, the guaranteed levels of access which countries must provide to agricultural products and textiles as a result of the Uruguay Round are essentially quotas by a different name. The import levels which the EU has negotiated with some former communist countries that have not joined the EU are another example.

The WTO's Agreement on Agriculture negotiated at the Uruguay Round allowed for a limited number of *tariff rate quotas* (TRQs), sometimes called *tariff quotas*. Access for imports under TRQs are restricted in the following manner. Imports up to a quantitative limit – the quota part of the TRQ – are allowed into the importer's market at a low or zero 'within-quota' tariff rate. Once the quota's quantitative limit is reached, additional imports are allowed in at a high 'over-quota' tariff rate. Thus, TRQs differ from import quotas in that additional imports are allowed in once the quota level is reached. Of course, it is possible to exclude all additional imports by simply setting the over-quota tariff prohibitively high. Allocation of the limited access provided by the quota portion of the TRQ suffers from all the same difficulties associated with import quotas, and firms wishing to export should be aware that without an allocation they will face the over-quota tariff if they wish to export. The TRQs may be renegotiated in future WTO rounds, and liberalization can entail: 1) lowering the within-quota tariff; 2) increasing the quota; 3) reducing the over-quota tariff; or 4) some combination of the other three. As the ramifications of these liberalization strategies are complex and depend on the situation in individual import markets, firms pushing for liberalization should be careful what they ask for – understanding the market in the importing country is crucial (Gaisford and Kerr, 2001; Khorana, 2008).

8.2.3　Non-tariff barriers

As formal barriers to trade such as tariffs and import quotas have been progressively reduced through the WTO, non-tariff barriers to the international movement of commodities have become much more common. This is for two reasons. First, nations put in place a large number of domestic policies and regulations when their markets were protected. With the removal of tariff protection, many of these now act to restrict trade. Often, new domestic regulations are put in place without full (or any) consideration of trade ramifications. Further, they are most often put in place to address a genuine domestic concern. As a result, negotiating their removal can be very difficult.

Second, the GATT had no effective means to deal with non-tariff barriers until the conclusion of the Uruguay Round. Hence, nations under domestic pressure to provide protection put non-tariff barriers in place rather than new tariffs. By doing so they avoided GATT-sanctioned retaliation. The Uruguay Round eliminated the use of some non-tariff barriers and put additional restrictions on the use of others. Their very complexity, however, makes their elimination extremely difficult. The form and shape of non-tariff barriers are constrained only by the inventiveness of the minds of bureaucrats, and providing a comprehensive list is not possible. As a result, only a selection of the major non-tariff barriers are discussed.

Variable levies

Variable levies are a tax on goods collected when they pass through an importing country's customs but, unlike tariffs, they are not preset at a fixed level. They are used to keep the domestic price isolated from changes in the world price. As the international price falls the size of the levy increases, and as the world price rises the size of the levy decreases. In effect, variable levies have the same stabilizing effect on domestic price as an import quota, without the bureaucratic problems associated with quota allocations. Distortions are minimized because imports will come from the least-cost supplier.

The most contentious use of variable levies was by the European Union. They were applied on agricultural imports (where, prior to the conclusion of the Uruguay Round, GATT disciplines were particularly weak) into the EU and were an adjunct to the **Common Agricultural Policy (CAP)**. While variable levies provided a high and stable price for farmers in the EU, all of the international price instability was borne by exporting nations. In fact, variable levies acted to increase exporters' price variability. Hence, the use of variable levies proved to be a very contentious trade issue. Many of the world's suppliers of agricultural commodities are third world countries that require an increased degree of stability to foster their economic development. In the Uruguay Round, the EU agreed to change its variable levies into either import tariffs or tariff rate quotas. The former are expected to have a stabilizing effect on world agricultural prices, while the latter still push much of the price instability on to exporting countries.

Export restrictions

While most trade-restricting measures relate to the protection of an importing country's markets from changes in international markets, as suggested above, there are circumstances where exporting countries wish to restrict the movement of commodities or products out of the country. While, at first glance, such behaviour may not appear as if it should be of international concern, both the short-run and long-run effects of such actions may be detrimental to the international trading environment and, ironically, to the interests of the exporting country.

Nations will want to restrict exports in situations where world supplies of the commodity are declining and, as a result, export revenues are rising. This may seem perverse behaviour. However, if the commodity in question is a significant input into major domestic industries or a food staple, then the exporter may wish to limit supplies leaving the country so that domestic prices can be kept low. Exports can be reduced by using export taxes or quantitative restrictions (Scholefield and Gaisford, 2007).

The short-run consequences of limiting the supply going to international markets further increase the price of the commodity in importing nations. For importers, this increases the hardship created by the shortage. The long-run effect is to increase protectionist pressures in importing countries. First, as the importer's security of supply is threatened by the actions of the exporter, subsidies or protectionist measures may be put in place by the importer to foster increased domestic supplies.

Second, the high short-run prices in the importer's country may encourage firms to invest in facilities to provide the product domestically. When the export restriction is removed at a later date, those who invested in the new facilities can be expected to lobby vigorously for protection. There can be little doubt that the failure of the Japanese to liberalize their agricultural trade can, in no small part, be attributed to the US soybean – a major input to livestock production – embargo of the early 1970s. Clearly, once the international shortage passes, the exporter may face reduced access to its traditional import markets.

Health, sanitary and phytosanitary regulations

These non-tariff barriers encompass a wide range of measures that relate to the physical condition of products when they enter a country. Every nation has regulations in place to ensure that products coming from abroad do not carry diseases that could be hazardous to the environment or to the health of humans, animals and plants. Further, regulations are put in place to ensure that domestic products are handled in a sanitary fashion to protect human health and that they are grown under conditions – *phyto* is a Greek term referring to plants – which are not hazardous to individuals or the food chain. Bans on the use of DDT provide an example of the latter. Exporters should expect to conform to importing countries' regulations. Regulations of this type are primarily applied to biologically based imports such as agricultural products, fish and timber products.

As these regulations address legitimate domestic concerns, they have proved extremely difficult to deal with effectively on an international basis. There is no doubt that protecting domestic livestock herds from foot and mouth disease in countries where it has been eradicated is a legitimate action by an importing country. It cannot be denied, however, that the ban on imports of livestock and fresh meat products from countries such as Brazil, where the disease persists, has considerable economic impact given the country's potential as an exporter.

The major problem with health, sanitary and phytosanitary regulations is that they may unnecessarily restrict imports. As standards in different countries are developed independently, they may become barriers to trade unintentionally. They can also be used opportunistically to restrict imports.

The major reason that differences in regulations become barriers to trade is that they can significantly increase transactions costs for exporters. For example, an exporter of meat products will have to comply with domestic sanitary standards by putting certain procedures in place which are then monitored by government inspectors. If the country to which the firm wishes to export requires different procedures – even if the eventual standard of health is the same – then both sets of procedures will have to be followed, resulting in increased costs. In some cases, scientific procedures may simply be incompatible, and a potential exporter must choose between the domestic and the export market. It may be impossible, for example, to design a slaughterhouse that can satisfy the regulations of both the domestic and a foreign market. This means that exporters must have separate 'dedicated' export facilities. Of course, the transactions costs may be cumulative if an exporter has more than one country it wishes to supply.

The tests needed to monitor compliance with the regulations have a scientific basis and require qualified personnel to undertake them. Problems may arise regarding the international equivalence of scientific testing facilities and the training of personnel. As a result, exporters may be required to pay to have inspection personnel trained and certified in the importer's country. The exporter may have to pay to have domestic laboratories inspected by foreign personnel and be required to bear any costs of modifying the facility. It may be that the importer requires that the tests be undertaken in specified facilities within its own country. The facilities specified might not have sufficient capacity to handle the volume of imports. The lack of facilities will have the same effect as an import quota. If the specified facilities in the importer's country are owned by the government, the charge for undertaking the procedures may be set artificially high. The effect is the same as a tariff.

Further, even if all the regulations can be met by the exporter, by simply altering the regulations frequently the importer can significantly increase transactions costs for the exporter. Facilities will have to be reinspected, staff training upgraded and testing facilities modified.

It should be clear that there is a wide scope for these types of regulations to be used opportunistically as trade barriers. Exporting firms shipping products covered by such regulations should take great pains to ensure that the importer's regulations are met, because refused loads may deteriorate in transit or may not be suitable for sale when returned to the domestic market. Further, exporting firms should monitor any proposed regulations so that a presentation can be made to the importer's government if the changes are likely to have trade-inhibiting effects.

Consumer protection legislation

As with health regulations, consumer protection legislation can become a barrier to trade because nations develop their standards and procedures independently. Exporters will incur increased costs if they must comply with multiple regulations. This increase in transactions costs may be sufficiently high so as to totally inhibit trade. While much consumer protection legislation acts only as an unintentional barrier to trade, it can also be used strategically to limit trade. As consumer protection legislation does address legitimate domestic concerns, it often becomes difficult to argue for its removal on international trade grounds.

Transactions costs can increase for an exporter as a result of simple differences in regulations such as labelling requirements. If the exporter's domestic market and export market have different labelling requirements, a shutdown of the production line may be required so that the changeover can be effected. This reduces the length of production runs, thereby increasing per unit cost. It also adds to the firm's down time. For a firm that exports to 20 different markets, these additions to cost may prove to be significant.

In some cases, extensive modifications may have to be made to the final product or the entire product redesigned. The safety features of automobiles provide one such example. Even small regulatory differences in the spacing of lights can require entirely new metal-stamping dies for the export market. Some European cars imported into California must have very expensive modifications to meet pollution and safety standards – the modifications can sometimes increase the landed cost of the car by 30 to 50 per cent.

Increased transactions costs can arise in a number of ways. In response to consumer concerns, the European Union banned the production and sale of meat from animals that had been treated with growth hormones. This ban was extended to imports. Canadian and US exporters wished to continue to use growth hormones in production destined for their domestic markets, and export volumes did not justify separate production systems for beef produced without the use of hormones (Kerr and Hobbs, 2002; Neeliah et al., 2011).

As with the case of health regulations, exporting firms should monitor proposed changes in consumer protection legislation in countries where they have export markets. If the proposed changes will increase the transactions costs associated with exporting, then concern should be expressed to the proper authorities, both in the importing country and with international trade policy officials in the exporting country's government.

Rules of origin requirements

Rules of origin requirements are imposed for two reasons: to directly restrict imports and to prevent tariff circumvention. The former normally arises when countries are attempting to foster industrialization. The case where a nation is attempting to prevent tariff circumvention is manifest when an importing nation is a member of a free trade area. As explained in Chapter 5, countries belonging to free trade areas are not required to have the same levels of external tariffs (e.g. the US, Canada and Mexico have different import tariffs on automobiles that are manufactured outside the NAFTA area). Goods can move freely between members of the free trade area, but goods may be imported from countries that do not belong to the free trade area at different rates of tariff. This creates a situation whereby high-tariff countries can have their tariffs circumvented. For example, country A in a free trade area may have a 30 per cent tariff on automobiles from country C, which is not a member of the free trade area. Country B, which is also a member of the free trade area, may have only a 5 per cent tariff on country C's automobiles. As goods can move tariff free between countries B and A, it becomes profitable to import country C's cars into country B, paying the 5 per cent tariff, and then trans-ship them to country A and pay no additional tariff. The cost of C's automobiles, including the 5 per cent tariff and the transactions costs associated with trans-shipment, may be considerably less than the landed cost of directly shipping automobiles from C to A and paying the 30 per cent tariff. As a result, the protection A has sought by imposing the 30 per cent tariff has been circumvented.

To overcome this problem, the high-tariff member of the free trade area will negotiate a rules of origin provision whereby goods moving from its trading partner must have a certain proportion of the value of the good added in the partner country.

Rules of origin requirements whose primary purpose is to foster industrialization are simply regulations specifying that a certain proportion of the value of a good sold in the country must have been added within the country. For example, an importer may require that 30 per cent of the value of any automobile sold in the country be added within the country. Typically, this might mean that a car can be imported as parts and local labour used to assemble it. Sometimes it may be that a certain proportion of the vehicle's components – maybe the engine – be sourced in the importing country. These types of rules of origin requirements are a means to capture additional value added for the importing country. Developing countries have often justified their use of these measures as being part of their overall industrialization strategies. The specific aim is to allow their industrial managers and labour force to become proficient at manufacturing.

Carrier of origin requirements

Carrier of origin requirements can be of two forms. An importing country may require that goods moving to its shores must be transported on ships registered in the importing country (a flag carrier) or on the importing country's national airline. On the other hand, an exporting country may specify similar requirements whereby goods exported must be moved on its flag carriers or airlines.

In the export case, it is a means for the exporting country to capture some of the benefits arising from the international transaction. It also provides a means for fostering domestic shipping interests in high-cost countries or indirectly supporting a national airline.

In the case of importers, flag carrier or national airline stipulations can act as a significant barrier to trade. Of course, they are also a means to capture additional benefits from international transactions. Specifying that goods must move by the importer's carrier may make it impossible for the exporter to access transport. If an importing country wishes to act strategically to protect certain industries, it may simply inform the exporter that no transport is available during the period when the exporter needs to move its goods. The effect is the same as an import quota. If the carrier is a nationalized firm, then the importing government may set the shipping or air freight rates prohibitively high. The effect is the same as a tariff.

Restrictions on government procurement

Over the period since the GATT was established in 1947, the governments of most countries have come to assume a much larger role in the economy (Gerber, 2000; Viju and Kerr, 2011). Most developed market economies have become mixed economies with certain sectors controlled directly by the government – health care, electricity generation, communications systems, automobile manufacture – although the degree of government involvement and the activities undertaken by government vary considerably. In addition, the concept of the 'welfare state' has been extended from the Scandinavian countries to a greater or lesser degree in all developed economies. To support these activities, government bureaucracies have grown apace. As a result, in many countries the government share of gross domestic product (GDP) can exceed 40 per cent.

Many of the developing countries that have received their independence since the formation of the GATT opted to follow a socialist path to development. This has meant that the government proportion of the modern sectors of their economies tends to be quite large, although moves to a more market orientation in many developing countries in recent years means that the share of the government sector has been reduced.

When goods and services are purchased from the private sector by government, it is usually accomplished through procurement contracts. In many cases, these contracts are allocated using a competitive bidding process. Whatever the means of letting contracts to supply the government, the application process is often restricted by legislation to firms owned by citizens of that country. When governments constitute such large proportions of total economic activity, these restrictions become major barriers to trade.

In certain circumstances, there may be legitimate reasons for restricting access to procurement contracts to the country's nationals. In particular, it may be desirable to have national defence contracts restricted. This protects the country from disruptions to weapons supplies and spare parts in time of war. Further, there may be some strategic industries where a country does not wish to be dependent on foreign suppliers, as this might make the country vulnerable to economic blackmail or even international sanctions in times of political disagreements with supplying nations.

For the great majority of goods and services purchased by government, no such national security case can be made. Restricting procurement contracts to nationals simply becomes a means of protecting domestic firms from international competition.

In parallel with but not part of the Uruguay Round, an Agreement on Government Procurement was reached. It constitutes part of the WTO. It is a voluntary plurilateral agreement with only a limited membership. About 20 developed countries – with the EU signing as one – and half a dozen developing countries are party to the agreement. The European Union has eliminated restrictions on government procurement within the Union, and the Canada–US Trade Agreement reduced the barriers to trade arising from government procurement contracts. The difficulties associated with removing barriers to foreign firms in government procurement contracts are discussed further in Chapter 18.

 REFERENCES

Gaisford, J.D. and Kerr, W.A. (2001) *Economic Analysis for International Trade Negotiations*, Edward Elgar Publishing, Cheltenham, UK and Northampton, MA, USA.

Gerber, J. (2000) National policies and the limits of international integration. *Journal of International Law and Trade Policy*, 1(1), 11–21.

Kerr, W.A. and Hobbs, J.E. (2002) The North American–European Union dispute over beef produced using growth hormones: A major test for the new international trade regime. *World Economy*, 25(2), 283–96.

Khorana, S. (2008) The development and relevance of tariff rate quotas as a market access instrument: An analysis of Swiss agricultural imports. *Journal of International Law and Trade Policy*, 9(2), 8–31.

Neeliah, S.A., Gorburdhun, D. and Neeliah, H. (2011) The SPS agreement: Barrier or catalyst. *Journal of International Law and Trade Policy*, 12(2), 104–30.

Scholefield, R. and Gaisford, J.D. (2007) Export taxes: How they work and why they are used, in *Handbook on International Trade Policy*, ed. W.A. Kerr and J.D. Gaisford, Edward Elgar Publishing, Cheltenham, UK and Northampton, MA, USA, pp. 237–47.

Viju, C. and Kerr, W.A. (2011) Protectionism and global recession: Has the link been broken? *Journal of World Trade*, 45(3), 605–28.

9

Control of the use of trade barriers

9.1 The need for multilateral controls

As governments will, at times, be forced to give in to domestic political pressure for protection, international agreements attempt to mitigate their effect through a variety of control measures. While these control measures must be voluntarily agreed to in an international forum, once in force they become difficult to ignore and, hence, can be a major influence on domestic decision makers. Obtaining a multinational consensus on control measures has proved very elusive and, as a result, many of the provisions for control were weak prior to the establishment of the WTO. An attempt at considerably improving the effectiveness of control measures was made during the Uruguay Round and was one of the major reasons for replacing the GATT organization with the WTO. Greater success at controlling the use of trade restrictions has sometimes been achieved by regional trading agreements. As members of regional economic groupings are likely to have more homogeneous economies and a smaller number of participants, controls are more readily agreed to. This can be a two-edged sword as, while regional agreements tend to reduce the total number of trade barriers, they may make it more difficult to reach agreement among regional groupings.

9.2 Measures to control the use of trade restrictions

As trade restrictions take many forms and affect imports in a variety of ways, no single method of control can be totally effective. As a result, a variety of measures form the multilateral basis for control of trade barriers.

9.2.1 Tariffication

The process of tariffication is the method that has been the main and preferred instrument of control at the WTO. Tariffication is the conversion of all non-tariff barriers, including import quotas, into tariffs that provide an equivalent degree of protection. Once tariffication of a non-tariff barrier has taken place, then the tariff becomes subject to the GATT tariff reduction negotiations at the WTO. Given the success of the GATT tariff reduction rounds, tariffication has proven to be an effective strategy for reducing barriers to trade.

Tariffication was chosen as the primary control measure for five reasons. Firstly, it allows direct comparison of different nations' levels of protection. Attempts by economists to calculate the rates of protection which non-tariff barriers and subsidies provide – their tariff equivalents – have often led to acrimonious debates over methodology and the technical competence of experts (Pinder, 1988). Tariffs are simple and easily understood. Secondly, tariffs are transparent. This means that the degree of protection is readily observable and, hence, exporting firms can easily take account of them in their business calculations. Thirdly, they cannot be used to discriminate among exporting countries without explicitly charging individual countries different rates. Most non-tariff barriers have sufficient administrative leeway to allow importing nations to discriminate. Fourthly, as they cannot be used in a discriminatory fashion, it will mean that the trade that remains will be undertaken on the basis of international efficiency – the low-cost exporter will be able to pay the tariff and remain the lowest-cost foreign supplier of the market. Fifthly, tariffication provides easily compared measures of protection when trade barrier reductions are negotiated. This greatly simplifies the process, as it prevents 'apples versus oranges' arguments at the negotiations.

Beyond nations' reluctance to move to tariffication because they wish to retain the opaqueness and opportunities for discrimination which non-tariff barriers provide, it may also be difficult to agree upon the tariff rate which provides an equivalent degree of protection to the non-tariff barriers it replaces. As non-tariff barriers such as import quotas provide different levels of protection as the international price rises and falls, determining the size of a tariff of equivalent value becomes a topic for negotiation and clearly a matter of timing. No common method of converting non-tariff barriers into equivalent tariffs has been agreed, and as a result in the wake of the Uruguay Round a number of countries were accused of 'dirty tariffication' whereby conversions took place at very high rates (Gaisford and Kerr, 2001; Swinbank, 2004). Still, these high rates are now transparent and can be targeted for reduction in future negotiations.

9.2.2 Harmonization

For many non-tariff barriers, tariffication does not provide a practical means by which trade-restricting effects can be removed. As different regulatory regimes pertaining to health, sanitary and phytosanitary matters or consumer protection act as unintentional barriers to trade, an alternative means to control their trade-restricting effects must be found. In other words, nations need regulatory regimes in place to protect their citizens, and the regimes simply cannot be removed and converted to a tariff. As it is the differences in regulations that cause trade distortions, one means of removing their trade-distorting effect is to remove the differences in regulations. This is the process of harmonization.

Harmonization means that nations agree to negotiate a redrafting of their individual regulations into one common set of regulations. They must also collaborate when drafting all new regulations. For example, the 1992 initiatives in both the European Union and the NAFTA have commitments to harmonize technical standards. A number of Uruguay Round agreements have harmonization provisions. In the Agreement on Sanitary and Phytosanitary Measures, for example, while harmonization is encouraged, nations are still effectively allowed to set their own standards. The Agreement on Technical Barriers to Trade, in a similar fashion, encourages countries to establish international standards for testing and certification procedures.

Harmonization requires long and arduous sets of negotiations. As many of the regulations are very technical in nature, the negotiations are often left to scientific and technical experts. Domestic firms that deal internationally should attempt to gain access to these discussions, because the changes that will inevitably arise as harmonization takes place may require significant alterations to existing procedures and/or new capital expenditures. In some cases, meeting the new common standards may prove to be prohibitively expensive even for firms that sell only in the domestic market. Firms should attempt to ensure that harmonization is accomplished in the least costly manner – something that the technical personnel conducting the negotiations may not always take into account. Harmonization of new regulations has often proved cumbersome and, hence, slowed the introduction of new regulations. Further, the process is often complicated by political systems that have multiple levels of government. Sub-national governments may have no direct role in the harmonization process and, hence, introduce regulations without understanding their international ramifications.

Regulatory harmonization can prove difficult and ultimately costly even when economies are at similar levels of development. When economies are at different levels of development, it may be beyond the fiscal and technical ability of developing nations to raise their levels sufficiently to conform to those of the developed country. As food safety and consumer protection are likely to be important to consumers, no lowering of developed countries' standards can be expected in negotiations. As a result, harmonizing multi-laterally may have to wait until considerable economic development takes place. Unfortunately, in some cases the absence of regulatory harmonization may be a major inhibitor of trade-led economic development.

9.2.3 Treating foreign firms as if they are domestic firms

When non-tariff barriers act to inhibit trade and where harmonization may not be appropriate or is prohibitively expensive, committing to treat foreign firms as if they are domestic firms may provide an alternative.

This should not be confused with the WTO principle of **national treatment**, whereby foreign firms will not be treated differently from domestic firms in terms of regulations. This has a much stronger interpretation. It means that citizens and firms from the country to which it is to be extended will, as far as commercial purposes are concerned, be treated as nationals of the country extending the treatment. Reciprocal extensions of such treatment are normal.

This type of treatment might be extended in the case where a country has carrier of origin requirements in place. As part of a regional trade agreement, it could extend national treatment to the carriers of other countries with which the agreement is concluded. This would mean that the carriers of partner countries could act as the means of transport for all goods that had been previously restricted to carriers of the extending country's flag.

In a similar fashion, this form of treatment can be extended to the bidding process for government procurement contracts. This would mean that a foreign firm bidding for the government contract would be treated no differently from a domestic firm. In a similar fashion, if countries have restrictions on foreign access to defence contracts or investment in sensitive sectors of the economy – energy, banking, utilities – this form of treatment can, for example, be extended to other members of customs unions or free trade areas.

It is important that potential exporters monitor the negotiation of bilateral or regional trading agreements to ensure that such treatment is extended to their activities. Agreements to remove tariffs and harmonize technical barriers to trade will not be sufficient to ensure access to all sectors of the trading partner's economy when legislation exists restricting those sectors or activities to the country's nationals.

9.2.4 Equivalence

The mutual granting of **equivalence** provides an alternative to harmonization when regulatory differences exist which act to inhibit trade. The granting of equivalence means that the standards used by foreign trading partners will be considered equivalent to those imposed on domestic firms. For example, it may be that automobile safety standards in two countries provide equal degrees of consumer protection but are met through different means. Harmonization might impose considerable capital costs on automobile manufacturers that would have to alter their processes to meet new common standards. The changes would, however, provide little gain to consumers. Granting equivalence to domestic regulations for cars manufactured to the trading partner's standards may be a cost-effective means of removing trade barriers. It may be even more important in the case of testing facilities and professional certification. Harmonizing testing facilities built under different regulatory regimes may prove prohibitively expensive. Further, harmonizing the professional certification of individuals involved in scientific testing may require reform of the entire education system, and individuals trained prior to harmonization may have to undergo expensive and long-term retraining. The granting of equivalence will reduce these costs.

The granting of equivalence will, however, require a process whereby the different regulatory standards and procedures are evaluated to ensure that the protection provided to a nation's citizens is not reduced. Further, in the absence of an agreement to harmonize future regulations, all new regulations established in one country would have to be judged as to the equivalence of their effect. Facilities and procedures that are granted equivalence have to be monitored over time by the granting country to ensure that standards are being maintained.

While, in the short run, the granting of equivalence for some activities may prove more cost-effective, in the long run harmonization will reduce monitoring and evaluation costs. An optimal solution may be to grant equivalence for some current activities while at the same time making a commitment to harmonization over the long run. Firms should take particular care that the granting of equivalence for foreign procedures does not extend an economic advantage to competitors from another country. Firms should lobby for the acceptance of these foreign procedures for use in their own domestic industry.

9.2.5   Safeguards

The safeguard procedures that have been included in the WTO act like a steam pressure release valve by allowing countries to escape from their WTO commitments when domestic protectionism becomes too strong for them to ignore. Safeguards also act as a containment vessel. While countries are allowed relief from imminent political problems, their actions do not perpetrate harmful beggar-thy-neighbour free-for-alls or force countries to leave the WTO entirely. The level at which this pressure release valve is triggered was raised at the Uruguay Round negotiations.

A WTO member is allowed to take a 'safeguard action' to protect a specific domestic industry from an unforeseen increase in imports which is causing, or which is likely to cause, serious injury to the industry. The Uruguay Round agreement sets out the criteria for determining serious injury. The trade restrictions put in place when the criteria for the existence of serious injury have been met can only be applied in a manner that will mitigate the effects of a serious injury. Given that domestic political pressure for protection can be intense when there is an unanticipated surge of imports and that the procedures for determining serious injury are time-consuming, safeguard provisions allow for a preliminary finding of serious injury. Any trade restriction imposed on the basis of a preliminary finding can remain in place for only 200 days.

Tariffs, as the least distortionary trade-restricting measure, are the protectionist policy which WTO members are encouraged to use in safeguard actions. Import quotas are allowed, but shares of the total import quota must be allocated to exporters on the basis of their past market shares. This is an attempt to uphold the principle of non-discrimination and to prevent an individual country's exports being targeted by an importing country. A safeguard committee operates under the auspices of the WTO and, if it decides that there are exceptional circumstances, then the shares of import quotas can be allocated in a manner that is different from that based on historical shares.

In terms of containment, safeguard trade restrictions can be in place for a maximum of only eight years, and then only if there is evidence that the protected industry is attempting to become more competitive with imports. Otherwise, safeguard restrictions can be in place for only four years. Once a safeguard trade restriction has expired or been withdrawn, then the importing country must wait two years before beginning proceedings to reimpose the safeguards. Trade restrictions cannot be reapplied for an additional period of time equal to the duration of the previous safeguard action.

A one-year waiting period is imposed if a previous safeguard trade restriction was applied for less than 180 days. Further, reimposition is allowed only if the restriction was not applied to the product more than twice in the previous five years.

The clear intent of safeguard procedures is to allow politicians a means to defuse protectionist pressure and to provide an incentive for the importing country to encourage its industry to adjust. An attempt is made to eliminate the possibility of strategic use of safeguards to forestall the need for domestic industries to adjust. Politicians can use the argument that uncompetitive firms have had their chance to change.

If the importing country adheres to the safeguard provisions when imposing a trade restriction, then other WTO members cannot ask for compensation for three years. The exporters adversely affected can negotiate with the importing country to receive compensation after that period. If no agreement is reached on compensation, then the exporter can impose restrictions of equivalent value on the exports of the original importer. No further beggar-thy-neighbour retaliation is allowed.

Safeguard actions pose a threat to firms in both the exporting country and the importing country. The former is more direct. The agreement on safeguards requires countries considering a safeguard action to announce its intentions and give public notice for hearings and other avenues for interested parties to present evidence. Firms involved in exporting should monitor the situation in their major markets closely and be prepared to take part in safeguard hearings. Otherwise, only the point of view of importing firms will be heard. Further, exporting firms should make sure that their governments are aware of pending safeguard hearings and lobbied to take part in the proceedings.

Firms that export different products from the country imposing an import restriction under a safeguard action may also suffer a loss of markets. This can occur in the case when the original exporting country exercises its right to retaliate when compensation cannot be agreed. It is likely that retaliation will be carried out either to maximize the impact in the country that initiated the safeguard action or to reduce protectionist pressure at home. Firms should realize when they are in industries that are likely candidates for retaliation. They should encourage their government to provide compensation. If this strategy fails, they should be prepared to lobby the retaliating government against the imposition of restrictions on their product.

9.2.6 Adjudication

As with any system of rules, those agreed upon by nations to regulate the international movement of commodities will be subject to differences in interpretation and may require clarification from time to time. When nations cannot agree on the meaning of what has been agreed to or on whether their actions conform to the existing rules of trade, then some form of adjudication is required to ensure the continuance of the arrangement. In some sense, the need for adjudication can be seen as a breakdown in the 'spirit of the GATT'. The result is, to a greater or lesser degree, a retreat to legalistic mechanisms.

The establishment of effective dispute mechanisms has proven to be one of the more difficult tasks associated with institution building in international trade. This is because it requires that nations agree to give up a measure of their sovereignty to some supranational institution. Restrictions on national sovereignty have been stoutly resisted by most politicians of almost any stripe, no matter what the country. Further, as the individuals who must constitute the adjudication authority remain citizens of some nation state, ensuring that those individuals act (and appear to act) in a non-partisan fashion can prove very difficult.

Prior to the WTO, the establishment of GATT panels to adjudicate disputes and the acceptance of the recommendations of the panels relied primarily upon the principle of consensus, including the acquiescence of the accused party. Hence, dispute settlement was dependent on the power of moral suasion both for getting a dispute to the panel stage and for ensuring compliance. The entire GATT dispute procedure was long and cumbersome, with the onus on the contending parties to find a satisfactory solution bilaterally. Only as a last resort were they to apply to have a panel struck. While panels were charged with the responsibility to work quickly, and most did, the process whereby countries reach the point where a panel could be asked for was often very long and drawn out. As the imposition of many trade-restricting measures arises from short-term strategic considerations rather than fundamental structural differences between economies, the slowness of the GATT dispute mechanism could not prevent opportunistic imposition of trade-restricting measures when relief from trade problems was sought. The slowness of the procedures also allowed them to be subsequently abandoned when a GATT panel's judgment appeared imminent. In many cases, countries did not bother to refer disputes to the GATT. A nation imposing trade-restricting measures could use the weakness of the dispute procedures to achieve its short-term goals.

Frustration with the GATT dispute mechanism was one of the major reasons for the establishment of bilateral and regional trade associations. These agreements often had much stronger dispute settlement mechanisms. As discussed in Chapter 5, the European Union has followed a judicial or legal approach to dispute settlement. Trade disputes among member countries are expected first to go through national courts. Appeals can then be made to the European Court. As a result, the entire process is cumbersome, costly and time-consuming. The major problem with the EU system, however, is that the European Court must rely on national courts and governments to ensure compliance with its judgments. In a number of cases this support has not been forthcoming or forthcoming only very slowly. The NAFTA took a non-legal approach. The dispute mechanism agreed to relies on arbitration rather than a judicial approach, and strict timetables for the arbitration process (Apuzzo and Kerr, 1988; Read, 2007). Procedures are explicitly set out for the selection of individuals for the arbitration panels so that biased arbitrators can be rejected.

The WTO took over responsibility for the adjudication of disputes from the GATT. A common set of dispute settlement procedures is applied to all areas of WTO responsibility, including trade in goods. The Uruguay Round Understanding on Rules and Procedures Governing the Settlement of Disputes (DSU) follows, to a considerable degree, the arbitration model set out in the NAFTA. Adjudication of disputes is administered by the Dispute Settlement Body (DSB) of the WTO.

The DSU has two major aspects which are common in arbitration – as opposed to judicial – procedures: 1) the use of neutral adjudicators; and 2) strict timetables for proceedings. In addition, a panel can be established on the basis of a complaint from only one party to the dispute. This removes one of the major weaknesses of the previous GATT dispute settlement procedures, which required the consent of all parties to the dispute before a panel could be set up.

Panels have three members who are not citizens of the countries in dispute. They are drawn from a list of people of appropriate background and experience maintained by the WTO. Appeals to panel rulings can be made to an **Appellate Body** composed of seven members, three of whom will hear any individual case. Countries can appeal only on the grounds that panels have not acted appropriately or on the basis of legal interpretations made by the panels. The actual case is not heard by the Appellate Body. The appeals procedure, which is new in the WTO, adds a legal element to dispute settlement, but the use of experts on panels is consistent with the original GATT concept of settlements based on economic rather than legal criteria. Over time, however, WTO dispute settlement proceedings have taken on an increasingly legalistic character that is not likely to be in the interest of businesses that wish to engage in international commerce – the arbitration model was originally chosen because it could provide economically and commercially workable solutions to trade problems rather than those based on legal precedent.

As protectionist pressures tend to build and then to ebb away, it was in the interest of politicians to break a GATT commitment and then attempt the strategic use of delaying tactics to prevent an adverse decision being brought down by a dispute panel. As a result, the DSU provides for rigid timetables for all aspects of dispute settlement from the point in time when one party notifies the WTO of its intentions right through to compliance with a panel's ruling. The first step is a request for consultations with the other country. Consultations must begin in 30 days or the complaining country can ask for a panel. When consultations are agreed to, if after 60 days no resolution is reached a panel can be requested. The two countries in dispute have 20 days to find mutually agreeable members for the panel. If they do not, the DSB will appoint the panel. Panels have three or six months to complete their work. After a panel issues its report, a maximum of 60 days is allowed before it must be accepted or rejected by the DSB. If one party wishes to appeal, the appeal must be made in this 60-day period. Appeals can take a maximum of 60 days. The parties must accept the panel report within 30 days of the release of the verdict on the appeal. If the judgment goes against the accused, then there must be a mutual agreement on implementation of the panel's recommendations in 45 days, or in 90 days if arbitration is required to determine the procedures for implementation. The entire procedure should take no more than 600 days. This is less than two years and, compared to the past experience in the GATT, where disputes dragged on for years, exceptionally short. The WTO dispute settlement mechanism appears to be a success, with its use increasing by a widening range of countries (Kerr, 2001; Read, 2007). The member countries have complied with panel rulings, with the notable exception of the EU's refusal to lift its ban on the import of beef produced using growth hormones (Kerr and Hobbs, 2002), although the speed with which compliance takes place can be frustrating to firms wishing to take advantages of business opportunities that arise from the reduction in import restrictions. The precedents set by the WTO panels should be monitored closely by firms engaging in international commerce.

REFERENCES

Apuzzo, A.M. and Kerr, W.A. (1988) International arbitration – the dispute settlement procedures chosen for the Canada–U.S. Free Trade Agreement. *Journal of International Arbitration*, 5(4), 7–15.

Gaisford, J.D. and Kerr, W.A. (2001) *Economic Analysis for International Trade Negotiations*, Edward Elgar Publishing, Cheltenham, UK and Northampton, MA, USA.

Kerr, W.A. (2001) Greener multilateral pastures for Canada and Mexico: Dispute settlement in the North American trade agreements. *Journal of World Trade*, 35(6), 1169–80.

Kerr, W.A. and Hobbs, J.E. (2002) The North American–European Union dispute over beef produced using growth hormones: A major test for the new international trade regime. *World Economy*, 25(2), 283–96.

Pinder, J. (1988) Country intervention indexes. *Choices*, Fourth Quarter, 28–9.

Read, R. (2007) Dispute settlement, compensation and retaliation under the WTO, in *Handbook on International Trade Policy*, ed. W.A. Kerr and J.D. Gaisford, Edward Elgar Publishing, Cheltenham, UK and Northampton, MA, USA, pp. 497–508.

Swinbank, A. (2004) Dirty tariffication revisited: The EU and sugar. *Journal of International Law and Trade Policy*, 5(1), 56–69.

10

'Fair' trade

10.1 Contingent protection

Contingent protection measures are used by governments in importing countries when they feel that firms in exporting countries are conducting their international commerce in a manner which is 'unfair' to its domestic firms. The idea of 'fair' trade defies a workable definition but remains a conceptual notion upon which many countries base their contingent protection. 'Fair' trade is often discussed in the context of the equally indefensible concept of the *level playing field*. Tariffs are applied to the goods of the exporter at rates that mitigate the perceived economic damage, and their removal is contingent upon the 'unfair' practices being halted. Contingent protection measures are applied in two cases – when dumping occurs and when trade-distorting subsidies are being used by an exporting country.

10.2 Dumping

In theory, dumping should be the international equivalent of business practices that are considered unacceptable even when firms sell only in their domestic market. The primary unacceptable business practice which dumping should attempt to address is the international equivalent of **predatory pricing** (Kerr, 2001; Lau, 2007). Predatory pricing is selling below cost to gain a strategic market advantage. As predatory pricing on an international scale has been difficult to prove, alternative tests that are supposed to provide a simpler means of identifying predatory pricing have been devised. These tests, while they may provide evidence of predatory pricing, do not necessarily do so and, hence, anti-dumping duties may be applied in situations which are not defensible in economic theory (Kerr, 2006; Lau, 2007). Having duties imposed serves the interests of firms in importing countries that are seeking protection.

International predatory pricing might be practised by an exporting firm to gain market shares or even market domination in an importing country. It could sell below cost in the importing country and sustain this practice by cross-subsidizing with profits from sales in the exporter's domestic market. This may be the tactic followed when the importing country has restrictions on foreign investment which prevent the less expensive strategy of acquiring market share by purchase or merger (McGee, 1958). Clearly, predatory pricing is detrimental to competing firms in an importing nation, and in many countries it would not be allowed if the predatory firm were a domestic competitor.

One definition of 'unfair' business practice used in dumping cases is selling at a price below the full cost of production, which is a pricing practice that is not illegal in domestic law – firms often lose money. Further, determining the full cost of production has proved elusive. Firms seldom produce only one output. Attempting to allocate a portion of the joint costs to the product that is suspected of being dumped is not a useful exercise. As there are no generally accepted international accounting rules, it only leads to contending groups of accountants. Further, securing the required cost information from a firm in a different country may be difficult if not impossible. Given the difficulties with calculating the 'full cost of production', it has become subject to widespread abuse as a protectionist measure (Kerr, 2006; Baylis and Malhorta, 2008). Vested interests have been able to prevail on their governments not to have the system improved at WTO negotiations (Kerr and Loppacher, 2004; Thulasidhass, 2012). It is important to realize, however, that 'selling below the full cost of production' does not necessarily mean that a foreign firm is using predatory pricing – most likely it is not, and imposing dumping duties is simply disguised protectionism (Kerr, 2001).

An alternative test which can be applied is whether or not the price in the importing country, allowing for transportation costs, is less than the price at which the commodity is marketed in the exporting country. In certain cases this could be evidence of predatory pricing. However, predatory pricing is not the only explanation for this 'evidence'. It is well known that a monopolist with the ability to keep markets separate will practise **price discrimination** (Schmitz et al., 1981). International boundaries provide an excellent means of keeping consumers apart. As a result, it may be the case that the optimum pricing strategy of the firm will be to charge a lower price in the importer's market. A monopolist, however, can be charging a price higher than the full cost of production. The importing country should not care if foreign firms wish to use monopoly pricing – charge higher than their true supply price – as this simply makes the importer's firms more competitive. In fact, if the monopolist were forced to set the price at its cost of production, it would lower its price. The lower price would be detrimental to firms in the importing country. Price discrimination is not an illegal business practice – everything from seniors' discounts to the use of coupons issued by supermarkets is price discrimination (Kerr, 2001). However, it may be to the advantage of firms in the importer's country to accuse the exporter of dumping using this definition. The tariff applied under anti-dumping provisions increases the price of imports to that which is charged in the exporter's domestic market.

It is also necessary to prove that the industry in the importing industry is 'injured' when dumping is taking place. As with the definitions of dumping, how injury is determined is left to the importing country's government to define. As a result, the methods used to determine injury have only a tenuous economic basis and are biased toward a positive determination (Kerr and Loppacher, 2004).

Clearly, the tests for dumping are flawed. In both cases – the selling below cost definition and the price discrimination definition – foreign firms are being held to a higher standard than domestic firms. When accusations of dumping are made they may simply represent opportunistic behaviour by importing firms rather than a true need for relief from predatory pricing. Firms that are exporting should carefully assess the risks associated with pricing strategies that could be construed as dumping. Further, companies facing import competition should monitor the pricing of foreign products. Prices of imports as well as those of the same product in the exporter's home market should be tracked. If the evidence suggests dumping, the information should be provided to the relevant government agency. Firms interested in engaging in international commerce should lobby their governments to work hard at having the definitions of dumping altered to truly reflect the unfair business practice of predatory pricing rather than the normal business practices of selling below cost or price discrimination. Currently, dumping is the WTO provision that is most open to exploitation by protectionists and significantly increases the risk of engaging in international commerce.

10.3 'Unfair' subsidization

Countervailing duties are the contingency protection measure used in the case of 'unfair' subsidies. The definition of what constitutes 'unfair' is well established. In the WTO, a countervailable subsidy is one which, firstly, is trade distorting and, secondly, has caused material injury to a domestic industry in the importing country. Trade-distorting subsidies are specifically disallowed, but there has been a long debate surrounding the difficult problem of defining a trade-distorting subsidy. In fact, all subsidies applied to traded commodities will distort international movements of products in the long run (Gaisford and Kerr, 2001). It has never been seriously contemplated that countervail should prevent governments from subsidizing.

Trade-distorting subsidies have been classified into three types in the WTO:

1. direct export subsidies;
2. domestic subsidies that indirectly enhance a country's export performance;
3. domestic subsidies that reduce or prevent the substitution of imported goods for domestically produced goods as inputs to production.

It is in the latter two cases that difficulties with definitions have arisen. Theoretical attention has focused on devising subsidies which will not elicit a supply response from domestic firms which either increases exports or reduces imports in the short run. The term used for subsidies that would be acceptable – that is, non-trade distorting in the short run – is **decoupled** (Kerr, 1988). Decoupled means that the level of subsidy is independent (decoupled) from the firm's level of output.

At the WTO negotiations, a pragmatic approach has been taken given the theoretical difficulties in defining decoupled subsidies. Subsidies have been divided among agreed categories based on whether they are considered countervailable or not. There is general agreement that subsidies that are not specific to a product or an individual firm are acceptable – or 'non-actionable'. Subsidies on research and development which are broad based, education subsidies, interest subsidies, assistance to disadvantaged regions and payments for upgrading facilities to meet new environmental standards are all considered non-actionable.

Prohibited subsidies are those whose payment depends upon the value or quantity of the goods exported or upon the firm receiving the subsidy having to purchase domestic goods rather than foreign goods. For example, to receive a subsidy a US firm might have to agree to purchase only American steel. If a subsidy is judged to be in the prohibited category it must be withdrawn immediately. Some exceptions have, however, been negotiated for agricultural commodities and developing countries. If a prohibited subsidy is not withdrawn, the complaining country can impose countervailing duties.

The third category – 'actionable' subsidies – is more complex. The agreement reached at the Uruguay Round stipulates that no member country should, through the use of its subsidies, cause injury to the domestic industry of another member country. For example, a subsidy paid to all smelters might lower the price of copper production sufficiently to allow significant quantities of copper to be exported to another country. Further, subsidies should not reduce the market access expected by a country as a result of a reduction of tariffs. For example, as part of its WTO commitments a country might agree to reduce its tariffs on coal. Firms in exporting countries could subsequently expect an increase in their coal sales. The country that reduces its tariffs, however, might introduce a subsidy on the transport of domestic coal that would just offset the effect of the tariff reduction. Hence, the increase in sales expected by the exporter would be nullified.

As any subsidy is likely to have some effect on trade volumes, to prevent nuisance suits over trivial trade distortions the concept of **serious prejudice** has been introduced. Serious prejudice is presumed to exist when an actionable subsidy exceeds 5 per cent of the subsidized product's value. When the subsidy level exceeds 5 per cent, if a country complains to the WTO it then is up to the subsidizing country to prove that the subsidy does not cause serious prejudice to the complaining member. Serious prejudice may prove difficult to define and, hence, easy to disprove in the case of an individual importing country. If a subsidy is proved to be actionable, the subsidizing country must withdraw the subsidy or remove the adverse effects. If it does not, countervailing duties can be imposed.

It is important for firms in importing countries to monitor the initiation of, or changes to, subsidies in the home countries of their major competitors. If the use of a prohibited or actionable subsidy is suspected, a representation can be made to the appropriate body in their own country. In a similar fashion, it is important that exporting firms work closely with domestic policy makers to ensure that new or altered subsidy programmes are not structured in ways which will lead to a request for countervailing duties from competing firms in their export market.

Firms taking subsidies from their governments should take care that they are not paid in ways that are considered actionable. It is the goods of the firm that received the subsidy that will have the countervailing duties imposed on them. Governments should be cognizant of the international constraints on their use of subsidies, but it is not always the case. Subnational governments, such as those of municipalities, may not. In any case, the onus is on the firm to ensure it has not been the recipient of an 'unfair' subsidy.

REFERENCES

Baylis, K. and Malhorta, N. (2008) Antidumping and market power in the agricultural sector, with a special case study of the fresh tomato industry. *Journal of International Law and Trade Policy*, 9(1), 38–50.

Gaisford, J.D. and Kerr, W.A. (2001) *Economic Analysis for International Trade Negotiations*, Edward Elgar Publishing, Cheltenham, UK and Northampton, MA, USA.

Kerr, W.A. (1988) The Canada–United States Free Trade Agreement and the livestock sector: The second stage negotiations. *Canadian Journal of Agricultural Economics*, 36, 895–903.

Kerr, W.A. (2001) Dumping – one of those economic myths. *Journal of International Law and Trade Policy*, 2(2), 1–10, www.esteyjournal.com.

Kerr, W.A. (2006) Dumping: Trade policy in need of a theoretical make over. *Canadian Journal of Agricultural Economics*, 54(1), 11–31.

Kerr, W.A. and Loppacher, L.J. (2004) Antidumping in the Doha negotiations: Fairy tales at the World Trade Organization. *Journal of World Trade*, 38(2), 211–44.

Lau, C.C. (2007) Antidumping: Theory and practice, rationales and calculation methods, in *Handbook on International Trade Policy*, ed. W.A. Kerr and J.D. Gaisford, Edward Elgar Publishing, Cheltenham, UK and Northampton, MA, USA.

McGee, J.S. (1958) Predatory price cutting: The Standard Oil (N.J.) case. *Journal of Law and Economics*, 1, 137–69.

Schmitz, A., Firch, R.S. and Hillman, J.S. (1981) Agricultural export dumping: The case of Mexican winter vegetables in the U.S. market. *American Journal of Agricultural Economics*, 63(4), 645–54.

Thulasidhass, P.R. (2012) Constructive methods and abuse of antidumping laws: A legal analysis of state practice within the WTO framework. *Journal of International Law and Trade Policy*, 13(2), 183–200.

Summary of Section III

While the institutions that attempt to provide rules under which international trade can be conducted may be badly flawed and a number of their existing rules open to opportunistic manipulation, they have proved both durable and relatively effective. Their effectiveness is not based on their formal legal status but rather on their very existence. Firms that act to blatantly disobey the rules will probably face increased transactions costs as the eye of international scrutiny is focused on them. Time and resources will be required to justify their actions and to provide information to domestic and/or international bodies. Governments which attempt to ignore their voluntarily agreed-to international commitments also face increased costs in terms of reduced international credibility and reputation. Further, concessions in other areas of economic or political interest may be more difficult to secure from other nations. The threat of these increased costs is sufficient to keep most international players within the 'spirit' of the agreed rules of trade.

There is a general consensus that rules for trade are needed. The lessons of the disaster of the 1930s are not lost on contemporary trade policy makers. The tug of war between a country's desire for sovereignty and the need for an orderly system for trade will continue. As the world economy becomes increasingly integrated, however, more and more vested interests are created in the continuation of the orderly conduct of international trade. It should also be kept in mind that vested interests in protectionism will always exist and, no matter what the rules, they will be actively seeking ways to circumvent commitments governments have made or, if possible, to convince governments to ignore their commitments.

Section IV

The economic actors which conduct international trade

Introduction to Section IV

The relative economic conditions in two or more countries create opportunities for engaging in international commercial transactions. The general rules within which international trade can be conducted are established under multilateral agreements or bilaterally between nation states. In addition, each individual country imposes laws and regulations relating to the conduct and administration of its international trade. In combination, this set of constraints represents the commercial environment within which international business activities can be undertaken. It is up to individual 'economic actors', however, to identify and act upon the opportunities for international trade which exist. These economic actors may be either private firms or government organizations. International transactions can take place between two private firms, between a private firm and a government organization or between two government organizations. These distinctions are important, because government organizations may have different objectives and operate under a different set of constraints from private firms. Depending upon the constraints faced by the individual economic actors, some opportunities for trade may be enhanced, while others may be reduced or eliminated. Even if a firm is not directly involved in international business, the international activities of firms and government organizations can alter its competitive position domestically. Hence, it is important to understand the economic actors that initiate and carry out international transactions.

International business must be approached from a very wide perspective. The traditional view of trade transactions being the exchange of goods between two firms located in different countries – commodity exports/imports – is far too narrow to encompass the range of activities that constitute international commerce. Some firms operate in more than one country – transnationals or **multinationals**. Expanding the definition of what is being traded to include 1) intellectual property, 2) goodwill (or reputation) and 3) services (particularly managerial services) helps to explain the activities of transnational firms. A foreign subsidiary run by a manager sent by the parent firm may simply be the export of managerial services from a nation where a particular form of managerial expertise is relatively abundant to a nation where it is relatively scarce. A transnational firm that manufactures new products or uses new processes in one country, which were invented in its research and development division in another country, is simply importing the output (intellectual property) of its research programme. Expanding the definition of exports/imports, however, does not help to explain why transnational firms exist.

As an alternative to setting up an operation in a second country, any firm that perceives an export opportunity has the option of simply operating in one country and selling to a firm in another country. Companies 'rent out' managerial services to independent firms in foreign countries. Patented processes are sold outright to foreign firms. Further, simply extending the definition of what is being traded does not explain the existence of the large number of intermediate forms of organizing international commercial activity that exist in between market transactions by national (those that choose to operate in only one country) firms in two countries and exchanges among the operations of a transnational firm. These intermediate forms of business organization include international joint ventures, licensing arrangements, franchising, and long-term contracts. In Chapter 11, the types of considerations which influence a firm's choice for the organizational form which it will use to exploit perceived international business opportunities will be examined in detail.

An additional choice faces national firms that have identified a profitable international business opportunity. They can choose either to export their products directly to foreign customers or to sell to companies that specialize in arranging international transactions. These 'trading houses' can operate in the exporting country or in the importing country, or they may be transnationals. They may be large trading **conglomerates** like those that have long been associated with Hong Kong (such as Jardine, Matheson & Co.) and Japan (such as Mitsubishi), or they may simply be small import–export businesses. There are national firms that are primarily concerned with the production of goods that undertake international transactions themselves, and there are others that choose to sell to intermediaries. What factors influence that choice?

The undertaking of international business is extremely complex and will vary with the nations involved, with what is being transacted, with the size of the market and with the partners to the transaction. As a result, a business must consider each transaction on its own merit. There are no fixed rules that can provide 'cookbook answers'. Section IV, however, provides a guide to some of the complex decisions facing business people wishing to engage in international commerce.

11
National firms and transnational firms

11.1 Do transnationals make sense?

At the start of the twenty-first century there were approximately 40 000 transnational corporations. There was a fivefold increase in the number of transnational firms from 1970 to 1990 (UNCTAD, 1993). These firms had 200 000 foreign affiliates. Approximately one-third of the global exports of goods and services are intra-firm trade between parents and affiliates.

The question of how international transactions are actually organized has not been an important concern of most economists who have been in the forefront of developing the theory of international trade. They have been interested in understanding the economic forces which create opportunities for trade and which can alter the international competitiveness of industries. Whether a trade opportunity is acted upon by a British firm selling to a French firm or by a British firm transferring some of its output to a subsidiary in France, the trade flow is the same. Relative profitability should determine whether a British firm sells directly to a French firm or sets up a subsidiary. The alternative means by which international transactions can be organized will differ in their costs, and these costs will be an important factor in determining the organizational form that is chosen by firms. Trade theorists of the neo-classical school, who are not concerned with the organizational form under which trade is conducted, simply assume that these 'transaction' costs are small enough to safely ignore. For most of the questions they wish to explore, little is lost in making this assumption. Transactions costs cannot be ignored, however, if questions concerning the organization of international commerce are to be answered.

11.2 The cost of organizing international transactions

The relationship between the costs of organizing international transactions and the types of institutions, for example bilateral contracts between national firms in different countries, transnational firms, joint ventures, international licensing agreements and so on, which actually coordinate those transactions is part of the more general question concerning when firms coordinate economic activities and when markets are used to coordinate economic activities. This approach to understanding the organization of economic activity has its roots in the work of Nobel Prize winner Ronald Coase (1937), who asked the question 'What determines the size of a firm?', where size is taken to mean the number of activities which come under the direction of a firm's management. Turning this question around, it becomes 'At what stage will markets – or some other mechanism – replace within-firm managerial orders as the means of moving products through the production and distribution system?' (Gaisford et al., 1994). A new 'school' of economic thought known as 'transactions cost economics' or 'new institutional economics' has arisen which attempts to answer these and other related questions. Some of the major authors identified with new institutional economics are Armen Alchian, Yoram Barzel, Stephen Cheung, Paul Joskow, Benjamin Klein and Oliver Williamson. A readable discussion of new institutional economics can be found in Cheung (1992) or Hobbs and Kerr (1999).

All of the methods that can be used to accomplish the vertical coordination of production and distribution require a commitment of resources and, hence, impose costs on a firm. When markets are used to organize vertical coordination, it is prices that provide the incentives for firms to sell products or to purchase inputs. Changes in prices force firms to re-evaluate their decisions. The constant re-evaluation of selling and buying decisions allows for the identification of the mix of business activities that will maximize profits. Firms using markets, however, must expend resources to acquire information on prices, to negotiate a deal with the selected suppliers or customers and to ensure that the deal is honoured. Such activities come under the general headings of information, negotiation and monitoring/enforcement costs.

Let us use the example of a car manufacturer to illustrate this point. Assume the manufacturer purchases the brake pads that are subsequently incorporated in its new vehicles. To select a supplier, purchasing personnel must first phone around to various potential suppliers to get rough price quotes – information costs. These price quotes must be evaluated. When a number of likely suppliers are identified, executives must spend time in preliminary discussions with those firms. Once a deal is struck in principle with a supplier, lawyers must be brought in to draw up the legal contract – all of these are considered negotiating costs. It may then be necessary for the car manufacturer to institute a programme of testing the brake pads supplied to ensure that they meet its specifications before they are installed in the new cars – monitoring cost. Testing is necessary, because the quality of brake pads cannot be determined through simple visual observation. If the seller used inferior metal then the pads would wear out too quickly and the car manufacturer would be forced to replace customers' brakes or lose them as future customers. Testing the brake pads before they are installed will be much cheaper than either of these alternatives. Still, resources must be expended on testing. If the quality of brake pads could be determined without cost then the buyer would simply not pay the stipulated price for them. They could only be sold at a lower price that reflected their inferior quality. As the price system does not work perfectly and costlessly, the seller may choose to act opportunistically and use inferior materials to increase its profits. To prevent the seller from exercising this option, the buyer must incur the costs associated with testing.

As an alternative to using the price system to acquire the required brake pads, and incurring the cost associated with using it, the car manufacturer could simply purchase the brake pad supplier. Its own managers could then ensure that brake pads of the correct quality specification were supplied to the car assembly division. This would save the cost associated with acquiring and assessing competitive prices. No negotiations would be required and no legal fees incurred, as there would be no need for a contract. Quality standards would be specified as part of the car manufacturer's internal quality control system. Vertical coordination would be accomplished through managerial orders given to employees.

If managerial orders were always a less costly way of accomplishing the tasks associated with vertical coordination, then firms would tend to expand until they were **vertically integrated** along the entire production and distribution chain. While this sometimes happens, it is clearly not the case for the majority of firms. This suggests that internally managing vertical coordination also has costs associated with it.

Managers charged with coordinating production or distribution activities within a firm require information upon which to base their decisions. This information is generated by the internal accounting system. Managers must ensure that this information is checked and verified. Further, employees have to be supervised to ensure that they efficiently undertake the tasks assigned by managerial orders. Without supervision, employees can exercise opportunities to 'shirk'. A manager may order that a truckload of brake pads be loaded for delivery to the assembly plant on Friday afternoon to meet a Monday morning automobile production deadline. Unless there is adequate supervision the workers may 1) leave before the job is completed or 2) work slowly, knowing that they will be retained and receive overtime pay to ensure that the Monday delivery can be met. Clearly a system of managerial orders also has costs associated with it.

Transactions cost theory suggests that, when it is more profitable to use a system of managerial orders to coordinate a production or distribution activity, then the firm will vertically integrate to internalize it. If markets can be used at a lower cost then the activity will not be internalized. Of course, in some cases both methods will be too costly and the activity will not take place.

A firm that decides to vertically integrate across international boundaries becomes a transnational firm. Goodwill, management skills and the use of intellectual property as well as the movement of goods can be coordinated internally across international boundaries. Doing business across international boundaries, however, can both alter the relative size of transactions costs and present firms with an array of new transactions costs which are not present when business operations are confined to one country. There are the obvious costs of currency conversion and of meeting the requirements of the importing country's customs regulations. The latter can add considerably to the costs and risks associated with doing business, particularly when over-zealous scrutiny of paperwork, tedious border inspections and capricious refusals of entry for cargoes are used as non-tariff barriers to trade. (For a discussion of one example of how the cost of these activities can affect firms' decisions to trade see Bruce and Kerr, 1986.)

Each country has its own consumer protection legislation that can force firms to alter production processes or to entirely redesign products. Foreign consumers may have different tastes that must be catered to. For example, most beef consumers in North America and Europe prefer lean meat. In Japan, for a variety of religious and culinary reasons, consumers prefer beef that has a very high degree of internal fat (Kerr et al., 1994). Successfully exporting to this lucrative Japanese **niche market** requires firms in beef-exporting countries to alter their beef-processing procedures, livestock production systems and even the genetics of the animals used in production. Meat plants wishing to supply Islamic countries must employ mullahs to conduct halal slaughter rituals. In Britain and Japan, cars are driven on the left-hand side of the road, while in Western Europe and North America they are driven on the right. Successful exporters in Japan and Britain had to design and engineer their cars to accommodate both right- and left-hand drives. (Car manufacturers in the US historically did not typically design their cars to accommodate right-hand drive mechanisms, which may explain better than any other reason their failure to export to the Japanese market. Of course, some US manufacturers solved this problem in the United Kingdom by establishing subsidiaries. Relatively flat domestic demand in recent years has, however, led US firms to engineer more of their vehicles to be adapted during production to drive on either side of the road.)

Tax regimes differ among countries, and time and resources must be spent to determine the correct mix of activities to be undertaken in each country. Tariffs may have to be paid. International shipments may require sturdier packaging. Executives may have to be given training in foreign business practices, and they and their families familiarized with a foreign culture.

European transnational oil companies operating in the Middle East, for example, provide intensive orientation programmes for their executives and their families before they move abroad. Expensive leave, travel and emergency health care packages must be offered to executives and professional personnel sent to many foreign postings. While the numerous additional costs of doing business internationally can be identified and factored into business decisions, the important question is how these costs affect how the firm chooses to conduct its international activities.

11.3 Capturing the returns to research and development

Some firms spend considerable resources on researching and developing new products and production processes. To recoup these costs, including the costs of failed research projects, companies must be able to reap the benefits. Otherwise, they will not be willing to invest in these activities. In the developed countries, where most of the world's research and development take place, governments have recognized that ensuring that firms can expect to receive the returns to their research and development activities is important for the process of economic growth. It does not matter how a firm captures the return on investment – by producing the new product or employing the new process in its own factories, by leasing the knowledge to another firm or by selling the knowledge outright. However, the ability to lease, sell or prevent others from benefiting from industrial espionage requires that the companies which do the research and development receive the property rights to the product or process. One method of assigning the rights to intellectual property is through the use of patents.

The success of patents as a means of providing firms with intellectual property rights depends upon the willingness of governments to enforce those rights (Boyd et al., 2003; Ball et al., 2013). When a foreign government rigorously enforces patents, firms can be assured that they will receive the benefits from the use of their knowledge in the foreign market. Intellectual property can be sold or leased. When property rights are not rigorously enforced by foreign governments, firms have an incentive to vertically integrate their operations into the foreign country so that they can maintain control of their property. (The term '**horizontal integration**' is often used to describe foreign branch plant operations which produce the same product as that which is produced by the firm in the home country. As we are expanding the definition of exports/imports to include intellectual property, goodwill and management services, branch plant operations are simply an alternative way of vertically coordinating exports, and to be consistent we will use the term 'vertical integration'.) Of course, the poor enforcement of property rights means that firms operating transnationally must expend resources to prevent industrial espionage in their foreign operation. This is often accomplished in subtle ways. For example, it may mean sending engineers or technicians from the home country to run the operation in the foreign country. If the knowledge is carried in their heads, possibilities for stealing copies of specifications and formulations are reduced. Further, individuals operating in a foreign environment may be less open to selling their knowledge – either through covert activities or by simply being hired away – than foreign nationals. If the knowledge is so complex that written records of specifications and procedures must be kept, or it is sufficiently simple to be acquired by observation, transnational firms will tend to hire and train local personnel. Managers sent from the home country may be more diligent at preventing industrial espionage than local managers.

While the intellectual property of domestic firms may be well protected, foreign-held patents and foreign operations may be considered fair game by courts or police. Hence, the system of justice has a *national bias*. Some companies spread a single industrial process among a number of countries so that no complete set of information on a process exists in any one country. This strategy reduces the incentive for industrial espionage or even confiscation of intellectual property through nationalization. Of course, each company must assess the loss of returns associated with selling or leasing its knowledge to firms in countries with poor enforcement of property rights against the extra cost of active measures to prevent industrial espionage. Clearly, firms may choose to become transnationals to increase the returns to the intellectual property that they own. Evidence of firms acting upon these types of incentives can be found in Buckley and Prescott (1989) and Davidson and McFetridge (1982).

Protection of intellectual property rights has been particularly poor in a number of developing countries (Boyd et al., 2003). In some countries, allowing local firms to treat the intellectual property of foreign firms as fair game has had the implicit if not explicit approval of the government. In many cases, however, the local government does not have the resources or capacity to enforce its laws relating to patents. Large numbers of transnational firms operate in these countries as a result. Little research and development work is, however, carried out. In some cases this has led to transnationals becoming a focal point for nationalist discontent, and policies have been put in place to restrict the activities of transnational corporations (Kerr and Anderson, 1992). One of the major problems associated with the liberalization of the former command economies of Eastern Europe, Russia and the rest of the former Soviet Union has been the absence of both a tradition of commercial law and the will to enforce newly proclaimed systems of commercial law (Hobbs et al., 1997).

11.4 Using goodwill to international advantage

A firm's goodwill relates to its reputation regarding the quality of the goods produced, the quality of the service provided or the trustworthiness with which it conducts its business affairs. One manifestation of goodwill is the firm's trademark. A firm that wishes to capitalize on its trademark internationally, that is, export its goodwill, has three forms of organization to choose from. It can export its products and prominently display the trademark on the product. It can also vertically integrate by setting up operations in the foreign country. Finally, it can rent its trademark to a firm in the other country through a franchise operation. Of course, in industries like fast food the first option does not exist, because the perishability of the product precludes its direct export. The decision regarding how to enter a foreign market will depend on the degree of protection given to trademarks and the costs of monitoring activities in foreign countries.

Low-quality counterfeits dissipate the firm's goodwill with consumers. If the laws restricting counterfeiting are poorly drafted or enforced, then a firm may choose to operate transnationally by establishing its own distribution system. By directly controlling distribution, substandard counterfeits cannot be passed off as trademark products. This has been a strategy followed by at least one major jeans manufacturer, Levi Strauss.

Franchises will be used when it is easy to monitor the quality of the product. If the holder of a franchise can cheat on quality, say by using substandard parts in electrical goods or lowering service standards in a franchised fast food chain, it can lower costs and enhance its profits in the short run. The firm selling the franchise loses goodwill over time as customers become less and less satisfied. Having the foreign operation run by a salaried employee reduces the temptation to cheat on quality. Firms like McDonald's prefer direct ownership to franchises in some markets. Where quality may be difficult to measure, such as in banking or for engineering consultants, direct ownership is more likely to be used.

11.5 Protecting vulnerable assets

An incentive can be created for firms to integrate transnationally in cases where a large degree of **asset specificity** exists in a good that is to be traded across borders. The incentive also exists when investment in production processes dedicated to individual foreign markets is required. Asset specificity arises when investments are made by one party which, once made, are limited in alternative uses. After the investment is made, the other party to the transaction may be able to 'renegotiate' the terms of the transaction to its advantage (Klein et al., 1978). Formally, this purposeful renegotiating of an agreement for economic gain is known as **post-contractual opportunistic behaviour (PCOB)** or **opportunistic recontracting**. For example, suppose a firm in an exporting country could negotiate a contract to supply a guidance system suitable only for installation in one particular type of aircraft made by a firm in another country. To produce this guidance system, however, the exporting firm might have to make a considerable investment in a production line that would have few alternative uses. Prior to making the investment, the firm would have to negotiate a price for the guidance system that would cover its production costs and at least a competitive return on investment. Once the investment is made, however, the buying firm has the opportunity to attempt PCOB. It has an incentive to renegotiate the price it pays for the guidance system because the selling firm has no other market in which to sell its guidance system. As long as the buyer will pay a price sufficient to cover the guidance system's production cost and to contribute something to a return on capital, the selling firm will be better off than if it is forced to cease production. Refusing to produce the guidance system unless it gets the original agreed price will mean higher losses, because the exporter will receive no contribution to return on capital. While it may be possible to attempt to seek enforcement of the original contract conditions in the courts, legal costs may be large, and litigation long and drawn out. When legal recourse must be sought across international boundaries, enforcement may be difficult (Wasylyniuk et al., 2003), and the legal process may suffer from national bias. Teece (1976) discusses a number of examples of opportunistic recontracting.

Firms in exporting countries, however, may well be cognizant of the risks of PCOB and build extra premiums into the prices they are willing to negotiate. The buying firm, on the other hand, by integrating backward into the exporting country can set up its own production facility and avoid these price premiums. Transnational operations in mining and other resource-based industries can be explained in this way. Specificity can also be present in consumer products. Special goods may be produced to satisfy a unique foreign taste and, hence, can be sold only at a discount in the country where production takes place. For example, the very fat beef preferred by Japanese consumers can be sold only at a considerable discount to consumers in exporting countries like the US, Canada and Australia (Hobbs and Kerr, 1991).

If product quality is costly to determine, buyers are faced with the possibility that sellers either are unable to deliver the required quality or may cheat on quality. Buyers may build in price discounts to their offer prices that reflect their perceived risks. At these prices, sellers may not realize sufficient profits and, hence, will not sell high-quality merchandise. As a result, no international trade will take place in high-quality products. If the buying firm decides to operate transnationally by purchasing the operation in the exporting country, then it can eliminate this risk by setting up a quality control system run by its own managers. Japanese importers complain that quality control is lax in both beef production and beef processing in exporting countries. Shipments are often refused. Negotiating a mutually acceptable contract price with risk-averse beef exporters has proved almost impossible. Some Japanese firms have purchased ranches and processing facilities in Australia and the US (Anderson et al., 1992). Exporting firms are likely to integrate forward and operate transnationally when the distribution of their product requires specific investments or if their product is subject to deterioration if improperly handled during distribution.

11.6 Exercising market power

If international **cartels** are outlawed, or if the cost of enforcing cartel arrangements is too high, then there may be an incentive to operate transnationally so that the full benefits arising from the exercise of market power can be realized (Casson, 1985; Ball et al., 2013). For example, if separate firms in a number of countries are producing and selling very similar products under monopoly conditions, each individual firm may have an incentive to attempt to increase its market by exporting to another country. In other words, the individual national monopolies would be broken by competition from imports. The resulting competition reduces total profits. Hence, there is an incentive for firms to cooperate to maintain their individual national monopolies. In many countries, however, joining a cartel is illegal. Even if cartels are legal, there may be large incentives for individual members to cheat. If detection of cheating is difficult, total profits of the cartel will be reduced. If production comes under the ownership of one firm operating transnationally, then it can order its individual national subsidiaries not to export. Basically, because the total potential profits of the transnational firm are larger than the sum of the potential profits of the individual firms, the transnational can afford to purchase the individual national firms. When circumvention of market sharing agreements is easy to identify and police, cartels will be the preferred form of industrial organization. Cartels may also be preferred when the purchase of national firms is prohibited. This is the case for international air flights where government-owned airlines have been prevalent.

11.7 Strategic use of transfer prices

Firms operating transnationally may be able to increase their profits by being able to take advantage of differences in tax rates among countries. Strategic use of internal **transfer pricing** across national boundaries can reduce a company's tax bill. Internal transfer prices are the reported accounting prices at which goods or services are transferred between different divisions of a company. Assume that an importing country taxes profits at a higher rate than the country where the exports originate. Increasing the reported price at which the exporting division transfers the product to a subsidiary in the importing country decreases the pre-tax profits made by the division in the importing country. At the same time, the high transfer price increases the pre-tax profits in the exporting division. These increased pre-tax profits are taxed at a lower rate, resulting in higher net profits for the firm. This will give the transnational corporation an advantage over separate firms engaging in transactions at the market price. Abuse of transfer pricing, whether real or imagined, has been one of the major criticisms of transnational corporations and has led to considerable friction with national governments.

Some countries have elaborate customs regulations that require firms to provide detailed information. Complying with these regulations is costly for firms. Even if the transfer of goods is undertaken at the prices that would prevail in the market, the transnational corporation may be able to charge a high price for management fees or other services whose true value may be extremely difficult for tax departments to estimate.

11.8 Long-term contracts

Long-term contracts can be used as an alternative to both transnational operations and arm's length export sales at spot market prices. Contracts may be less costly than operating transnationally when the importer's legal system is well enforced, is relatively inexpensive and does not have a bias toward national firms. Contracts work well when the relationship between the exporting and importing countries is harmonious, the prices of the traded goods are not volatile and the market environment is sufficiently well understood so that the contract can be specified to account for most contingencies. Compensation for breach of contract should be included in the contract. Long-term contracts are less costly than one-off export sales when guarantees of ongoing sales are required to justify investments in scale-based cost-saving technology. When fraud is easy to detect but hard to prove in court, problems with opportunistic breach of contract can be eliminated by choosing to produce the required commodity through a transnational operation. When exchange rates are unstable or markets unpredictable, it will be difficult to specify all contingencies in a contract. Greater reliance will be placed on one-off export sales.

11.9 Joint ventures

International **joint ventures** arise when capital or expertise from firms in different countries is combined to mutual advantage. In equity joint ventures, both parties contribute capital. When one firm contributes only expertise, it is a technical joint venture. In both cases, profits are shared on the basis of the contribution of the partners. Joint ventures differ from licensing arrangements or franchises in that any profits are shared, whereas the holder of the licence or franchise can keep all profits once the fee is paid.

By drawing on two sets of expertise, costs can be reduced. Business practices and customs differ among countries. A firm with an opportunity to sell its product in another country could choose to integrate forward by operating transnationally but would then have to make a considerable investment in learning local business practices and customs. Mistakes can be costly. Many examples exist of attempts to transfer advertising campaigns to foreign markets where they have, at best, had no impact and, at worst, greatly offended local consumers. Western business people who are used to writing complex contracts have had great difficulty adjusting to Japanese business relationships based primarily on trust built up over a long period of time. Of course, the problems encountered by Japanese automobile firms when they attempted to transplant their personnel management practices to the US and

Europe have been the subject of a number of movie comedies. Having a joint venture partner can eliminate these costly learning periods. Further, governments may be more predisposed to providing grants and subsidies when a local partner is involved in a venture.

Joint ventures are distinct from mergers in that they are set up with a specific task in mind. When the task is accomplished or the venture is no longer mutually advantageous, it can be terminated without the difficulties associated with dividing the assets of fully integrated firms. Both parties share in the profits and, therefore, each has less of an incentive to act opportunistically than if they were separate firms. The incentive to cheat is not, however, totally eliminated. This means that time and resources must be expended to monitor the activities of partners. Further, while the cost of learning how to conduct business in the foreign economy is eliminated, managers seconded to the joint venture may have to learn to work with partners who have very different business practices. These cultural differences can often endanger the success of joint ventures. The fact that many governments have had to force foreign firms into joint ventures suggests that these transactions costs are not trivial.

Joint ventures may be terminated because the objectives of firms change over time. By observing its joint venture partners, the exporting firm may learn enough about the local market to feel sufficiently confident to undertake the distribution of its product directly. On the other hand, if the joint venture involves production, the local partner may learn a sufficient amount about the process to set up its own production facility. Hence, joint ventures carry the risk that future competitors will be created. The relative cost of direct transnational operation will have to be weighed against the risk of creating future competition.

Owing to the ease with which they can be dissolved, joint ventures represent a means by which the transactions costs associated with abandoning international operations can be reduced. If a transnational firm makes it known that it wishes to shut down its operations in a country, the local government may attempt to prevent the loss of economic activity by restricting capital repatriation or threatening confiscation. If entry into a foreign market is perceived as risky, it may be prudent to enter the market via a joint venture operation. If the foreign joint venture proves to be not worthwhile, it may be sold at a discount to the local partner. There is less likely to be a problem with capital repatriation after a sale to a local partner.

If partners in the host country are considered too untrustworthy, the host country's economy is considered too unpredictable or the host government restricts repatriation of capital, equity joint ventures may not be advisable (Middleton et al., 1993). There may still be scope for technical joint ventures, where the host country partner puts up the capital and the exporting partner provides technical or managerial expertise through seconded staff. Profits are shared on a pre-agreed formula. A commitment of staff is made, but they can be easily withdrawn if the venture proves to be untenable.

11.10 Greenfield investments versus acquisitions

Firms will probably incur additional organizational costs when they choose to operate transnationally. Providing correct incentives and monitoring employees to prevent shirking will probably prove more difficult, and hence more costly, as cultural differences increase (Davidson and McFetridge, 1985). As a result, transnational operations may be more efficient when cultural differences are small. A firm wishing to enter a foreign market must also consider whether it wishes to enter the market by acquiring a firm in the host country or setting up an entirely new subsidiary – a **'greenfield' investment**. If the latter alternative is chosen, more mistakes are likely, and learning the foreign market will take longer. If the former method of market entry is chosen, then the firm inherits a local corporate culture that may not mesh well with its own.

11.11 Limits on foreign direct investment

As transnational corporations may have a competitive advantage over domestic firms, governments might wish to limit their activities (Kerr and Anderson, 1992; Ball et al., 2013). These restrictions act to limit foreign direct investment (FDI), as discussed in Chapter 1. If firms decide to organize themselves as transnationals, it suggests that this is the most profitable means of conducting their international commerce. Restrictions on FDI have similar trade-limiting effects to direct limits on the movements of goods and services. These restrictions can take many forms. There may be limits on the total amount of FDI. FDI may be restricted to certain sectors of the economy. Joint ventures with local firms may be required. Limits on the repatriation of profits can be imposed. These **trade-related investment measures (TRIMs)** have been addressed with limited success both in bilateral negotiations and at the WTO.

For a number of years Canada required all FDI proposals over a certain value to be vetted by its Foreign Investment Review Agency. The agency seldom, if ever, used its powers to deny an application. However, the paperwork required for the review process imposed additional costs on potential investors, and the process caused delays. Its public nature also informed Canadian firms of potentially profitable business ventures. Foreign firms, particularly in the US, felt that these procedures caused them to lose profitable opportunities. Canada agreed to significantly reduce its powers of scrutiny in the NAFTA.

The Uruguay Round also addressed the issue of TRIMs. The WTO will oversee the Agreement on Trade-Related Investment Measures. Regulations which require that local inputs must be purchased by transnationals or that restrict the volume or value of imported inputs they can purchase must be eliminated over fixed periods of time. The agreement, however, is weak, as it fails to deal with direct restrictions on investment and domestic regulations that may limit the business strategies of transnationals.

Clearly, the choice of organizational structure which firms use to expand into foreign markets depends upon a large number of factors, which all carry different costs. The continued existence of a wide range of international commercial arrangements suggests that no single type of arrangement offers consistent advantage. Further, how firms conduct international commerce evolves over time. Hence, it is important that firms engaging in international business should be willing to consider alternative organizational structures. Regular evaluations of these alternatives should be carried out.

 REFERENCES

Anderson, C.L., Hobbs, J.E. and Kerr, W.A. (1992) Transactions costs and the benefits of trade: Liberalizing the Japanese importing system for beef. *Asian Economic Journal*, 6(3), 289–301.

Ball, D.A., Geringer, J.M., McNett, J.M. and Minor, M.S. (2013) *International Business*, 13th edn, McGraw-Hill, New York.

Boyd, S.L., Kerr, W.A. and Perdikis, N. (2003) Agricultural biotechnology innovations versus intellectual property rights: Are developing countries at the mercy of multinationals? *Journal of World Intellectual Property*, 6(2), 211–32.

Bruce, C.J. and Kerr, W.A. (1986) A proposed arbitration system to ensure free trade in livestock products. *Canadian Journal of Agricultural Economics*, 34(3), 347–60.

Buckley, P. and Prescott, K. (1989) The structure of British industry sales in foreign markets. *Managerial and Decision Economics*, 10, 189–208.

Casson, M. (1985) Multinational monopolies and international cartels, in *The Economic Theory of the Multinational Enterprise: Selected Papers*, ed. P.J. Buckley and M. Casson, Macmillan, London, pp. 60–97.

Cheung, S.N.S. (1992) On the new institutional economics, in *Contract Economics*, ed. L. Werin and H. Wijkander, Blackwell, Oxford, pp. 48–65.

Coase, R.H. (1937) The nature of the firm. *Economica*, new series, 4, 386–405.

Davidson, W.H. and McFetridge, D. (1982) *International Technology Transactions and the Theory of the Firm*, Working Paper No. 106, Amos Tuck School of Business Administration, Dartmouth College, Hanover, NH.

Davidson, W.H. and McFetridge, D. (1985) International technology transfer mode. *Journal of International Business Studies*, Summer, 5–21.

Gaisford, J.D., Kerr, W.A. and Hobbs, J.E. (1994) Non-cooperative bilateral monopoly problems in liberalizing command economies. *Economic Systems*, 18(3), 265–79.

Hobbs, J.E. and Kerr, W.A. (1991) Japanese beef importing system changes may be less useful than first appeared. *Journal of Agricultural Taxation and Law*, 13(3), 236–57.

Hobbs, J.E. and Kerr, W.A. (1999) Transaction costs, in *The Current State of Economic Science*, Vol. 4, ed. S. Bhagwan Dahiya, Spellbound Publications, Rohtak, pp. 2111–33.

Hobbs, J.E., Kerr, W.A. and Gaisford, J.D. (1997) *Transformation of the Agrifood System in Central and Eastern Europe and the New Independent States*, CAB International, Wallingford.

Kerr, W.A. and Anderson, C.L. (1992) Multinational corporations, local enterprises and the political economy of development – some basic dynamics. *Journal of Economic Development*, 10(1), 105–24.

Kerr, W.A., Klein, K.K., Hobbs, J.E. and Kagatsume, M. (1994) *Marketing Beef in Japan*, Haworth Press, New York.

Klein, B., Crawford, R.G. and Alchian, A. (1978) Vertical integration, appropriable rents, and the competitive contracting process. *Journal of Law and Economics*, 28(2), 297–326.

Middleton, J., Hobbs, J.E. and Kerr, W.A. (1993) Poland's evolving food distribution system: Joint venture opportunities for British agribusiness. *Journal of European Business Education*, 3(1), 35–45.

Teece, D.J. (1976) *Vertical Integration and Divestiture in the U.S. Oil Industry: Economic Analysis and Policy Implications*, Institute for Energy Studies, Stanford University, Stanford, CA.

UNCTAD (1993) *World Investment Report 1993: Transnational Corporations and Integrated International Production*, United Nations, New York.

Wasylyniuk, C.R., Bessel, K.M., Kerr, W.A. and Hobbs, J.E. (2003) *The Evolving International Trade Regime for Food Safety and Environmental Standards: Potential Opportunities and Constraints for Saskatchewan's Beef Feedlot Industry*, Estey Centre for Law and Economics in International Trade, Saskatoon, www.esteycentre.com.

12

Private firms and state trading agencies

12.1 Government involvement in international commerce

In many countries the conduct of international commerce has, to some degree, been removed from the private sector and placed in the hands of the government. **State trading agencies** are often set up. Sometimes these agencies are broad based, handling a large number of products. More often, they are specialized to a limited range of commodities. Their degree of autonomy from the international trade ministry or other government departments with an interest in international commerce varies considerably. In some cases, they operate almost as profit-maximizing private firms, while in other cases they are instruments of government policy. Dealing with state trading agencies can present special problems for private firms wishing to import from, or export to, countries where they operate. Even where state trading agencies do not have a monopoly over a nation's commerce, they can alter the profitability of a transaction organized between private firms by granting concessionary trade terms to competitors. Further, transactions between state trading agencies in two different countries may not take place on a commercial basis and, hence, may affect the profitability of privately organized international transactions. Even if a private firm does not deal directly with state trading agencies, it is important to understand the motivations of these agencies and the parameters which determine their operating practices.

State trading agencies have been established to achieve a variety of political objectives. These objectives determine, in part, how state trading agencies interact with foreign firms and how they influence the international trading environment.

12.2 State trading agencies in command economies

In the command economies that were established in Russia and its empire after the communist revolution and subsequently in Eastern Europe, Asian communist states and Cuba, all international trade was in the hands of state trading agencies. International commerce was an arm of state foreign policy. State trading agencies, however, simply reflected the organization of communist economies, where all but the smallest of private enterprises were banned (Mises, 1981; Henderson and Kerr, 1984/85; Considine and Kerr, 2002). Some of these state trading enterprises have survived the transition of their economies from economic organization based on command to markets.

12.3 State trading agencies in mixed economies

Many countries whose economies are not based on central planning and vertical coordination based on command put at least a portion of their international trade in the hands of state trading agencies. Many developing countries established state trading agencies to replace the transnational corporations that controlled their international commerce. These transnationals were often able to exploit their market power to the detriment of local producers. State trading agencies may also have been established to provide local exporters with a degree of market power in international markets. The Canadian Wheat Board, which was once responsible for Canadian grain exports, was established with this objective. If they are run on a strictly commercial basis, state trading agencies may simply be extremely hard bargainers. Dealing with them will be similar to what might be expected from a private firm in a monopoly position.

In other cases, state trading agencies may be more closely linked to the diverse goals of government policy and, hence, may not make their decisions on strictly commercial criteria. This is particularly true for state agencies that deal in arms, munitions and strategic materials. The success or failure of negotiations between a state trading agency and a private firm in another country may well depend on such diverse criteria as the firm's employment practices, its environmental record, its investment portfolio, the countries with which it has commercial relations or the politics of the country where its head office is located. It is important that firms dealing with state trading agencies understand these non-commercial criteria. Otherwise, a great deal of negotiation time and effort may be expended to no avail. Firms may have to assess whether the potential profits from the transaction would justify altering their practices. To achieve political ends, governments may also be willing to accept lower rates of return or to subsidize the losses of state trading agencies. As a result, private firms that compete with state trading agencies in international markets may face prices or other conditions offered by a state trading agency which they cannot compete with.

State trading agencies may also be established when a country's demand for foreign exchange chronically exceeds the supply at the official exchange rate. In such cases, foreign exchange will have to be rationed. A government may feel that by establishing a state trading agency it can, through the direct control over the composition of imports that the agency can provide, use its limited foreign exchange to the best advantage. Often, this means giving priority to capital goods rather than consumer goods or the import of food staples rather than luxuries. Dealing with these types of state trading agencies may be long-drawn-out processes, as the demands for foreign exchange required for the particular transaction must be weighed by the agency against all other transactions. What appears to be a mutually advantageous international transaction when judged on commercial criteria may not be concluded because it fails to qualify under the criteria the agency uses to prioritize the use of foreign exchange.

Private firms should be cognizant that they must be willing to commit larger amounts of resources to the negotiation process than may typically be necessary in a transaction with another private firm. The state trading agency may simply be attempting to keep the negotiations going until sufficient reserves of foreign exchange are available for the transaction to qualify for funds. Further, because its negotiation costs are high, the state trading agency may be interested in negotiating only large-scale deals. Small firms may be effectively shut out of the market, a point that may not be obvious at the outset of discussions. Small firms should be careful not to put too much effort into a proposal until they are sure that the state trading agency is sufficiently interested to seriously pursue negotiations.

12.4 Payment in kind

When a state trading agency is responsible for only a few commodities or it is not directly involved in the allocation of foreign exchange reserves, its officials may not be able to acquire sufficient foreign exchange to finance the agency's import requirements. As a result, they may be encouraged to arrange international exchanges that do not require formal commitments of foreign exchange. These are usually some form of countertrade arrangement whereby the exporter agrees to import a specified quantity or value of product from the state trading agency's country as payment. These *payment-in-kind* arrangements require no foreign exchange.

Private firms considering entering into countertrade arrangements may be faced with considerable transactions costs. The costs associated with breaching contracts may also increase considerably. For example, an exporter may contract to design a factory and supply production engineering services in a foreign country. The host country may fear that if the firm were to be paid in cash it could behave opportunistically and under-engineer the facility. Only sub-quality goods could then be produced. On the other hand, if as part of the contract the exporter agreed to accept part of the factory's output as payment, it would have an incentive to ensure that high engineering standards were adhered to. Many countertrade agreements are based on this type of reciprocity and can be seen primarily as an aid to enforcing contracts (Williamson, 1985; Hennart, 1989).

Countertrade has, at times, accounted for approximately 20 per cent of the international exchange of goods and services, and state trading agencies continue to play a considerable role in some transition and developing economies. Hence, private firms interested in international commerce may forgo profitable opportunities if they refuse to consider countertrade arrangements. They must, however, be very careful to assess the transactions costs that will arise in the process of arranging and fulfilling the commitments made. These costs must be considered in the firm's decision-making process.

There are three basic types of countertrade agreements:

1. barter: goods for goods;
2. buy-backs: agreeing to purchase a portion of the output resulting from the goods or service inputs provided to an importer;
3. counter-purchase: where an equivalent value of unrelated goods must be purchased in return for securing the export order.

Each of these types of agreement will impose different transactions costs on the private firm entering into an agreement with a state trading agency.

12.4.1 Barter

If the countertrade arrangement is a **barter** agreement whereby a specified set of goods and/or services is exchanged for another specified set of goods and/or services, the original exporting firm will have a number of new tasks to undertake. First, it must assess the market value of the goods offered in exchange. In some cases this may be relatively straightforward. If the goods on offer are already present in the home market of the firm that will receive the goods (or some other third market which can be assessed), then valuation can be determined from market prices. However, if the goods on offer have no presence in the firm's home market then valuation may be difficult. Official prices in the supplying country are not likely to provide a reliable guide, as they may be determined directly by the government or produced under a considerable subsidy. Prices may not reflect market forces but instead foreign exchange distortions. To determine value, quality must be verified. In some cases samples offered by state trading agencies cannot be relied upon to provide a true representation of production quality. Until a reasonably accurate valuation is made, negotiations on the quantity to be exchanged cannot be concluded.

The receiving firm may not have had any experience in marketing the product on offer, for example a heavy engineering firm having to find markets for aspirin. Once an agreement is concluded, the firm that has agreed to accept the return products offered in a barter agreement must make arrangements to take delivery. This may involve arranging transport. Further, the original exporting firm may have no experience with importing, and additional expertise may have to be hired. The firm may then be faced with finding a market for the goods, incurring market entry costs and possibly establishing a distribution network. The goods may not arrive in convenient quantities and may have to be stored until they can be sold over time. They may have to be repackaged or further processed to meet the requirements of local consumers.

Of course, the firm receiving the goods in exchange may not wish to undertake these activities itself, particularly if the product line is not one with which it is familiar. In this case the product may be sold to another firm, but at a discount. Barter arrangements appear to be the least popular form of countertrade. The associated transactions costs are sufficient in magnitude to make such arrangements unattractive (Banks, 1983). Stories of firms desperate to make an export sale that were subsequently lumbered with shoddily produced and unreliable computers or unpalatable canned meat are sufficiently common to suggest that firms should be extremely careful when considering entering into a barter arrangement with a state trading agency.

12.4.2 Buy-back agreements

Buy-back agreements usually entail the exporter supplying capital equipment and/or technical expertise for use in a new or upgraded production facility. A share in the future output from the facility is taken in payment. Raw material inputs may also be provided, with repayment taken in the form of a portion of the output produced.

Buy-back agreements can also involve considerable hidden or unanticipated transactions costs. In some cases, the output produced may fit well within the exporting firm's activities and, hence, transactions costs are low. A steel producer that provides technical expertise to a new steel mill under a buy-back arrangement may well be able to integrate the additional steel received into its existing distribution system without much difficulty. On the other hand, a firm which produces paper-making machinery may have no experience with the marketing of paper. Arranging for the disposal of the output received in payment may require considerable additional expenditure. It is likely that the buy-back arrangement was suggested by the state trading agency in the first place because it did not have a ready market for the paper.

Even if the product received as payment in a buy-back arrangement fits well within the exporting firm's operation, there still may be problems with scheduling deliveries. This can be a significant problem if the product received in return is an input into further production. If the facility in the other country cannot keep to its agreed production schedule then alternative supplies may have to be arranged, often at higher costs. If the output is specialized to the production of the receiving firm – suggesting high switching costs – production may be disrupted. For example, if a car manufacturer provided engine-making machinery and expertise to produce engines for a particular line of its vehicles, no suitable alternative engine may be available if production in the engine plant is disrupted or the rate of production fails to meet a priori expectations.

If these problems were encountered in normal business transactions between private firms, the purchaser of the engines would have a number of alternatives. If management at the engine plant was perceived as the problem, then the car manufacturer could buy up the engine manufacturer and install its own management. This may not be possible when the deal is made with a state trading agency. Even if an alternative supply can be found in the case of a disruption in production, the firm is still bound to take the pre-specified quantity of output. A mismatch between the now available supply of the input and orders for the final output could be the result. Further, if the firm receiving the inputs has overestimated demand for its final output, it may be forced to carry excessive inventories of the agreed input because of the fixed quantities in the agreement.

Even if the product received in return is not an input into the exporting firm's production, problems may arise if the product does not meet the originally specified quality standards. The firm can refuse to accept the resulting output but is then in the position of not having received payment for the goods or services originally provided. If the state trading agency chooses to dispute the firm's claims regarding quality, then redress will have to be sought in the courts. State trading agencies, however, may receive preferred treatment from national courts. This is particularly true when state trading agencies are an integral component of government economic policy and courts are not independent.

12.4.3 Counter-purchase arrangements

Counter-purchase arrangements consist of two cash transactions without the need for foreign exchange. The exporter receives payment in the importer's local currency or credits equal to the pre-agreed value of goods or services that the exporter provides. These must be spent within the state trading agency's country. As the firm is allowed to select the items it takes in return, counter-purchase arrangements are more flexible than barter or buy-back agreements. The firm, however, is still faced with identifying suitable products to purchase and with arranging for import and eventual disposal.

If international trade is entirely under the control of a country's state trading agencies, the payment portion of the counter-purchase agreement will also have to be arranged with a state trading agency. The agency may attempt to restrict the range of products to which the firm has access – possibly to goods which are in surplus or which it finds difficult to sell internationally because of poor quality. Further, the state trading agency will have full information on the amount that the exporting firm must spend. If the goods on offer do not have a transparent domestic market, the state trading agency may be able to manipulate prices to reduce the firm's expected returns.

Many of the problems faced by private firms in their dealings with state trading agencies relate to the agency acting opportunistically. There are a number of reasons why this type of behaviour is more prevalent in state trading agencies. Countertrade exchanges tend to be large-scale one-off arrangements. The most important inhibitor of opportunistic behaviour is the threat of loss of future business. This is not a major concern in the case of arrangements that are not to be repeated. Further, as state trading agencies are not necessarily motivated by profits, the threat of the loss of future profits will weigh less in the decision-making process. As state trading agencies may be large, private firms may find themselves dealing with a different set of negotiators for each transaction. As a result, personal relationships and mutual trust may fail to develop.

Even if the official policy of the state trading agency is to not act opportunistically, the advancement of bureaucrats in state trading agencies may not be based on long-term results. Hence, they can have an incentive to act opportunistically to maximize their own personal satisfaction – a **principal–agent** problem. (Principal–agent problems relate to providing incentives for employees or other agents to act in ways which those setting the objectives – the principals – desire. In bureaucratic organizations like state trading agencies where measuring employees' output, such as promoting repeat business over a number of years, is particularly difficult, opportunities for employees to act in ways different from those desired by the principals are likely to be numerous. For a discussion of principal–agent theory see Strong and Waterson, 1987.) Further, state trading agencies in countries with strong socialist or nationalist traditions may perceive private firms or foreign businesses as socially undesirable and, hence, opportunistic behaviour towards them as being politically acceptable.

Firms should not be surprised when extra transactions costs arise from countertrade arrangements. Market-determined prices, payment in money and a fully convertible currency are considered necessary conditions for efficient international trade. These conditions are seldom manifest when state trading agencies are party to international transactions. Firms should take particular care to plan for additional costs when dealing with state trading agencies.

 REFERENCES

Banks, G. (1983) The economics and politics of countertrade. *World Economy*, 6, 159–81.

Considine, J.I. and Kerr, W.A. (2002) *The Russian Oil Economy*, Edward Elgar Publishing, Cheltenham, UK and Northampton, MA, USA.

Henderson, R. D'A. and Kerr, W.A. (1984/85) The theory and practice of economic relations between CMEA member states and African countries. *Journal of Contemporary African Studies*, 4(1/2), 3–35.

Hennart, J. (1989) The transaction cost rationale for countertrade. *Journal of Law, Economics and Organization*, 5(1), 127–53.

Mises, L. von (1981) *Socialism: An Economic and Sociological Analysis*, 3rd English edn, Liberty Classics, Indianapolis, IN.

Strong, N. and Waterson, M. (1987) Principals, agents and information, in *The Economics of the Firm*, ed. R. Clarke and T. McGuinness, Basil Blackwell, Oxford, pp. 18–41.

Williamson, O.E. (1985) *The Economic Institutions of Capitalism: Firms, Markets and Rational Contracting*, Free Press, New York.

13

Production firms and trading houses

13.1 What is a trading house?

Some firms specialize in organizing the international movement of goods. These import/export firms or '**trading houses**' act primarily as intermediaries between producers in exporting countries and users or distributors in importing countries. Trading houses may operate in one country or transnationally. If the trading house does not operate transnationally, it may deal exclusively with individual trading houses in other countries or a limited number of agents. In some cases, firms that started as trading houses have vertically integrated backward or forward into production or distribution activities and are virtually indistinguishable from transnational conglomerates. They may, however, still be referred to as trading houses. A producing firm which is thinking about expanding sales by entering a foreign market has a choice of directly exporting itself or using a trading house to expand its sales. Trading houses, however, should be distinguished from customs brokers or shipping agents that are used by firms only to facilitate the actual transnational movement of goods between countries.

The firm that is considering using a trading house may have the option of selling its product directly to the trading house or having the trading house act as its agent. This decision depends on the degree of control that the firm wishes to retain over its product in the marketing and distribution stages. In the case of the largest trading houses, a joint venture arrangement may be considered. As a result, the product expertise of the firm wishing to enter the foreign market can be directly combined with the trading house's knowledge of the local market. Importers can also be proactive in using the trading house to aid in the search for foreign suppliers.

13.2 Why use a trading house?

Trading houses are a means to reduce the transactions costs associated with entering a foreign market. Their ability to reduce transactions costs will be determined by a number of factors, including the characteristics of the product that will be exported, the characteristics of the market to be entered, the characteristics of the firm wishing to enter a foreign market and the importance of the potential market to the exporting firm.

Trading houses act to reduce transactions costs by providing a convenient grouping of services. They may also be able to take advantage of economies of scale. Hence, they play a similar role to department stores or warehouse discounters in a domestic market. There are considerable costs associated with entry into a foreign market – costs of identifying potential customers from a distance, travel costs for personnel, verification of the potential customer's reputation, compliance with foreign government regulations, and identification and selection of foreign legal, banking, taxation and other business support services. Trading houses are able to spread these costs over a large number of transactions. Further, once a trading house has been in operation for a considerable period, it is not faced with the costs associated with learning-by-doing that a firm which decides to enter a foreign market directly will have to incur.

13.2.1 Product characteristics

Some products lend themselves better to being sold through a trading house than others. When a firm does not need to retain control of the product in the marketing and distribution stages a trading house may be cost-effective. Generic products which do not need any advertising support can be sold to trading houses. It is then up the trading house to locate a distribution system. When marketing a brand name is important to a product's success in a foreign market, the exporting firm may benefit from direct contact with the distributors. The experience that the exporting firm has gained in marketing its products in the home market can be utilized to full advantage in this case. Of course, advertising and other promotion strategies may have to be tailored to the local market. Close cooperation may be required between the exporter and foreign distributors. When brand reputation is important, the firm may also wish to maintain control over distribution. Foreign distributors that do not properly care for, display or price the exporter's product to advantage can be dropped. For example, a firm may base its promotional activities on creating a quality image for its brand. The foreign distributor may try to capitalize on the quality image to its own advantage by selling the product at discount prices. This will attract additional customers to its premises and add to the sales of the other products it carries. The process of discounting, however, may cheapen the image of the product with consumers and act against the interests of the exporting firm. Selling the product to a trading house means that this form of control is lost.

'Stand-alone' or 'self-contained' products are more amenable to sale to a trading house than those which carry a large after-sales service component. After-sales services such as maintenance, repairs, spare parts, warranty work and replacement of defective units require specialized knowledge of the product which a trading house is unlikely to have and would find costly to invest in. As a result, firms wishing to export these types of products may well find it more efficient to set up their own transnational distribution organizations.

If the exporting firm perceives that the product it wishes to enter a foreign market with is 'risky' in terms of its possible acceptance in the market, then selling to a trading house may be a way to formally eliminate the risk. When approached, the trading house will contact its offices or agents in the target country to investigate the potential market. This should include an assessment of the risks associated with attempting to sell the product in that market. The trading house should be able to do the assessment at lower cost than the producing firm because of its experience in the country. Risks can be spread over the entire range of products that it trades in. Certainly, the trading firm will take account of the risks when it determines the price it will pay for the product, but it does assume the risk. Of course, this will be more important for producing firms that are small or where the foreign market is expected to be a large proportion of the firm's revenue.

When the producing firm is confident that its product will receive ready acceptance in the target market, then instead of selling the product to the trading house it may have the choice of using the trading house as an agent. This would mean that the producing firm will have access to the trading house's expertise in the target market but will retain ownership of its product. The producing firm, however, assumes any risks associated with sales of its products. The trading house will simply charge a fee for its services. Of course, a producing firm's relationship with a trading house need not remain static. A producing firm may, at the initial stage of market entry when perceived risks are high, choose to sell directly to the trading house. If the market develops successfully and the risk level falls, the trading house can then be hired as an agent. At some point the market may become sufficiently developed for the producing firm to wish to consider direct sales to foreign distributors or to establish a transnational distribution operation. Hence, a trading house can be a useful stepping stone to full market entry over the long run.

13.2.2 Market characteristics

The characteristics of the market to be entered – or more correctly the degree of difference between the market targeted for entry and the markets with which the producing firm has experience – will be important in determining whether a trading house is used. If the target market's consumers are similar to those in the producing firm's home market, if business practices are similar, if there are no major language difficulties and if the interaction between business and government is undertaken under the same philosophical basis as in the home country, then it may be a simple matter to conduct business directly with foreign firms. Basically, the cost of learning how to deal with the 'foreignness' of the market will be low. Mistakes, and the losses associated with them, will be reduced. When these differences are large, however, trading houses become a much more cost-effective means of conducting international commerce.

For example, in the interface between East Asian businesses and Western business, trading houses have taken a major role. In some cases, they have come to dominate trade. This is particularly true in Japan, where *sogo shosha* such as Mitsubishi and Mitsui are major forces in the national economy. The ten largest Japanese trading companies handle approximately 50 per cent of Japan's exports and 60 per cent of imports. The largest firms have in excess of 100 overseas offices. Further, owing to their extensive international networks, these trading companies conduct a considerable proportion of their business by arranging commercial transactions between firms in third countries (e.g. between the Philippines and Peru). The major Japanese trading houses have developed a wider expertise that includes insurance, banking, distribution, marketing and management support plus air, ocean and land transport. They have extensive networks of subsidiaries and many business partners. They also have close relations with the Japanese government.

The Japanese trading companies arose, and still prosper, because business practices developed very differently in Japan and there is still a shortage of Japanese who understand and feel comfortable dealing with Western business people. There are considerable differences between Japanese and Western culture, in methods of conducting business and in particular business etiquette. While the study of Japanese business techniques became popular in the wake of the spectacular Japanese success in the 1970s and 1980s, previously very little was known about Japan. Japanese education was very inward looking, and foreigners were discouraged from living and working in Japan. The Japanese written language, which is based partially on characters rather than an alphabet, requires a very large investment in time for foreigners to learn. In the period when Japan was beginning to trade with the world, most European and American firms were unwilling to make the investment necessary to learn about the Japanese market. The task fell to the Japanese to develop trade links. Trading companies were the most efficient way to organize the limited quantity of Japanese sufficiently versed in Western methods to be of use in facilitating trade. Even today, there are few Western firms that will spend the resources necessary to understand the Japanese market well enough to operate there directly.

Many Western firms have lost lucrative opportunities because they attempted to conduct business in Japan in the same fashion as in the West. In many cases the Japanese were offended, often in ways Western firms were never able to comprehend. Many Japanese firms have had similar experiences when they attempted to enter Western markets. For example, Japanese business relies much more heavily on building relationships based on trust and much less on contracts than their Western counterparts. Japanese business people often feel pressured into concluding business deals before they feel they can trust Western business people. On the other hand, Western business people feel that the Japanese waste time and won't close a deal. Western firms are more hierarchical in their decision structure and, hence, are able to make decisions quickly. Japanese firms seek to make internal decisions by consensus, a much slower process.

Trading houses such as Jardine, Matheson & Co. and Hutchison Whampoa developed in Hong Kong, primarily to facilitate Western trade with China. They handled the problem of the cultural interface by internalizing it within the company's structure through the use of local Chinese **compradors**. These employees or exclusive agents were able to develop the personal relationships upon which most business in China is based. Any cultural conflicts were kept within the firms. The costs associated with misunderstandings were minimized through trust built up over long years of cooperation based on mutual benefit.

Keeping the cross-cultural relationships few and long-standing meant that investment costs of cross-cultural education were minimized for both the Europeans and the Chinese. In a similar fashion, the lifetime employment practices of Japanese firms made the considerable investment required of Japanese employers to train staff to deal with foreign firms more worthwhile than similar investments made by Western firms for their more transient employees to learn about Japan.

The wider the cultural gulf between two countries, the larger the investment that will be required to directly trade successfully with the other country. A trading house can provide a cost advantage when this gulf is large. Identification of the right trading company to suit the particular requirements of the firm wishing to enter the foreign market may, however, require a considerable degree of investigation. Some trading houses are very specialized, while others are broad based. Individual trading houses offer different ranges of services. Hence, there will be a matching process that may take considerable time to arrive at. Some trading companies act transnationally, while others operate nationally. The latter may deal with a limited number of trusted agents in the foreign country. Again, the reason for the limited number of contacts is related to the investment time required to identify potential agents that can be trusted. Smaller or less well-established trading companies may not have as effective or reliable foreign agents.

For some commodities, it may be virtually impossible not to use a trading house. This is because moving the commodity requires specialized handling equipment or because some industries' markets are relatively closed. The international transfer of grain, for example, is almost exclusively controlled by grain trading firms like Cargill or Bunge.

13.2.3 Characteristics of the exporting firm

Many of the costs associated with directly entering a foreign market, either through direct distribution or by trading with foreign firms without a trading house to act as an intermediary, can be considered **indivisible** or lumpy. This means that they are not related to the quantity of output sold. Business travel, negotiation time, business communications, paperwork, and investments in machinery or other technology to comply with foreign customs regulations may be the same whether 100 or 50000 items are sold. Clearly, the more units of output that are sold for export the lower the per unit costs of these activities. As a result, using a trading house may be much more cost-effective for firms wishing to sell a small volume. If, over time, the market expands and develops, then a threshold may be reached where the firm might wish to consider dispensing with the use of a trading house.

13.2.4 Importance of the market

If a firm expects the market to be an important or long-term outlet for its product, it may wish to undertake the expense of direct market development from the outset. This is because using a trading house will mean that the firm will avoid the process of learning about the foreign market. In other words, it will become reliant on the services of the trading house and its contacts and agents. If the agents are closely tied to the trading house, then it may not be possible to deal with them independently when the producing firm decides that market volumes could justify dispensing with the services of the trading house. Even if retailers or other end users can be identified and contacted, they may not wish to damage their relationship with the trading house by dealing directly. Further, they may simply not trust the unknown producing firm even if they have direct experience with the commercial potential of the product itself. The production firm will be no further ahead than it was originally. The possible disruption to the normal distribution systems when the production firm attempts to enter the market independently may be costly.

13.3 Questions of culture

Clearly, the decision whether or not to use a trading house as the means to accomplish a firm's international ambitions is a complex one. Firms should not, however, underestimate the value of the services that a trading house can provide. Many production firms have not taken seriously the different ways business is conducted around the world. Even simple differences in language can cause loss of sales or ruin a major promotional launch. One car manufacturer spent considerable effort to invent a catchy name – at least to the ears of an English speaker – for one of its new models. In the process it inadvertently picked a word which was suggestive of poor performance in Spanish. The launch of the car in Spain and Latin America was a disaster. Even when the same language is spoken, subtle differences in usage can thwart a marketing effort. The best salesman for a British manufacturer of writing materials and related products could not understand the cool reception and lack of orders he received from a sales trip to visit the rather staid firms in the US stationery industry. It was not until he was long back in the UK and having a beer with an American friend that he discovered that the full range of rubbers he was offering US customers was taken to be a range of condoms – the American term is 'eraser'.

Business can involve a good deal of entertaining. The firm in a host country has a chance to trot out a range of culinary delicacies. Unprepared Western business people in Asia have caused great offence by refusing oriental delicacies such as dog or live seafood. Eating with the left hand in Arab countries gives great offence. British firms have offered Muslim visitors ham and Hindu buyers beef. The results have been the same, offence, loss of a mutually beneficial transaction and the possibility of gaining a reputation which will have a detrimental effect on wider business prospects. There is no single culprit in these situations – both the buyer and the seller needed to spend the resources to be better briefed. To understand when no offence is intended and that there are always ways to politely refuse is only efficient business practice.

Cross-cultural problems do not arise only in direct business dealings. Firms have sent employees with a fondness for alcohol to countries in the Middle East where consumption of alcohol is banned. The wives of Western businessmen are often unprepared for the restraints put on women in some Muslim countries. Most problems can be avoided by careful preparation and screening of those who are to deal with foreign clients. The best salesperson in the local market may be the wrong person to send abroad. All of these screening and training activities add to the costs of organizing successful foreign transactions. As is often the case with advertising or other forms of marketing, these activities may be treated as a cost rather than an investment by company management. A company's international division will probably require considerably higher investments per sale, particularly in the early days of entering a new market. The division may have a difficult time justifying these investments to senior management who are familiar only with the types of activities required in the home market.

There are many means by which the transactions costs of entering or operating in a foreign market can be reduced if a firm decides not to use the services of a trading house. First, it may be possible to hire personnel with valuable human capital. The children of immigrants from the country where market potential has been identified can often be particularly useful in helping to bridge the cultural gap. They are likely to have an appreciation of both cultures and to be able to explain the obvious pitfalls or faux pas to be avoided. Often they are bilingual and can be used for the direct conduct of negotiations. Even when they are not fully knowledgeable of their parents' former country, they are unlikely to require the same investment to 'get up to speed' as someone from an entirely different culture.

A firm should take care, however, before it hires the children of immigrants. For example, the children of Japanese who have immigrated to the US are often treated with suspicion by the Japanese. Similarly, while it may be an asset to have employees who are conversant in the language of the country to which exporting is to take place, this will not always be the case. It has been suggested that Japanese business people prefer to negotiate with foreign business people through a translator. The translation process allows them a longer time to formulate their responses.

Culture can often be used to advantage. Business people, particularly when they are new to a foreign environment, may be uneasy and unsure. A friendly face can get them relaxed or even leave them open to exploitation for commercial advantage. Japanese firms have been known to send one of their own employees who is a native of the visitor's country to meet the visitor at the airport on arrival. The task of the employee is to find out when the visitor has booked the flight home. Once this information is obtained from the 'friendly face', the firm's operation is coordinated so that the visitor is kept busy – touring the plant, meeting large numbers of apparently senior executives, and being entertained in expensive restaurants and bars. A few preliminary negotiation sessions may be arranged but nothing substantive. All the while the clock is ticking and the visitor, who has an employer who has spent a lot of money on the trip and who will expect results, begins to politely ask when serious negotiations will begin. All manner of stalling tactics are used, unsettling the visitor even more. Finally, an hour or two before the plane leaves the Japanese make some form of offer. The visitor, out of time and with nothing to show, will, it is expected, be willing to grant terms favourable to the hosts. Investing in the 'friendly face' can yield a high return.

13.4 The cost of identifying new markets

One of the major investments faced by a firm that chooses not to employ the services of a trading house is locating prospective buyers or suppliers in foreign countries. This **cost of search** is recognized as formidable both by business organizations such as chambers of commerce and by governments. As a result, both provide a number of services aimed at lowering this transactions cost for individual firms. Trade shows and fairs provide a relatively low-cost means of bringing large numbers of buyers and sellers together in one place. This lowers the cost of search for both parties. These gatherings, however, add a considerable element of competition. Buyers or sellers are able to directly compare the firms they may wish to deal with. Chambers of commerce provide a low-cost means of identifying the dates, locations and requirements of trade shows. Further, there are organizations that specialize in individual product lines – electronics, toys, wine, sporting goods, etc. – which offer more focused gatherings.

Firms wishing to have an exhibit at an international show need to research both the expected clientele and the most effective means of communicating their message. A display that is considered very effective in the home market may fail to communicate in a foreign market. It may appear amateurish when compared to the sophisticated offerings of firms with considerable international experience.

Many governments have programmes aimed at helping firms wishing to enter foreign markets. The programmes attempt to lower the costs of searching out customers. Embassies in foreign countries have commercial attachés and other staff whose job it is to become familiar with the country's markets and commercial practices. They develop contacts with foreign business people. They can often be useful in identifying potential customers and getting an initial meeting organized. Governments also arrange formal visits for groups of business people where a large number of potential contacts are arranged. Often these trips are wholly or partially subsidized. Visits for potential foreign customers can be organized. Commercial attachés can often aid in the process of evaluating a potential customer. They may know the foreign firm's reputation or will be able to suggest organizations in the foreign country that can provide an evaluation.

Banks which specialize in international transactions or which operate transnationally can also often provide information that can aid in the evaluation of the reliability of potential foreign customers. They may also provide insights into business practices, as well as assessments of political risk. They will be familiar with the regulations affecting the international transfer of funds.

Of course, the very wide range of services provided by chambers of commerce, governments and merchant banks are also provided in various forms by large trading houses. When one considers all of the activities which must be undertaken by each individual firm that chooses to organize its own international activities, it is not difficult to understand why trading houses have been so successful. As the globe has shrunk because of better communications and lower travel costs, the world business community has become more cosmopolitan. The widespread emulation of the American model of business education is reducing differences in business practices. International trading houses may find their competitive advantages eroded. The costs of organizing international transactions, however, are ever changing, and the dynamics of world markets will continue to evolve. New markets and new technologies may arise where trading houses will be able to deliver their services at a cost advantage. Firms trading in other markets may no longer choose to employ their services. Firms engaging in international commerce will have to continue to consider whether or not trading houses provide the least-cost means of accessing foreign markets.

Summary of Section IV

There is no one model of a successful international firm – one that has its product or service consumed in more than one country. Successful firms range from small one-person import/export businesses run out of an individual's home, to large conglomerates like Mitsubishi, to focused specialized firms like McDonald's, to government operations such as the national oil company of Saudi Arabia, to universities, to franchised dancing schools. The means by which they organize the vertical coordination required to accomplish international transactions is also extremely varied – spot markets, franchises, subsidiaries, agents, contracts, joint ventures, countertrade and licences. This continuing and probably increasing diversity suggests that firms, both those considering entering a foreign market for the first time and those that have been involved in international commerce for centuries, need to evaluate carefully the method that they will use to conduct international commerce. As with any business venture, long-term success will depend on the ability of the firm to adapt to new market opportunities and changes in its costs.

International commerce has additional costs associated with both the identification of market opportunities and completing transactions. Even if a firm does not directly organize its international commercial activities but rather employs an intermediary, it must still be cognizant of these costs to evaluate the value of the services of its agent. The volume of international trade and commerce has been growing at a more rapid rate than most domestic economies. This suggests that foreign markets are worthy of more than a casual glance. Given the nature of the additional transactions costs involved, evaluations need to be done carefully.

The process of entering a new foreign market will be the most costly phase of international commerce. Once foreign markets are successfully entered, the special activities required will become familiar and routine. There will always be the additional costs associated with currency exchange, customs regulations and staff training. Products will have to be altered or modifications made to service activities to satisfy foreign tastes. Differences in business practices and cultures will always present a challenge. They need to be dealt with within the rational framework of expected returns on investment. The key is to realize that most 'problems' will arise because insufficient investments were made in investigating those practices which make foreign transactions different from those in the familiar home market.

Section V

Institutions that facilitate international trade

Introduction to Section V

Transactions between firms in two countries will almost always be more expensive than similar transactions within one country. These international transactions costs can be sufficiently high that firms may seek out alternatives to directly exporting their products to firms located in other countries. These alternatives include joint ventures, licensing, franchises, vertically integrated transnational operations and selling to a trading house. Direct exporting, however, remains one of the most important methods of conducting international business. A number of institutions have developed over the long evolution of international commerce which act to reduce the transactions costs associated with organizing the movement of goods between firms located in different countries. These are primarily private sector institutions that charge a fee for their services. These fees must be taken into account when decisions regarding direct exporting are made. Direct exporting will be the mechanism used to undertake international business activities if the transactions costs associated with direct exporting are less than those associated with the alternatives.

A number of problems face the direct exporter once a tentative agreement has been negotiated with a foreign customer. It is important to stress that this is a point in time when only an agreement in principle regarding the transaction has been reached. Part of the final negotiations will relate to the specific institutional instruments that will be used to ensure that the transaction is completed to the satisfaction of both parties. Direct export opportunities which appear to be mutually beneficial for both parties often fail to take place because agreement cannot be reached on how to complete the transaction.

The three major problems facing a potential exporter are:

1. How is the transaction to be financed?

2. How are the goods to be physically moved from the exporting firm to the importing firm?
3. How are any disputes to be resolved?

These potential problem areas should be addressed prior to any transaction taking place – whether it is the simplest of domestic transactions or complicated international contracts.

For example, consider a simple transaction at a vegetable market – a customer negotiating the purchase of tomatoes from a vendor. Once a price and quantity have been agreed to, there are implicit, if not explicit, rules that exist to facilitate even this basic transaction. The transaction is financed by the direct exchange of currency. This ensures that the seller gets paid. Unless the buyer and seller have developed a relationship of mutual trust over a long association, credit is seldom extended and payment by cheque not acceptable. This is because the transactions costs associated with the seller verifying the creditworthiness of the buyer, or with chasing down the buyer if payment on the cheque is stopped, are simply too high. The buyer carries the tomatoes away from the stall, removing any need on the seller's part to arrange transport.

Disputes are minimized because the buyer is allowed to visually inspect the tomatoes that will be included in the purchase. Caveat emptor (or buyer beware) applies to other aspects of the tomatoes' quality which the buyer cannot detect during the visual inspection. The quality of a tomato eventually consumed in the home of the consumer can be affected by the treatment it receives by the consumer after the exchange and over which the seller has no control. Hence, to prevent disputes, the implicit rule of caveat emptor normally applies to this type of transaction.

Transactions are, however, seldom so simple. Payment terms are negotiated based on letters of credit, and 30–60 days for payment are pre-specified. Who pays for and arranges transport is subject to negotiation. Formal contracts are drawn up which attempt to carefully set out the exact conditions of the transaction and to outline an agreed course of action if problems arise. Contracts are an attempt to reduce the probability of disputes and the eventual costs associated with resolving them. If disputes do arise, they are ultimately solved by litigation in the courts. For international transactions, these potential problem areas become more complex and potentially more costly.

The increase in costs associated with international transactions arises for a number of reasons. Firstly, there is no international commercial law supported by a supranational legal system. As a result, if one party fails to live up to the terms and conditions of an international contract, the costs associated with solving the dispute rise and the risk of not achieving a satisfactory outcome increases. Secondly, as both the distances and the time involved between when the goods are shipped and when they are received in the buyer's premises tend to increase with international transactions, the potential for problems to arise while goods are in transit increases. Even if distances are short, time can be added because of the need to clear customs. Thirdly, two currencies will be involved in the transaction, and this will complicate the negotiations surrounding payment. Fourthly, establishing the trustworthiness of the other party to a transaction is likely to be more costly when it has to be done at a distance and across cultures. While these costs and risks cannot be eliminated, specialized international institutions exist to help reduce both the costs and the risks. In most cases, a range of services exist from which firms can choose. Costs vary, and finding a mutually satisfactory mix of services is a subject for negotiation between exporter and importer.

An exporter is faced with the problem of ensuring that payment will actually be received for the product sold to the foreign firm. In the best of all worlds, the exporter would be paid in its own currency deposited in its domestic bank by the importer prior to the shipment of the goods. There would be no risk for the exporter. This procedure, however, may not be acceptable to the importer because, once the exporter has received payment, the importer is vulnerable if the exporter chooses not to honour the contract and fails to ship the goods. The importer may attempt litigation in the courts of the exporting country, but legal costs may be prohibitive and the courts may be biased in favour of their own country's firms. Faced with this prospect, the importer may simply refuse to conclude the deal. On the other hand, the exporter may not be willing to risk shipping its goods and trusting the buyer to pay once the goods have been received. The exporter would be faced with litigation costs and the possibility that the importer's national courts are biased. A number of alternative means of payment have been devised which reduce the ability of firms to act opportunistically. These will be discussed in detail in Chapter 14.

Most international transactions involve a time lag between when a deal is negotiated and when the goods are finally delivered. Problems can arise as a result of the need to convert payment from one currency to another. This is because exchange rates are not normally fixed. Even when they are fixed, the possibility of devaluation always exists. A change in exchange rates over the time lag between conclusion of the contract negotiations and receipt of the goods will mean that one party may not receive the amount that it expected. A change in the exchange rate can wipe out the profits expected in the international transaction. The perceived exchange rate risks may be high enough for one party to prevent a successful conclusion to negotiations. Again, private market mechanisms exist which can reduce these risks, but at a cost.

Specialized enterprises have developed to facilitate the movement of goods between countries. There are institutions that help to reduce the transactions costs faced by firms wishing to export using sea or air transport. Air freight forwarders act to consolidate the shipments of a number of exporters so that bulk rates can be secured for their customers. Unique documents have been developed to standardize and facilitate the movement of sea freight. International insurance markets exist, and apportioning of liabilities among carriers, warehousers and the contracting clients is relatively standardized. Firms involved in exporting are faced with choices of transportation and insurance that must be weighed carefully when an export sale is being negotiated. It is often necessary to use customs brokers to facilitate the passage of goods across borders. The price negotiated in the contract can be used to apportion these costs between buyer and seller. For example, f.o.b. prices mean that the seller is responsible for all costs up until and including when the goods are loaded aboard the aircraft or ship that carries them abroad. This means that the costs of transport via the international carrier, insurance costs and the costs of delivery to the buyer's premises are paid by the buyer.

However, c.i.f. prices mean that the costs of international transport and insurance are paid for by the seller. Prices can also be quoted on the basis of 'ex works', where the importer takes responsibility for all aspects of the transaction after the product leaves the premises of the exporter. Prices may also be quoted 'as delivered' to the premises of the importer. Some firms may be able to negotiate better rates than others for transport and insurance. As a result, these aspects of the transaction need to be carefully negotiated.

As there is no system of international commercial law enforced by a supranational organization, national courts remain the last resort for legal recourse in the case of a contract dispute. The slowness, costs and possibility of national bias associated with the use of courts have led to international arbitration being provided by the private sector as a cost-reducing alternative. Arbitration by neutral parties can be chosen at any time by the mutual agreement of the disputing parties. International contracts often specify the use of arbitration if a dispute subsequently arises.

The costs of organizing international transactions tend to be higher than those associated with strictly domestic transactions. Firms, however, have the option of using a number of institutional arrangements that have developed in the private sector to reduce the costs faced by any firm wishing to undertake international transactions. The key is to choose the right mix of instruments to minimize these costs given the particular circumstances surrounding the transaction.

14

Financing international transactions

14.1 Arranging for payment

The financing of international transactions has three elements:

1. arranging for payment;
2. securing foreign exchange;
3. reducing the risks associated with changes in the exchange rate.

The most important of these is arranging for payment.

When considering export transactions, one of the most important points of negotiation is ensuring that payment is received. The converse, of course, is to ensure that the goods paid for are actually received. When a business deal is negotiated with a firm located in a country that has a different business ethic, with a firm whose personnel are not well known and where recourse to the court system is costly at best and biased at worst, an exporter is prudent if it worries whether it will be paid. The transaction is simply open to opportunistic behaviour on the part of the other party to the contract. Full insistence on payment in advance, however, leaves the importer open to opportunistic behaviour. The exporter may simply fail to ship the goods once it has been paid. While this may appear to be a pessimistic view of business practices, the very existence of a number of elaborate mechanisms which attempt to overcome the problem of ensuring payment suggests that examples of firms choosing to behave opportunistically are sufficiently numerous to have created a demand for these services.

The probability of non-payment is most acute when the business arrangement being negotiated is not likely to be repeated. If future mutually advantageous deals are probable, then neither side in the transaction has an incentive to act opportunistically by failing to pay (or failing to ship) the goods. Repeat business is the best insurance policy against opportunistic behaviour. It also allows time for the parties to become familiar with each other and to establish a relationship based on mutual trust. If such a continuing relationship can be built up over time, the costs of ensuring payment will be minimized.

14.1.1 Open account

The least costly method of organizing payment is an **open account** system. The exporter simply ships the goods and invoices the buyer, with payment being due at a specified time after the goods are received. The importer pays with its own cheque, and the only costs are the bank clearing charges. Of course, this is similar to most domestic transactions. The exporting firm must, however, be willing to pay any charges associated with technical problems related to payment and suffer the consequences for cash flow of any delays. Communicating with foreign banks and tracing down any problems with payment, even when the buyer is not behaving opportunistically, will increase costs. Open account, however, is probably a reasonable method to use with foreign customers with whom one has built up a successful ongoing business relationship.

If a firm uses an open account billing system and the buyer refuses to pay, the cost may be greater than in the case of a similar situation in the domestic market. This will be true even if litigation costs are no higher and the national courts in the buyer's country are not biased. For example, over the period that the goods are in transit, the foreign firm may become insolvent or simply change its mind and refuse to accept the goods. The exporter still owns the goods but is faced with the choice of either finding another foreign buyer or bringing the goods home. Finding another buyer in a foreign country may take considerable effort and expense (e.g. to fly out sales personnel). Making alternative arrangements may take considerable time and, as a result, storage costs will be incurred. If the goods are to be brought home, then the extra cost of international transport and insurance may have to be borne. In some cases, the import tariffs and customs duties associated with importing the goods back into the country will have to be paid. The final result may be that it is less costly to sell the goods off at a considerable discount in the original country of destination.

Outright refusal to pay may not be the preferred strategy for firms that have to consider the prospects of future business relations. Buyers, however, may still have considerable latitude to act opportunistically by attempting to renegotiate the agreed price. For example, the buyer may claim that the goods have not arrived in the condition specified in the contract and refuse to take delivery. The buyer may then propose a price reduction. It may be very costly for the exporter to verify the condition of the goods (e.g. flying out company personnel on short notice may be prohibitively expensive). The exporter, faced with either finding another buyer or transporting the goods home, may find the original buyer's reduced price offer the least costly alternative (Kerr et al., 1990; Ball et al., 2013). The buyer is speculating that the seller will be sufficiently unsure about the validity of its claim for future deals not to be affected. The great majority of international arbitrations relate to disputes over the condition of delivered goods and the appropriate price discount. This suggests that verification problems are common.

14.1.2 Documentary collection

Banks specializing in international transactions provide a range of services that can be used to reduce the risk of non-payment. One method is to arrange for *documentary collection*. The bank acts as an intermediary between the seller and buyer. The buyer cannot gain control of the goods unless payment is made. As a result, the opportunity of refusing to pay once the goods are received is removed, increasing the seller's security. Once a deal is negotiated, the seller ships its goods and then takes the documents that will secure the release of the goods from either the shipping company or a warehousing firm in the buyer's country to its bank. The bank then sends the documents to a bank in the buyer's country which it considers to be reliable. When the goods arrive, the buyer is notified. The buyer must make payment to the bank before it can receive the documents that will release the goods. The buyer takes the documents to where the goods are held, presents the documents and takes delivery. The bank in the buyer's country forwards payment to the seller's bank. The bank charges a percentage of the shipment's value for this service.

Risks still remain for the exporter. As there is normally a time lag between when the goods are shipped and when they are received, the buyer may decide that it no longer wishes to purchase the goods. Hence, the buyer may simply not attempt to claim the documents from the bank in its country. The result is that the seller has incurred all the cost of shipping its goods and, effectively, has no buyer. The seller's bank may be instructed to make a protest through a notary public that the bill is not paid at maturity, but that is the extent of its obligation. Neither bank provides any guarantee of payment. The 'protest' can form the basis of litigation, but the seller is still faced with the costs and risks of litigation in a foreign country. One way an exporter can reduce its potential losses is to negotiate the quoted price on an f.o.b. basis. This means that the importer pays for the cost of international transport and insurance and, hence, will be less likely to walk away from the shipment. At the time that the shipment must be paid for, however, the cost of transport and insurance represent a **sunk cost**. Based on its perception of the current market the buyer may still not want to accept the goods.

If the importer does not collect the documents, the exporter is faced with finding and conducting negotiations and paying storage or demurrage charges. The alternative is to pay for the goods to be transported back to the seller's country.

To provide a measure of standardization, and hence to reduce the costs of becoming informed about documentary collection procedures, the International Chamber of Commerce, a non-governmental organization supported by business, has developed *Uniform Rules for Collections*. Its conventions are followed by most banks dealing in international transactions.

14.1.3 Documentary letters of credit

Documentary letters of credit represent the next level of security for ensuring payment in international transactions. This is because the buyer's bank and possibly a bank in the seller's country act as guarantors of payment. A list of pre-specified conditions, however, must be met. Documentary letters of credit have two aspects. Firstly, there is a letter of credit whereby the importer's bank guarantees payment if the exporter fulfils a set of pre-established criteria by a certain date. Secondly, there is a package of pre-specified documents that provide the evidence that the seller has fulfilled its contractual obligations.

Once a contract is agreed upon, including the list of documents which will act as the proof that the exporter has fulfilled its obligations, the importer contacts its bank to draw up a letter of credit, which specifies the amount to be paid to the exporter. The importer's bank guarantees payment to the exporter. It is the bank's responsibility to secure payment from the importer. The letter of credit also sets out the documents that the exporter must provide the bank with before payment can be made.

The documents required to complete the transaction will vary depending on the nature of the goods. The exporter must provide proof that the goods have actually been shipped – bills of lading for sea transport, railway consignment notes, waybills for trucks, air waybills for air freight, and so on. An invoice that provides a complete description of the goods will be required. The accuracy of the description may have to be verified by independent experts. This provides the importer with assurance that the exporter is actually shipping what is required. This is very important, because the bank deals only in documents and in no way guarantees the quality or quantity of the goods actually shipped. If the documents conform to the requirements specified in the letter of credit, then the bank will make payment. The bank has no interest in whether the goods shipped conform to the specifications agreed in the contract. Hence, it is important that the documents required in the letter of credit reflect the goods envisioned in the original contract. If the exporter is to arrange insurance for the shipment, then proof of insurance will be required. Documents that provide evidence of health inspection may be required for shipments of food and live animals. Independent chemical analyses may be required in the case of potentially dangerous goods.

The documents required can be complex. It is the responsibility of the bank to scrutinize the documents carefully before releasing payment. If there is a discrepancy in the documents that the bank does not detect, then the buyer can refuse to pay the bank. In one study of documentary letters of credit, 50 per cent of the documents failed to conform to the pre-established conditions on first presentation to the bank (Paliwoda, 1991). At best, having to amend the documentation to ensure compliance can delay payment. Rectifying discrepancies can be expensive, however, if the goods have already been shipped. In some cases, it may mean cancellation of the contract. The bank can attempt to contact the buyer to determine if the discrepancy is acceptable. Payment will be made, however, only once the bank is completely satisfied. The extra costs associated with these documentary discrepancies mean that the exporters must exercise considerable diligence to ensure that the documents are correct. Otherwise, what is supposed to be a low-risk transaction will still be subject to a considerable degree of risk.

Even if the documents conform to the pre-established criteria, there are different types of documentary letters of credit, each of which involves different degrees of risk. **Revocable credits** can be cancelled by either the exporter or the importer at any time before the documents are presented. This means that the exporter is at risk if the goods have already been shipped or if the order has been produced to a buyer's unique specifications. In the former case, the exporter will still own its goods, but they will be in a foreign country without a buyer. In the latter case, the exporter will be in possession of goods that may be of only limited use to other customers and, hence, can be sold only at a discount. Revocable credits should be used only when the seller is sure of the buyer's need for the goods.

Irrevocable credits cannot be altered unilaterally by either party. The conditions can be changed only by the mutual agreement of both parties. In normal commercial conditions, irrevocable credits are sufficient to ensure that the seller will be paid. The importer's bank acts as a guarantor.

Irrevocable credits, however, may not provide sufficient security of payment if the exporter is concerned about the ability of the importer's bank to fulfil its role. This concern may arise because of problems with the bank's solvency or because of a high degree of political risk in the buyer's country. It may be possible to arrange for a bank in the exporter's home country, or a reputable bank in a third country, to guarantee payment. This is called an *irrevocable* **confirmed credit**. Obtaining this guarantee may not always be possible if the bank that the exporter asks to provide the guarantee perceives that the risk is too great. The exporter's bank, however, may be better able to assume the risk than an individual company and, hence, be willing to provide the service. It can spread the risk over a large number of international transactions in a number of countries. Further, the bank in the importer's country may be far more reluctant to default to a major international bank than it would be to default to an individual exporting firm. Defaulting to another bank could threaten its ability to engage in international transactions in the future. In some cases, the same considerations may influence the actions of government agencies allocating foreign exchange. They may be more reluctant to refuse foreign exchange that is to be paid to a foreign bank than if payments to an individual foreign company are involved.

While irrevocable confirmed credits ensure that the exporters get paid, they do not protect the importer that is dependent upon particular suppliers. While the buyer will not have to pay for goods that are not shipped, if the exporter simply fails to show up with the documents by the specified time – does not ship the goods – then the importer is faced with a breach of contract. It will be forced to search out alternative suppliers and to initiate legal proceedings for breach of contract in the seller's country.

The precautions that have to be taken to ensure against either an involuntary failure to pay or opportunistic behaviour by buyers may appear excessive. Approximately 20 per cent of exports are facilitated through the use of documentary letters of credit, suggesting that businesses feel that the risks are real. Table 14.1 shows the percentage of UK export transactions facilitated by documentary letters of credit in different parts of the world. Clearly, transactions with firms in developing countries are perceived as having a larger risk of non-payment than those entered into in developed countries. Even for the best markets, however, approximately 10 per cent of transactions incorporate this financial instrument. Letters of credit may cost 0.25 per cent of the value of the shipment, but volume discounts are available in some cases.

Table 14.1 Use of documentary letters of credit for transactions between the UK and selected other regions

Region	Percentage of UK exports that use documentary letters of credit
European Union	9%
Rest of Europe	20%
North America	11%
Latin America	27%
Middle East	52%
Asia-Pacific	43%
Africa	49%
Asia	46%
Australia and New Zealand	17%

Source: SITPRO (2003, p. 9).

To reduce the cost of acquiring information, the private sector has developed widely accepted rules for drawing up and using documentary letters of credit. These rules are provided by the *Uniform Customs and Practice for Documentary Credits* of the International Chamber of Commerce.

14.1.4 Factoring and discounting

In some cases, exporters may not wish to wait for payments from importers, particularly when long delays are involved. Further, they may not be willing to attempt to collect foreign debt themselves. They may find it simpler to pay someone else to deal with these inconveniences and for them to assume the risks involved. The large international banks have institutionalized these functions through subsidiaries known as factors.

For firms that simply suffer from cash flow problems, factors provide a discounting service for international transactions. The exporter turns its invoices over to the factor in return for an immediate payment, which can be equal to 75 per cent (or less) of the invoices' face value. When the invoices are due they must be repurchased by the exporter at face value. The foreign buyer continues to pay the exporter directly. If the foreign buyer fails to pay the debt, securing payment is still the responsibility of the exporter. The buyer may not even know that its invoices have been discounted.

When the exporting firm has no interest in being involved in collecting bad debts or payments in arrears from foreign customers, it can use the service called **factoring**. In this case, the firm acting as the factor becomes responsible for collecting foreign debts. The exporter continues to invoice the foreign buyers, but the buyer pays the factor directly.

The factor keeps a running ledger of the invoices, informs the buyer when it is in arrears and is ultimately responsible for any bad debts. A limit to the amount of invoice debt the factor will accept will be negotiated. This limit will depend on the degree of risk perceived by the factor. Factors are particularly useful for firms that have small export sales or are new in a market. Factors are experienced in determining the creditworthiness of firms in foreign countries. They have staff – or hire foreign firms – to collect accounts in arrears. If export sales volumes are small, the costs of carrying out these activities themselves may be prohibitively high for exporters.

The factor charges a commission for its services and discounts the value of the invoices based on its assessment of the risks involved. The exporter, however, receives immediate payment, while the factor may be willing to accept invoices with terms of payment of up to 180 days. Transactions costs may also be reduced for the exporter because it only has to deal with one factor instead of a large number of foreign customers. As each country will have a particular degree of risk, its own institutional rules and a unique business culture, staff savings can be significant when the exports of the firm are spread over a large number of small markets.

Factoring, however, may create other problems for the exporter. The buyer may take offence at having its creditworthiness implicitly questioned when the seller chooses to use factoring. Further, a factor may be less knowledgeable regarding the special circumstances which may arise in an industry than an exporter who is directly involved. As a result, importers may feel that factors are less sensitive to their problems than an exporter. They may not choose to do business with the exporter at a future date. As a business relationship grows, the need for factoring declines. An exporter must weigh the risk of destroying the possibility of developing an ongoing business relationship against the risk of a relatively unknown importing firm failing to pay.

The decision to use the services of a factor as a means to overcome problems with cash flow should be considered carefully. Given the high costs associated with foreign market entry, exporting should not be approached as a short-term opportunity. A severe cash flow constraint might suggest that the time is not right to initiate a programme of export sales. The discounts and fees charged by factors will lower the profitability of exporting in the short run. This may mean fewer resources are available for developing products better suited to foreign tastes and, hence, reduce profits in the long run. If the firm is unable to service a growing market because the upper limit on the value of invoices established by the factor is reached, then the firm may not be able to fully service the market. The exporter's reputation as a reliable supplier could suffer, and future developments in export markets could be negatively affected.

14.1.5 Forfaiting

Discounting and factoring are arrangements for problems that arise from short-term delays in payment. The delay in payment that is acceptable to factors will seldom exceed 180 days. Many export arrangements, however, are based on payment schemes set out in long-term contracts. This will often be the case when capital goods such as industrial machinery are being exported or when the construction period is very long, as is the case with power plants, railways, hydroelectric facilities and factories. Foreign buyers are allowed to make payments over time. The buyer may, for example, need to sell some of the output produced with imported machinery to pay for the machinery. A problem arises only when the foreign buyer cannot enter international capital markets directly to obtain financing for the imports. Often, this constraint is the result of restrictions on accessing capital put in place by the buyer's government. Further, past actions of the importer's government might have led lending institutions to believe that commercial transactions with firms in that country were too risky. In particular, special arrangements have been required for long-term contracts with developing countries. It should be emphasized that the risks or constraints discussed here arise from conditions outside the control of the importing firm. Commercial criteria must first be used to assess the ability of the importer to fulfil its contractual obligations.

The exporting firm has two problems: it needs to reduce the risk of not being paid by the buyer and it needs to secure the means to finance the deal over the life of the contract. These two services are combined by firms that engage in **forfaiting**. The term arises from the French term *à forfait*, which implies the forfeiting of rights. The forfaiter accepts a risk by giving up recourse to the exporter for repayment of a loan used to finance an export contract. Most firms that offer forfaiting services are located in Switzerland, Austria, Germany or the United Kingdom.

The need for this type of service arose from changing commercial conditions. In the late 1950s the capital goods markets changed from a seller's market to a buyer's market. In addition, the process of decolonization led to an increase in the number of capital importing markets, where political risk levels were high. Command economies also began to purchase Western machinery and equipment. The strictly controlled capital and foreign exchange markets of command economies meant that exporters required access to long-term export financing if they were to be able to successfully negotiate a sale. In response to this demand, forfaiting evolved to provide a medium-term means for exporters to finance the credits required by importers. Typically, if the services of a forfaiter are required, financing will be needed for approximately 80 per cent of the export sale. To ensure good faith on the part of the importer, immediate payment of 20 per cent of the value of the contract is normally required.

The forfaiter acts as the guarantor of last resort against non-payment by the importer. The exporter receives financing for the arrangements in the contract and is freed from having to undertake collection activities if the importer defaults on its payments. It receives immediate payment against the importer's promises to pay in the future. The forfaiter both discounts the value of the promissory notes and charges a commission for its services. Transactions financed through forfaiting are complex and involve at least five parties:

1. the exporter requiring financing;
2. the importer, which promises to pay for the goods and services provided by the exporter;
3. the importer's bank, which must provide a guarantee for the importer;
4. the forfaiter, which acts as the guarantor of final recourse;
5. an investor, usually an international bank, which purchases the importer's promises to pay at a discount from the forfaiter.

A typical forfaiting arrangement is organized as follows. The importer and exporter agree to a schedule of deliveries and/or work over a number of years. Payments on a fixed schedule are agreed subject to a forfaiter being willing to finance the undertaking. The exporter obtains a commitment from the forfaiter for financing. The forfaiter offers the exporter a fixed discount rate on the future receipts and agrees to make payment to the exporter upon receiving the importer's promises of payment. The importer draws up a number of promissory notes against the delivery of the goods and services. The importer then arranges an **aval** with a bank acceptable to the forfaiter. This is the only guarantee that the forfaiter has against its loan to the exporter, because it has forfeited its rights to seek repayment from the exporter if the importer fails to honour its promissory notes. This guarantee must not be conditional on the exporter fulfilling its part of the arrangement with the importer, because the forfaiter has no right to seek repayment from the exporter. Hence, the importer's bank must assess the trustworthiness of not only the importer but also the exporter.

Once the aval has been arranged, the importer delivers the endorsed promissory notes to the exporter. The exporter endorses the promissory notes, delivers them to the forfaiter and receives the previously agreed discounted payment. The forfaiter endorses the notes and sells them to investors on international money markets. The investor holding the promissory notes presents them to the importer at the appropriate point in time and receives payment. If payment is not forthcoming, the investor presents them to the importer's guaranteeing bank and demands payment under the terms of the aval. Only if both the importer and the importer's bank default will the investor present the notes to the forfaiter which has guaranteed them. The forfaiter pays the investor and then must attempt to obtain payment from the defaulters.

The forfaiter is fundamentally a country risk specialist, which must assess the risk that the notes will not be honoured by the importer's bank. Forfaiters also assemble packages of discounted promissory notes that will be of interest to investors. The offerings of forfaiters represent a high-yield component of an investor's portfolio. Forfaiters tend to limit their commitments to offerings of promissory notes whose due date is in less than seven years. Presumably, they find it difficult to assess risks with a sufficient degree of accuracy for longer periods into the future.

The discount rates applied by forfaiters are determined by the cost of money in the Euromarket for the period of financing. The additional fee which the forfaiter charges ranges from 0.1 to 0.125 cent per month (1.2 to 1.5 per cent per year). The exact rate will be determined by the forfaiter's assessment of the degree of risk in the importing country.

This long and detailed discussion of forfaiting arrangements underlines the difficulties which are associated with assuring payment for some international transactions. Clearly, it is an extremely complex system, which the parties to a transaction would seek to avoid. This suggests that, when forfaiting is used, the perceived political risks must be significant.

To fully understand the services that forfaiters provide – and that exporters are willing to pay for – it is necessary to examine a transaction in detail. Before entering into a contract the exporter must make a commercial assessment of the likelihood that the importer will pay. If that assessment is not positive it is unlikely that the deal will be acceptable to the bank chosen by the importer to provide the guarantee. In other words, the bank must have a positive assessment of the importer's willingness and ability to pay prior to the contract being signed. The bank must also assess the likelihood that the exporter will fulfil its contract obligations. The 'investor' must assess the reputation of the forfaiter before it will accept the discounted promissory notes on offer. Hence, the only risk that the forfaiter must assess and set fees against is the risk that the importer's bank will fail to honour the conditions of its aval. While it is true that banks do fail because of poor management, this does not happen sufficiently often to justify the fees charged by forfaiters. The real question is why an exporter would choose to pay for the services of a forfaiter if it could obtain the same unconditional guarantee for the promissory notes from the importer's bank. Over £2 billion of exports are financed by forfaiting each year, suggesting that the problem of political risk requires closer examination.

14.1.6 Political risk

Political risk arises when normal international business practices may be adversely affected in the future by political events. It may involve a change in the relationship between a firm operating in a foreign country and that country's government. It may arise because the government of a foreign country can no longer guarantee the peace and security required for the smooth functioning of businesses. Political risk may also arise as the result of a deterioration in the political relations between the governments of two firms engaged in an international transaction.

Governments can adversely affect businesses, including banks, by imposing regulations that reduce profitability. Changes in legislation or poor economic management can adversely affect the operations of firms. Examples might be government legislation restricting access to foreign exchange or its inability to control inflation. Governments can affect ownership rights through expropriation.

If a nation's government is faced with insurrection or social unrest, firms may find it increasingly difficult to conduct business. Politically motivated strikes may prevent workers from arriving for work. The transport of inputs or outputs may be affected. Fuel, electricity and water supplies may be disrupted.

Governments may also lack the ability to enforce commercial law. This will mean that the cost of doing business will rise. Without strong enforcement of commercial law, there will be fewer constraints on opportunistic behaviour. If promises to pay cannot be enforced, transactions will have to be undertaken in cash. The use of cash payments is both cumbersome and time consuming. Doing business in cash also means that business people are easy targets for hold-ups. If robbery and theft cannot be controlled by the police force, then firms will have to spend additional resources to secure their premises and hire private security guards. For example, most firms in the Philippines employ large numbers of security personnel. When the government cannot guarantee the commercial environment, a fertile ground is created for organized crime to regulate the conduct of business. Of course, organized crime extracts a heavy price for this service. In Russia, for example, firms must pay *protection money* to organized crime if they wish to operate in peace.

Corruption is another source of political risk. If government officials do not fear prosecution for demanding bribes, the cost of doing business will increase, as they are able to charge privately for the services they are paid by the government to provide. Firms dealing with corrupt officials become subject to their whims. While relatively formal rituals may evolve to facilitate the payment of bribes, firms may suddenly find their activities at risk if government personnel change and new rituals have to be established. Further, firms that have been actively engaged in bribery may find themselves under investigation if the government initiates an anti-corruption campaign. If the firm is involved in corruption in high places, a change of government may find the firm identified with the old regime and the subject of investigation by the new government.

When governments clash, long-term commercial arrangements may suddenly be at risk. Restrictions may be put on payments to firms or individuals in the country with which there is a dispute. The assets of the other nation's citizens may be frozen. Business travel may be restricted. Direct air flights may be suspended between the countries, adding to the cost of transportation. Border inspections and customs clearance may become more difficult and time consuming. The movement of certain goods may require special licences or may be banned entirely. In some cases, the international community may impose sanctions on governments whose behaviour it considers unacceptable. Sanctions were placed on Iraq until the Second Gulf War and on Iran for its perceived pursuit of nuclear weapons capability. All of these events can make it more difficult for firms to live up to their previously agreed commitments. They may not be able to continue with existing mutually profitable business arrangements with firms in the other country.

Assessing political risk requires that firms expend resources to acquire information. Some easily available proxies for the economic performance of governments can be found in the ratings given to government bonds by firms such as Standard & Poor's. As the assessment of political risk is complex, however, a number of specialized private firms have entered the market selling this service over recent years. Firms that are in the process of negotiating a major foreign contract may well wish to employ such a firm. The hiring of these firms on a short-term basis may be more effective than keeping political risk specialists on the staff. The assessment of political risk, however, is to a considerable degree an art rather than a science and, as a result, the quality of the work produced may be difficult to assess. A firm has no recourse if the assessment is not accurate. When the services of a forfaiter are employed, for example, the forfaiter has a direct interest in the results of its assessments because of the guarantees it provides.

The range and complexity of private sector mechanisms that exist to ensure that payment is received when international transactions are entered into suggest that the risk of non-payment is high. In addition to private mechanisms, many governments provide guarantees of payment – export financing guarantees. In some cases they can be obtained at lower rates than those commercially available. In other cases they may be available for situations where the private sector is unwilling to accept the risk. Often government guarantees can be used to secure private sector financing. Securing government funds or guarantees, of course, is a skill in itself, and firms may have to expend considerable resources to be successful. Further, governments tend to move at a pace which is frustrating for firms attempting to take advantage of an exporting opportunity.

14.2 Acquiring foreign exchange

One of the major complications arising in international transactions is that at some point one of the parties to the transaction will have to convert the currency it uses in its own country into the currency of the country of the other firm. This has two aspects. The first is the costs and problems associated with converting or acquiring foreign currency. The second relates to the problems created when rates of exchange change over time. As many international transactions involve a time lag between when a deal is concluded and when payment is finally made, there is the possibility that changes in the exchange rate can reduce the profits expected from the transaction or even turn a profitable transaction into one where a loss is incurred. There are, however, institutional arrangements whereby firms can protect themselves against adverse movements in the exchange rate. Problems associated with changing exchange rates and the actions firms can take to protect themselves from these changes will be discussed in section 14.3. The problems and costs associated with the acquisition of foreign currency will be dealt with here.

No universally acceptable international currency has evolved, even though the existence of such a currency would considerably simplify international commerce. The costs, in terms both of the fees charged for currency exchange and of the delays that may surround the acquisition of foreign currency, should not be underestimated. For example, prior to the establishment of the euro, a popular exercise for the press in the European Union, where currency markets are very advanced, was to illustrate these costs by starting with some nominal amount, say £100 in a British bank. The currency then followed an orderly progression through the banking systems of the then 15 member states of the EU with the conversion commissions and other bank charges deducted at each stage. Typically, very little remained of the £100 when the cycle was completed with the re-deposit of the residual amount in a British bank. The complete cycle of transactions often took more than six weeks. The example certainly overstates the unit cost of converting currencies, because there is usually a lump sum charge per transaction made by a bank as well as a percentage commission. Even these lump sum charges, however, may become important constraints to some types of international businesses, such as online retailers, because of the large cost each consumer faces when having to arrange international payment.

The movement to an internationally accepted currency has been resisted by national governments, because the loss of currency sovereignty means that they would have much less control over their national economies. Macroeconomic policies, particularly the ability to establish independent interest rates through the use of monetary policy, require a national currency.

In the past, gold may have come close to serving as an independent international currency. Up until the early part of the twentieth century, international contracts were typically delineated in gold and, while national currencies existed, they were freely convertible to gold. While the exchange rate between the local currency and gold could change over time, the costs of exchange were minimized. This gold standard system of exchange worked reasonably well in an era when national governments were much less involved in macroeconomic management of the economy. The restrictions that the gold standard places on governments' freedom of action made the system no longer acceptable. Of course, gold is costly to transport, and its purity must be verified. Gold is also far too cumbersome to be used to finance the volume of international transactions that currently exist.

At times, other currencies, such as the US dollar, have gained considerable international acceptance. Using a single currency as an international standard allows the country which issues the currency considerable freedom in its economic policy. Other countries may be adversely affected. Even in subgroupings of states such as the European Union, where most internal trade barriers have been removed and the transactions costs associated with currency exchange were high, the movement to monetary union and the creation of the euro have been hotly debated and stoutly resisted by some countries. In the wake of the 2008 financial crisis, the euro has become contentious in some heavily indebted countries because it limits governments' freedom of action.

14.2.1 Convertible currencies

The simplest way for a firm to eliminate the costs associated with currency conversion is to impose all of the costs on the other party to the international transaction. An exporting firm, for example, could insist that all payments be received in its national currency. All of the costs of currency conversion would be paid by the importer. Of course, the ability to get the importer to agree to assume those costs depends upon the relative bargaining position of the two parties during negotiations. If the exporter's competitors are offering to accept payment in the importer's currency, then it may not be possible to require payment in the seller's national currency.

In the long run, the costs of exchanging currencies will be reflected in the prices which firms are willing to pay or must charge. Even if it is possible to impose the costs of currency conversion on the other party to the transaction, it may not be desirable to do so. Banks or other financial institutions in different countries may charge different rates to convert currency. Further, firms dealing in large quantities of foreign currency will be eligible to receive preferred rates. By accepting the task of currency conversion and, hence, reducing transactions costs, the firm with the ability to secure a preferred rate will be able to make the entire deal look more attractive.

14.2.2 Controlled access to foreign exchange

While there are direct costs associated with exchanging currencies in economies where currencies are freely convertible, there may be far larger indirect costs imposed on international transactions when currencies are not freely convertible. Governments may wish to control access to foreign currency for a number of reasons. They may wish to control the international purchases of individuals for ideological reasons or to prevent the transfer of assets out of the country. In most cases, however, control over the acquisition of foreign currency is used to ration shortages of foreign currencies. If a government is following a macroeconomic policy that fixes its exchange rate at a level where the demand for imports exceeds the value of exports which foreigners are willing to purchase, then some form of foreign exchange rationing will be required. This means that the domestic currency is overvalued relative to the particular foreign currency. If market forces were allowed to operate, the cost of purchasing foreign currency should rise. The government may not wish to allow the price of foreign currency to rise, because it will increase the price of imports, including some whose prices the government wishes to keep low for political reasons. In a number of African countries, the government keeps down the price of foreign currencies so that food can be imported at low cost to feed the people in large coastal cities.

If a government deliberately overvalues its currency, there is excess demand for foreign currency at the official exchange rate. Governments must develop mechanisms to apportion the limited quantities of foreign exchange among those who wish to acquire it. This usually means that the government designates some imports as having a higher priority than others. For example, capital equipment, essential inputs for industrial production and food staples may be designated high-priority items. Luxury consumer goods and tourist trips abroad will be given lower priorities. Only when all the demands for foreign exchange for higher-priority imports have been satisfied will foreign exchange be allocated for lower-priority items.

Even if the products that constitute an import transaction are in the high-priority category, the agency charged with rationing foreign exchange will have to be satisfied that the products fall into the priority category. At the very least, extra paperwork will be involved, and there will be delays until bureaucratic approval is received. If the goods involved in the deal have been designated as lower-priority items, then the entire transaction may be considerably delayed until the country's foreign exchange position improves sufficiently for an allocation to become available. For some goods, this position may never be reached, and the deal cannot be completed. Failure to complete a transaction can be particularly costly when the exporting firm is producing a product to meet an importer's unique requirements. There may be no alternative market for the product.

Governments may not be willing to consider allocating foreign currency to the importer until the goods are actually received. If an allocation of currency is not subsequently made, then the exporter is faced with the choice of bringing its product back home or abandoning it. Even if currency is eventually made available, the exporting firm may suffer from cash flow problems as a result of the long delays. The risks associated with non-convertible currencies need to be anticipated by firms wishing to engage in international transactions.

If the official exchange rate is set at a rate where the domestic currency is overvalued relative to a foreign currency, there will be excess demand for the foreign currency. **Black markets** will arise. As the foreign currency is in short supply, the black market conversion rate will be such that it takes more units of domestic currency to acquire the same quantity of the foreign currency than at the official rate. Conversely, this means that more domestic currency can be acquired for a unit of foreign currency on the black market. In effect, this makes goods priced in local currency more attractive. Importers will wish to purchase more goods than at the official exchange rate. Firms may, however, be tempted to use the black market to acquire imports.

Of course, using the black market is illegal, and the importing firm must weigh the risks of being caught and assess the likely penalties. These decisions become particularly difficult when competitors have decided to use the black market to acquire imports.

As there can be a considerable incentive for importers that can see an importing opportunity but are unable to obtain an official allocation of the currency needed to import to use the black market, governments are likely to put in place stringent regulations relating to the acquisition of foreign currency. These restrictions will require proof of the rate of exchange used to finance the transaction before the goods can be imported. As a result, additional time will have to be spent arranging proof that currency was exchanged at the official rate.

Governments that do not wish their citizens to acquire foreign exchange may set up elaborate mechanisms to inhibit the functioning of black markets. The government of China, for example, for years operated a system of dual currencies – one which was convertible and one which was not. This meant that all business people visiting China had to purchase convertible Chinese currency at the official rate. Every transaction to purchase local Chinese commodities became a challenge, because individual Chinese would refuse to give change in convertible currency, even if they had it (Kwaczek and Kerr, 1986). Officially they were not allowed access to the convertible Chinese currency. The only alternative was to seek out official tourist stores that dealt in convertible Chinese currency, a time-consuming activity. The net result was that Western business people were likely to spend more in China than they otherwise would have. The cost of doing business in China was increased. Adding layers of complexity to currency exchange will inevitably add to the cost of doing business internationally.

14.3　Changes in exchange rates

In the past, most countries followed fixed **exchange rate** policies. Currently, however, countries tend to embrace flexible or 'floating' exchange rate regimes. The exchange value of the currency is determined, at least within certain limits, by the forces of supply and demand in international money markets. This change has made international transactions more complex for firms.

Under a fixed exchange rate policy, the rate at which a nation's currency could be exchanged for each other currency was set by the government. If demand by foreigners for the nation's currency exceeded the supply provided by domestic firms seeking to purchase foreign currencies – implying that the relative price of the domestic currency should rise – then the government or its central bank would sell additional domestic currency into the international money markets. Foreign currency was received in exchange. This foreign currency formed the country's foreign exchange reserves. If the supply of domestic currency in international markets exceeded the demand for the currency at the fixed price – implying that the relative price of the domestic currency should fall – then the government would intervene in the market by using its foreign exchange reserves to purchase domestic currency. In this way the fixed rate was maintained.

14.3.1　Fixed exchange rates

Fixed exchange rate regimes meant that, except in exceptional circumstances, firms did not have to be concerned about changes in the exchange rate between the point in time when a deal was agreed and when payment was received. The exceptional circumstances, however, could have devastating consequences. The system worked well as long as the fixed rate reflected the underlying economic forces in the two economies and exports equalled imports – including flows of monetary capital – over the long run. If the demand for imports consistently exceeded the exports which could be sold to foreigners, then the amount of domestic currency being supplied into the international market to finance imports would exceed the demand for the currency by foreigners to purchase exports. As a result, the government would be consistently running down its foreign reserves to defend its currency. Foreign reserves, however, are not inexhaustible. Once they have been exhausted, the government could no longer defend the rate at which the exchange of currencies was fixed. When this occurred, the government was forced to devalue the currency, that is, fix the rate at a new level.

Devaluations tended to be quite large changes in the exchange rate. As a result, one party to an international transaction – agreed prior to the devaluation but where payment did not take place until after the devaluation – was certain to lose. Hence, while fixed exchange rates in most instances simplified international transactions for businesses, when a devaluation appeared likely international transactions became extremely risky. As a result, mutually profitable business deals were often put on hold for long periods when a government appeared to be having difficulties with its foreign exchange reserves.

Devaluations were common in the 1930s. After the Second World War, the US and the UK took the lead in designing new international monetary institutions – known as the **Bretton Woods system**. The International Monetary Fund (IMF) was its central organization. The Bretton Woods system was a fixed (pegged) exchange rate regime. While devaluations were still possible, they could not be used as part of strategic macroeconomic policy. The IMF managed a pool of gold and currencies that could be allocated to countries faced with devaluation. The system of pegged exchange rates could not be sustained, and in 1973 the exchange rates of the major industrial nations began floating.

Fixed exchange rates restrict the ability of governments to pursue independent macroeconomic policies. Some governments still attempt to follow fixed exchange rate regimes by pegging the value of their currency to the currency of a major country – probably the US dollar or the euro. In most developed economies, however, the exchange rate is allowed to float. Central banks may, at times, actively intervene in the exchange markets by buying and selling foreign reserves. They intervene to prevent wide swings in currency values or to support the currency at levels which the government feels represent psychological thresholds for business confidence.

14.3.2 Flexible exchange rates

Variable exchange rates complicate international commercial activity. Changes in the exchange rate must be anticipated for each international transaction. Given the delays involved in organizing the international movements of goods, almost every transaction will be subject to a degree of exchange rate risk. The movement by governments to **flexible exchange rates** with the collapse of the Bretton Woods system led to the development of a number of institutions that allow firms to manage this risk.

The exchange rate may, of course, move to the advantage of the firm that is arranging payments. There will be a period between the placement of an order and when payment is due. A buyer in an international transaction can choose to use the **spot** (or current day's) **rate** to acquire the required foreign currency at any time. However, if the firm is risk averse, a number of alternatives to this speculative behaviour exist.

Currency accounts

Banks often offer **currency accounts** as one of their services. This allows the firm to open a bank account in foreign funds, removing the risks and costs of exchanging currency for every transaction. Currency accounts are particularly useful when a firm is both selling and buying in a foreign market – so that there are both inflows and outflows of foreign currency. The firm can choose to exchange currency only when taking profits, which can often be delayed until the exchange rate is favourable. Of course, if the account moves into a deficit position then funds may have to be transferred to it when rates are unfavourable. Currency accounts, however, are not particularly useful for firms involved in one-way trades, for example exporting but not importing, or when foreign transactions are undertaken on an intermittent basis.

Foreign exchange contracts

Banks also offer **forward exchange contracts**. These can be used most productively at the point in time when firms are negotiating the price at which an international transaction will take place. A forward exchange contract is a promise by the bank to purchase or sell foreign exchange at a specified rate on a certain date – the future date when payment on the contract must be made. The advantage of forward exchange contracts is that the firm knows the future exchange rate it will face. This exchange rate can be used in determining what price to set. The bank assumes the risk that its quoted **forward rate** is not the actual exchange rate at the time when payment comes due.

Fixed-date contracts are useful only when the date when funds must be exchanged is known perfectly. It may not be possible, however, to know the exact day when a customer's payment will arrive. A **limited option** contract allows currency to be exchanged at any point within a 30-day period. The 30-day period might commence in three months' time.

Unrestricted **option** contracts are also available. They allow currency to be exchanged on any day over the life of the forward exchange contract. Of course, the exchange rate offered in limited option and option contracts is adjusted to reflect the risk which the bank is assuming by providing this degree of flexibility.

Borrowing foreign currency

Firms may also have the option of borrowing foreign currency. An importer may borrow foreign funds from its own bank on the day that negotiation of the contract is concluded. The current exchange rate is, of course, available to the firm. The borrowed foreign currency can immediately be exchanged for the firm's local currency, meaning that the known 'spot' rate becomes the effective exchange rate for the transaction. The domestic currency could be invested or applied against debts owing in the domestic currency. As foreign currency payments arrive over time from the customer, they can be used to repay the foreign currency loan. The interest rate on the foreign currency loan will reflect the rate of interest applicable in the foreign country whose currency is being borrowed. This is because this is the rate at which the bank will have to borrow the currency offered in the loan. Of course, large banks are able to borrow foreign currency at rates lower than individual firms, which hence is the reason that they are able to offer the service at advantageous rates.

Hedging currency on the futures market

The exchange rates at which banks can offer a foreign exchange contract will be established in the **futures markets** for foreign exchange. Futures markets for some agricultural commodities have existed for over 100 years. They represent formal markets where individuals can exercise their opinions about prices in the future. As the future cannot be seen clearly, differences in opinions regarding future prices are natural. When opinions are sufficiently strongly held regarding future prices, individuals may be willing to speculate financially based on their opinions. Speculators have no interest in actually selling or acquiring the commodities on whose price they are speculating. They are interested only in capitalizing on their skill at predicting prices. The formalization of speculation in futures markets provides a service for those who have an interest in reducing the risk associated with storing commodities for future sale or acquiring commodities at some time in the future. This activity is known as **hedging**. Basically, speculators assume the risks for those who wish to hedge on the futures market. Of course, if their speculations are correct, they will receive any windfall gains.

Under a flexible exchange rate system, a foreign currency is simply another commodity whose price is uncertain in the future. Futures markets in foreign exchange developed as a result of the movement from fixed to flexible exchange rates (Powers and Vogel, 1981). Assume a firm is about to enter into a foreign contract where payment will be made at some date, for example six months, in the future. It can, through a broker, buy or sell a futures contract to purchase foreign currency. Contracts are for standardized amounts of currency. At the date of maturity, the futures contract is closed out and no foreign exchange is actually taken delivery of. The spot market is used to acquire the foreign exchange needed to pay for the goods exported. Losses on the spot market should be offset by gains in the futures market or vice versa. The net result is to fix the rate of exchange for the original transaction involving goods.

A firm may wish to use the futures market rather than a bank to manage its exchange rate risk. The ability to buy and sell futures contracts increases the firm's flexibility in dealing with exchange rate risks and also removes the bank as an intermediary – of course saving the bank's charges. Hedging currencies, however, may be advantageous only for major users of foreign exchange, owing to the large size of individual futures contracts (Gillis et al., 1992). (A detailed explanation of the workings of a futures contract can be found in Gillis et al., 1990.)

Problems associated with payment are endemic in international transactions. Even when a foreign firm's willingness and ability to pay on time are not in question, the risks associated with variable exchange rates will remain. A large number of institutions have evolved in the private sector which allow firms wishing to engage in international commercial activities to reduce the transactions costs and risks associated with arranging for payment. If the institutions did not reduce transactions costs they would not survive. Identifying when to use a service provided by an individual institution is the challenge for firms engaging in international commerce. The mechanics of some of these institutional arrangements are extremely complex, and evaluating the worth of the various services available is no easy task. Most contingencies can be addressed through the use of one or more of the existing institutional arrangements. It is still up to the individual company to determine which events have a sufficient probability of occurrence to warrant the use of a particular service.

 REFERENCES

Ball, D.A., Geringer, J.M., McNett, J.M. and Minor, M.S. (2013) *International Business*, 13th edn, McGraw-Hill, New York.

Gillis, K.G., Yoshida, S., Hobbs, J.E. and Kerr, W.A. (1990) A futures market for Japanese beef imports: Is it the next logical step? *Kitami Daigaku Ronshu*, 24(3), 33–67.

Gillis, K.G., Jameson, K. and Kerr, W.A. (1992) Transnational hedging – an added complexity for feedlot management in Canada. *Journal of International Farm Management*, 1(3), 81–91.

Kerr, W.A., Hobbs, J.E. and Gillis, K.G. (1990) Reducing the risk of exporting to Japan: The development of market information, in *Selling Beef to Japan*, ed. D.K. Elton, W.A. Kerr, K.K. Klein and E.T. Penner, Canada West Foundation, Calgary, pp. 171–91.

Kwaczek, A.S. and Kerr, W.A. (1986) A note on the current Chinese experience with Gresham's law. *Economic Notes*, 15(1), 134–48.

Paliwoda, S.J. (1991) *International Marketing*, Butterworth-Heinemann, Oxford.

Powers, M. and Vogel, D. (1981) *Inside Financial Futures Markets*, John Wiley & Sons, New York.

SITPRO (2003) Report on the use of export letters of credit, 19 June, http://www.sitpro.org.uk/reports/lettcredr/lettcredr.pdf.

15

Moving products between countries

15.1 The movement of goods and international transportation

As with the financing of international trade, a large number of specialized institutions have developed to facilitate the international movement of goods. Their effect is to reduce the transactions costs associated with physically transporting goods between countries.

Transporting goods between countries can take place using four medium – ships, aircraft, rail and road vehicles. The bulk of internationally traded goods is carried by ships, although one should not overlook the use of road and rail transportation, which often accounts for a high proportion of the trade carried out between countries on the same continent. The carriage of goods by air, although small in volume terms (2 per cent), is large in terms of value (30 per cent). Two modes of transport (shipping and air transport) will be discussed in this chapter, as they account for the movement of the major portion of the value of internationally traded goods.

15.2 A taxonomy of seaborne trade and cargoes

Cargoes can be of several types depending upon the type of shipping service used to carry them. The two most important categories are **bulk cargoes** and **general cargoes**. Bulk cargoes tend to be raw materials or semi-processed commodities.

Bulk cargoes can, in turn, be broken down into liquid cargoes, such as petroleum, gas and chemicals, and dry cargoes, such as grain, iron ore, coal, bauxite and phosphate rock. Both these types of bulk cargoes are carried in specialized ships, for example tankers in the case of liquid cargoes. They tend not to be packaged, but rather protected by the hull of the ship. Loading and unloading can be carried out by specialized equipment, but by and large the operations are simple and routine.

General cargoes are made up of goods such as consumer products and machinery. The size of general cargoes is usually smaller than bulk cargoes, and they often require specialized packaging and handling. Recently, with the expansion of trade in certain manufactured goods such as cars, specialist ships have been built for their transport. As a result such goods can almost be treated as bulk commodities.

The modern-day bulk carrier has taken over the role of the latter-day **tramp freighter**; it sails between ports picking up and dropping off cargoes, hardly ever enters its home port and may never visit its nation of registry.

15.2.1 Ships and shipping services

To transport goods by ship between countries, exporters and importers usually use the services of maritime brokers to acquire the appropriate vessels to carry their cargoes. The majority of cargoes are carried by independent shipping companies, since very few exporters or importers own their own vessels.

For the transportation of dry bulk cargoes, commodity dealers and others wishing to ship these commodities can approach shipowners directly. More commonly, however, these two parties are brought together by **ship-brokers** via the **Baltic Exchange** in London (Cochran, 1994). As with any market, the Baltic Exchange provides a convenient and effective cost-reducing place for sellers and buyers to exchange information. Brokers provide a service that matches buyers' requirements with the vessels available.

The Baltic, like many of the other City of London institutions, traces its origins back to a coffee house. When it was established in 1744, the bulk of the trade its customers dealt in was with the Baltic states, hence its name. The Baltic Exchange employs more than 1000 people, buys and sells more than half of the world's tonnage in a market worth $50 billion and handles 30 per cent of all dry cargoes and half the crude oil. Deals struck on the 'floor' stipulate the cargo to be carried, its size, the terms of carriage and the rate, which is expressed in US dollars. The rules and regulations governing membership of the exchange, its ability to resolve disputes between members and its use of standardized contracts reduce the risks associated with international carriage.

The Baltic Exchange also plays a major role in tanker charters for liquid bulk transportation. Specialized brokers and agents, working mainly in London but also in New York and other minor regional centres, also arrange shipping on behalf of the shippers and shipowners. As with dry bulk carriers, it is unlikely that tankers ever see their home port or nation of registry.

Bulk carriers are very similar, if not identical, and their characteristics and the reputation of their owners are well known to all. The rates at which ships are hired are reported daily. This availability of information at little cost suggests that the market for dry bulk and liquid carriers approximates that of the economists' model of **perfect competition** (Metaxas, 1971). Standardization, low-cost information and the large number of brokers mean that both shipowners and potential shippers do not have to spend time and resources identifying customers or shipowners and determining their reputations. Transparency pricing reduces negotiation costs.

In contrast, the system under which general cargoes are transported is made up of a number of well-organized international cartels (Ademuni-Odeke, 1988). General cargoes are carried by ships that have a fixed route and a timetable that applies to both arrivals and departures. These timetables are adhered to irrespective of whether the vessels are fully loaded or not. This is the so-called **liner trade**, since a company's vessels ply a particular route or line. The liner trade is often arranged around **conferences**, which are essentially cartels formed by the companies involved in certain routes. The conference sets rates of carriage, conditions for transportation, routeing and timetabling. By controlling the membership of the cartel and maintaining other barriers to entry, that is, restricting specialized port facilities to the members of the cartel, the conference is often able to restrict competition. The justification for restrictive competition is that in return shippers face lower transportation risks. To have their goods transported, exporters and importers can approach the liner companies directly or again use brokers. More and more general cargoes are carried in containers that interface with other transport modes – railcars and trucks.

The majority of liner conferences were formed in the latter part of the nineteenth century and the early part of the twentieth. The transformation of European colonies into independent states and the rise of economic nationalism led many countries to question the composition of the conferences, since the shipping companies of developed market economies dominated their membership. As a result, and to improve their development prospects, many less developed countries began to seek access to these conferences on behalf of their shipping companies. In many ways this was a logical move:

ships are not very sophisticated pieces of capital equipment – the technology is not very complex and the human skills required can be obtained without too great a financial outlay. In other words, a developing country with a modicum of capital and human resources can fairly easily acquire a comparative advantage in shipping services. Through the UNCTAD, developing countries began to put pressure on the conferences for access under a specific code of conduct (Ademuni-Odeke, 1988). This code of conduct proposed that trade between two countries should be split between the ships of the nations involved on a formula. This code has met with a great deal of opposition, principally from the US and the EU, which viewed it as anti-competitive.

The EU has also examined the workings of two major conference agreements to ascertain whether their price fixing and capacity controls are anti-competitive. The European Commission has been interested in the Transatlantic Agreement and the Europe Asia Trades Agreement, which were signed in 1993 to stem the large losses incurred by shipowners on these routes. At the time, these agreements accounted for just over 70 per cent of the container trade between Europe, the US and the Far East. European users of these routes argued that the practices of these conferences raised the costs of carriage, which adversely affected the competitiveness of their goods (Walters, 1994).

The relatively small size of consignments of manufactured goods and the specialist packaging often required for their transportation make them ideal for transport in containers. The advantage of **containerized carriage** is that the consignment can be loaded off the ship on to a lorry or railcar and transported to the factory or warehouse or directly to the retail outlet having once cleared customs. By carrying goods in containers, shipowners are able to use large vessels that give economies of scale. These modern-day liners contrast not only in size but also in structure to those seen up until the late 1950s and early 1960s. Small consignments were carried on a number of decks within their hulls – the so-called 'tween deckers'. Some of these older ships are still used on routes that have not been containerized, although these routes are becoming fewer and fewer.

15.2.2 The chartering of ships

The hiring of ships is referred to as **chartering**. There are several types of chartering, varying not only in the length of the period for which a vessel is hired but also in the nature of the shipment involved.

The simplest form of charter is the **single voyage charter**, where a ship is hired to carry a particular amount of cargo between ports and either a lump sum is paid or a rate established per ton carried. A *trip charter* is similar to a single **voyage charter** but involves payment on a per day (or **per diem**) basis. Shipowners often prefer this type of charter, since they are paid a rate even if delays occur.

Longer-term arrangements also exist, which involve the hiring of a vessel or vessels for specified periods of time, that is, three months, one year, five years and so on. These arrangements can be carried out on the basis of a **consecutive voyage charter**, which is like a single voyage charter except that the vessel is hired for a number of specified voyages carried out one after another. The **time charter** involves the ship being made available for a specific period of time and allows the charterer to employ the vessel between any ports required. Sometimes a company may want to hire a vessel, use its own crew and operate it as it wishes. This form of hiring is known as **bareboat chartering** and has been used by transnational oil companies as a way of increasing the size and flexibility of their fleets. Owners of large fleets sometimes strike deals with the owners or purchasers of bulk commodities to transport a fixed amount of cargo between ports. These so-called **contracts of affreightment** allow owners to maximize the utilization of their fleets, as individual vessels are not specified. The shipowners are, however, often required to specify the size of each shipment and the time of delivery.

It can be seen from the variety of contracts of carriage available that the international shipping industry provides considerable flexibility for those needing to export. This flexibility minimizes the difficulties involved in transporting goods over great distances. For cargo owners wishing to have regular deliveries, time charters, contracts of affreightment and bareboat charters are particularly useful not only in guaranteeing regularity of delivery but also in allowing transportation costs to be known in advance. This is important when prices are being negotiated in an export contract.

Single voyage and trip charters are more useful to exporters that need to supplement their own capacity or where the product to be transported is highly seasonal or affected by other factors such as market fluctuations and political factors. This flexibility allows firms to take advantage of short-term export opportunities without making a major investment or long-term commitment in ships.

From the shipowner's point of view, the longer-term charters provide revenue stability. Single voyage and trip charters can, on the other hand, be very lucrative, especially when market conditions lead to a shortage of ships.

15.2.3 Conditions of carriage and service

As was indicated above, the prices of carriage or freight rates are determined largely by the open market. These rates, however, are quoted on a particular basis, dependent on the amount of service to be provided. The most common forms of price quotation are:

1. free on board (f.o.b.);
2. free alongside (**f.a.s.**);
3. cost, insurance and freight (c.i.f.).

Free on board, as discussed in Chapter 8, means that the exporter or seller of the good pays for the loading of the vessel and guarantees that the goods were placed on the vessel damage free. The purchaser or importer pays for the insurance and the unloading of the vessel. Free alongside implies that the seller places the cargo alongside the vessel in good condition. After that, the goods are the responsibility of the buyer, which must incur loading costs and other costs such as the insurance involved in the safe importation of the goods to their final destination. Cost, insurance and freight indicates that the price of the good includes the cost of transportation, the insurance premium and the cost of the goods. In other words, the seller meets all the charges that are necessary to ensure the carriage of the goods to their destination in good condition. Those negotiating to ship cargo should carefully assess costs of ship loading, insurance and so on and compare them to the pricing option available. When considering arranging these services privately, firms should be careful not to underestimate the potential monitoring costs.

15.2.4 The insuring of cargoes

An interesting feature of ocean transportation is that the carrier is not responsible for any loss or damage to the cargo unless negligence can be proved. As a result shippers, exporters and importers need to acquire insurance for their goods. This is usually taken out with underwriters who specialize in this work. **Marine underwriting** is a very complex area and tends to be carried out by the larger insurance companies and specialized institutions such as Lloyd's of London. Again, to ease the procedure, standardized contracts are used to cover one consignment or a series of consignments. Transactions costs for firms are, as a result, reduced.

15.3   Air freight and transportation

As has already been mentioned, air freight accounts for only a very small proportion of the international movement of goods. In value terms, however, about one-third of international trading is accounted for by air freight. It is one of the most rapidly growing forms of transport. The reasons for this are fairly straightforward. The current inability of aircraft to lift great weights and their high running costs mean that they are inappropriate mediums when it comes to transporting low-value bulky items. Aircraft are occasionally used in emergencies to transport heavy items, but in general they are not used for the transportation of such goods. In contrast, aircraft are an ideal mode of transport when it comes to high-value, low-density products such as diamonds, cut flowers and specialized tools. Most importantly, of course, air freight is used when the speed of delivery is important.

15.3.1   The growth in air cargo

The growth in air transport can be accounted for by two principal factors: the ability of modern aircraft to carry heavier loads of 30 tons or more in the case of jumbo jets and the increase in demand for high-value, low-density products. Other factors that are also of importance include:

1.   the reduced transit time of air transport when compared to sea;
2.   the location of airports near to important markets or centres, which may not be the case with sea ports;
3.   the ease of cargo transfer between aircraft.

All these factors reduce the costs of shipment. Direct transportation costs, however, may not be the only item that might give air freight an advantage over other forms of carriage. For example, lower transit times can translate themselves into lower inventory and stock requirements. The ease of shipment and lower journey times can lead to lower insurance costs. Finally, in the case where products are perishable or need to be shipped to a market quickly to take advantage of high prices, air transport may be the only mode of transport. Courier companies have seized the advantage provided by air freight in the market for small packages. Economies of scale that arise from high volume in delivery systems have given them a competitive advantage in the movement of these packages.

15.3.2 The supply of air services

Aircraft are provided on either a scheduled or a chartered basis and therefore are akin to the services provided by shipowners; however, the regulation of air transport by countries has shaped the industry's structure, and as a result it differs considerably from sea transport.

Nation states have taken a very active role in the regulation and promotion of their national airlines and, hence, a whole series of complex bilateral agreements exists between countries. These agreements control the number of flights between nations, the airports where foreign access is permitted and whether foreign airlines are allowed to pick up and carry passengers and cargo within a country's domestic market. These agreements do not have seagoing counterparts. It has usually been the practice to allow ships of any nation access to ports except when hostilities exist between nations or where cargoes are deemed to constitute a danger to the country.

Most of the major airlines offer cargo services, and there are also some specialized cargo-only carriers. The bulk of air freight is offered on a scheduled basis so that shippers know exactly the times of departure and arrival. This enables a reduction in the uncertainties associated with transport. Where volumes do not warrant specialized cargo-carrying aircraft, consignments are transported in the holds of regular passenger aircraft. As the volume of air freight has increased, specialized airports have arisen both to reduce competition with passenger traffic and to circumvent the advantages given to national carriers at major airports.

The chartering of aircraft is usually confined to cases where the cargo requires specialist handling facilities or where access is required to areas which do not have regular scheduled flights. As with sea transport, the chartering of aircraft is carried out via brokers who bring together cargo interests and aircraft owners. Again, some of these arrangements are facilitated on the Baltic Exchange.

 REFERENCES

Ademuni-Odeke (1988) *Shipping in International Relations*, Avebury, Aldershot.
Cochran, I. (1994) *The Baltic Exchange*, Lloyd's List Publications, London.
Metaxas, B.N. (1971) *The Economics of Tramp Shipping*, Athlone Press, London.
Walters, J. (1994) EU shipowners sail into ill wind. *Observer Business News*, 19 (June).

16

The settlement of international commercial disputes

16.1 Why disputes arise

All but the simplest of international transactions will involve the use of a contract. Almost all international movements of commodities will take time to organize and involve the delivery of goods or services to a specified place in another country. Of course, many international transactions will be complex, and include:

1. specifications for quality and other performance criteria;
2. dates for delivery and payment;
3. arrangements for transportation, insurance and payment of customs duties;
4. penalties for non-performance of the contract's provisions;
5. appropriate remedies in cases when the contract provisions cannot be fulfilled through no fault of the parties to the transaction.

It is not possible, however, to account for all future contingencies when the contract is being drawn up. In legal terms, this means the contract is not complete. As a result, there will be circumstances when the contract provides no guidance as to the appropriate remedy. Lack of completeness in contracts can also provide the opportunity for one party to act opportunistically.

Even when contracts appear to cover a set of circumstances, firms may disagree in their interpretation of events. While commercial disputes can often be settled by private discussions between the two parties, in some cases no agreement can be reached privately. The dispute must then be settled by a disinterested third party. In the case of disputes between firms in one country, two options are generally available – litigation through the courts or commercial arbitration. Arbitration is arranged through the private sector, while litigation takes place under the auspices of the nation's judicial system and is, hence, backed by the state. This means that the state can use its powers to enforce the settlements imposed by the courts. In the case of arbitration, the decision to abide by the decision is largely voluntary.

There will be times when those who lose an arbitration will not comply with the decision. In some cases, national courts will act to enforce the decisions made by arbitrators. If national courts will not enforce the decisions of arbitrators, the party seeking redress will be forced into using the courts to judge the original complaint. Given that recourse to the courts is the ultimate step, why do firms – particularly firms involved in international commercial activity – tend to choose arbitration to settle their disputes rather than the courts? The answer is complex and forms the basis of this chapter.

16.2   Differences in national legal systems

The major reason arbitration is the preferred method of settling international commercial disputes is that there is no supranational legal system to which governments are willing to delegate the powers of their courts. As a result, national courts remain the final adjudicators of commercial disputes. Institutions such as the European Union's European Court have begun to take on the role of a supranational court for firms operating within the Union, but such institutions remain the exception. For the most part, countries guard the sovereignty of their courts very closely.

Commercial law and court procedures vary considerably among countries. Even when the legal systems in two countries are based on the same set of legal principles, differences will arise over time because all legal systems are continually evolving. The absence of a supranational legal system means that firms wishing to enter into international transactions are faced with choosing which country's legal system to use if a dispute arises.

The fundamental problem is that a legal decision brought down by the courts in one country cannot be enforced in another country. Assume the firms were agreed that the courts in the exporter's country were to be used to settle disputes. If the importing firm refused to pay and a verdict was brought down against it in the courts, the judgment could not be enforced in the country of the importer. Hence, the exporter would have no assurance that it would be paid when it entered into a contract. On the other hand, if the importer's court system were agreed to, then if in the importer's opinion the exporter failed to fulfil the terms of the contract a judgment in the courts of the importer's country could not be used to force the exporter to comply. The importer would have no means of ensuring the exporter's performance when the contract was signed.

It might be possible to draw up two contracts for each transaction – one for each country. Differences in national legal systems, however, are significant enough to make it virtually impossible to construct parallel contracts that will convey the same intent and be interpreted in the same way. Subtle differences in the meanings of words in two languages can lead to alternative interpretations. Even if the same language is used, the legal interpretation of words can differ between countries. Attempting to construct two contracts would lead to considerably increased legal costs and would not lead to a satisfactory convergence between the two contracts. As a result, this practice is uncommon.

Even if firms are not concerned about the willingness of the other party to the contract to abide by a ruling made by another country's national court, firms may be concerned about national bias in the courts. In many countries, the courts are not an independent arm of government but are rather considered as an integral part of the government's policy-making machinery. As a result, they may actively promote the interests of their nation's firms to the detriment of foreign firms. Even when courts are independent of government, individual judges may not act in an unbiased fashion towards foreign firms. Further, courts and judges may not be free from corruption and, hence, may be induced to act in the interests of their own nationals. It may even be the case that a firm may not trust its own courts, feeling that they may be 'in the pocket' of foreign firms. As a result, the firm may wish to seek an alternative to the legal system in its own country.

Negotiations over which national court system should be used to settle contract disputes are likely to be protracted. This may raise the transactions costs of reaching a contractual agreement to unacceptable levels. International arbitration is a transaction-cost-reducing method to settle disputes when contracts involve parties in two or more countries.

International arbitration relies on the willingness of parties to a dispute to submit voluntarily to both the process and the decisions of an arbitration. If either party refuses to submit to arbitration, then national courts remain the means by which disputes must be adjudicated. Agreement to proceed to arbitration can be delayed until a dispute actually arises. Often, however, the parties agree in the contract to proceed to arbitration if a dispute arises. The actual forum within which the arbitration will take place can also be stipulated in the contract. Even if arbitration is agreed to voluntarily in the contract, firms may choose to act opportunistically and refuse to abide by the agreement if a dispute arises. Arbitration is not backed by the power of the state, unlike the case with rulings from national courts. Firms may even allow the agreed arbitration to proceed and, if the decision reached by the arbitrator is not to their liking, they can refuse to abide by the ruling. Some national courts do operate to enforce arbitration rulings but, if nothing else, this will involve considerable legal costs. Arbitration will always be open to opportunistic behaviour by one of the parties.

Opportunistic behaviour by firms that have voluntarily agreed to use arbitration for the settlement of disputes is not, however, common. If it were, it is unlikely that international arbitration would enjoy the popularity that it does. Most firms perceive it to be in their best interest to have an efficient and unbiased means to settle disputes. As disputes will arise from time to time, firms need a means whereby the disputes can be settled. Refusing to live up to a commitment to submit to arbitration can harm prospects for future business dealings between the two firms. Even if the firm does not contemplate future business dealings with the party with which it is in dispute, failure to live up to its arbitration commitments can lead to a loss of reputation. Contracts will be more difficult to negotiate with other firms in the future.

16.3 International arbitration versus national courts

International arbitration provides a solution to the problems associated with differences in legal systems. Arbitration procedures tend to be flexible, thereby allowing the concerns of both parties to be taken into account when the structure of a particular arbitration is agreed. Further, elaborate and transparent procedures exist to allay any concerns relating to bias.

The use of international arbitration has other advantages in the resolution of disputes. Litigation through national courts may not be particularly suited to the needs of international commerce. Litigation tends to be a very slow process. Firms may suffer from problems with cash flow or disruptions to production while they await a decision from the courts. Business records, accounts and technical standards are likely to vary among countries. The particular standardized formats used by businesses may, in part, be the result of regulations of national courts regarding the preparation of evidence. Having records transformed to comply with the rules of evidence in another country may add considerably to the time required for litigation. Arbitration proceedings can be organized to allow for more flexible rules of evidence.

The period of time allowed for the completion of an arbitration can be specified in a contract. In the case of perishable commodities, the two sides can agree to abide by the decision of a single independent inspector charged with making a decision on the spot. It is often possible to have an arbitration decision reached for a relatively complex case in six weeks – a case that might normally be three years or more in litigation.

Litigation can also be very expensive. Lawyers' fees can be sufficiently high to deter at least some firms from pursuing their cases. This can bias proceedings if one party to a transaction is large and well financed. Hence, the threat of litigation can be used strategically against a smaller firm. Arbitration proceedings can often be conducted without lawyers. Even if there are legal issues that require the services of lawyers, as arbitration procedures tend to involve much less time than litigation, lawyers' fees are reduced.

As courts are public institutions, their proceedings tend to be transparent. All citizens may have access to courtrooms, not just the interested parties. In many disputes, discussions of the technical details of products or processes are involved. Firms may not wish their trade secrets to be discussed in open court for fear of the information becoming available to their competitors. Arbitration proceedings can be conducted in private, thus safeguarding the confidentiality of information.

Most judges tend to be lawyers by training. As a result, they may lack the technical sophistication to judge a commercial dispute that involves complex engineering, scientific or managerial concepts. Even if expert witnesses are used in the courts, judges may not be able to understand their arguments or assess the quality of their information. Further, litigation tends to be adversarial, with the lawyers from each side presenting their best case to a court which is largely passive. It is up to the lawyers to manage their case in such a way that the judge reaches the desired decision. Arbitrators, on the other hand, are selected on a case-by-case basis and can be chosen for their technical expertise. Arbitration procedures may also allow arbitrators to take a proactive role – questioning witnesses, seeking clarification and calling in experts of their own. As a result, an arbitration decision is much less dependent on the relative skills of the lawyers preparing the case.

In some countries, courts have little flexibility when awarding claims. As litigation is an adversarial system, arguments are heard and the court may decide on an all-or-nothing basis. The claimant either wins or loses its case. The inability to fulfil the conditions of a contract, however, may not be the responsibility of only one party. Arbitrators are able to make decisions on the basis of reasonable business practices and can apportion the responsibility accordingly.

In international arbitration, the concerns of firms relating to national bias are handled through a number of mechanisms. The care and attention taken to prevent bias in international commercial arbitration suggest that it is an important concern of businesses. While international arbitration can be carried out by an individual arbitrator, it is common practice for panels of arbitrators to be used – often of three or five members. If, for example, a three-member panel is used, each party will nominate one arbitrator, with the third, who will act as the chairperson of the arbitration panel, being jointly chosen by the two parties or some disinterested third party. A normal procedure would be for the two parties to attempt to find a third arbitrator who is acceptable to both. If a suitable third arbitrator cannot be agreed upon then a disinterested third party will make the choice. Often, the two parties will use the services of an international arbitration centre that maintains lists of potential arbitrators. It is also common for individual parties to be able to reject at least one or more of the independent body's choices for the chairperson of the arbitration panel. The arbitration rules chosen by the parties may state that the chairperson cannot be a citizen of the home country of either of the contending parties. Allowing the firms to nominate their own member(s) of the panel provides assurances for the nominating party that their arguments will receive a fair hearing in the proceedings.

It is also common for the procedures for selection of arbitrators by the disputing parties to include time limits. If the time limit is exceeded, the independent body under which the arbitration is taking place will select the arbitrators. This prevents firms from acting opportunistically to delay or thwart proceedings by failing to appoint arbitrators.

National bias is also prevented by allowing for a choice of venues for the arbitration – presumably a mutually acceptable neutral country. Selection of the venue is often decided as part of the negotiations leading up to the signing of the contract.

Arbitration can also allow the parties to choose the legal system whose principles will govern the arbitration and by which the decision will be interpreted. This may be the legal system of either claimant or a third legal system that is acceptable to both parties. It is not uncommon for a dispute between companies whose home offices are in the US and Japan to be heard by an arbitration panel in Sweden with a Brazilian chairperson and the proceedings interpreted according to Swiss commercial law.

The decisions of arbitration panels are usually made public, and arbitrators must provide the reasons for their decisions. This allows firms to assess both the technical ability and the fairness of individual arbitrators. This improves the ability to make informed choices when choosing arbitrators. In national legal systems, judges tend to be assigned by the state. The parties to the dispute have no input into who will try their case. Arbitrators who do not provide decisions that are both technically competent and unbiased will not be selected and over time will be dropped from the list of available arbitrators.

While these procedures appear to be complex, they can be seen primarily as transactions cost reducing compared to firms being unable to agree on which national court will be used for litigation. This reduction in costs allows a mutually beneficial international transaction to proceed.

Critics of arbitration suggest that it provides less protection for individual rights than national courts. The primary means of protecting individual rights in the courts is the use of **due process**. The flexibility of arbitration procedures, whereby the rules are selected for convenience, fails to provide the same degree of protection as is the case with formal litigation. Firms voluntarily selecting to use international arbitration over the use of litigation are giving up the additional protection provided by national courts for the lower transactions costs associated with arbitration.

Firms choosing to use arbitration are not, however, totally protected from the interference and possibly bias of national courts. National courts may choose to overturn or augment the decisions of arbitration decisions if:

1. they are seen to contravene in a fundamental way the intent of domestic legislation or the principles of justice that the courts apply;
2. third parties might be adversely affected by the arbitration decision;
3. the arbitration decision is not in the national interest.

Arbitration can take many forms, and there are other avenues of dispute resolution which are near to arbitration. Expertise, for example, can be used as a form of arbitration. The power of experts may, however, be more limited. The parties to a dispute can agree to appoint an *expert* to judge the quality of goods with regard to whether they fulfil the specifications set out in the contract. The expert's opinion may not, however, be binding. If the opinion is given as evidence to an arbitrator, then the expert is not serving an arbitration function. If it is agreed that the expert's opinion will be binding on the parties without further interpretation or if the expert is also empowered to adjust the price of goods to reflect their true quality, then he or she is also acting as an arbitrator. A distinction is sometimes made between this type of arbitration, where only technical aspects of quality are being decided, and the type where arbitrators provide legal interpretations. National courts seldom choose to interfere when the arbitration deals solely with technical issues of quality. Courts are more inclined to intervene when matters of law are concerned, if for no other reason than to prevent the erosion of the state monopoly on justice.

Once arbitration is voluntarily agreed to, it is binding on the parties to the dispute. *Conciliation*, on the other hand, is not binding on the parties to the dispute until a mutually acceptable solution is found. Arbitrators may be asked to decide cases in a manner that is concerned with equity rather than strictly according to legal principles. Hence, the decision may be similar to that which would be reached by conciliation. By agreeing to arbitration, however, firms agree to be bound by the decision even if they would not voluntarily accept it.

While arbitration may be used as a replacement for national courts for cases that could have been brought before the courts, arbitration may also be used to decide on problems which could not be brought to the courts. Arbitrators can fill in gaps in contracts or alter their conditions to reflect changing circumstances. In some legal jurisdictions, contract law does not allow the courts to intervene to complete contracts or to alter their terms.

If a contract is not complete, then a mutually beneficial commercial arrangement may be threatened by the inability of the parties to agree on a mutually acceptable solution. While a solution may have been mutually agreed upon during the negotiations leading up to the signing of a contract, at some later date the circumstances may have changed. At that point in time, firms may have made unequal resource commitments. For example, a food processor may have signed a long-term contract with an importer to provide a specialized line of confectionery products that would not be marketable in the processor's domestic market. To fulfil its contract the processor must make a considerable investment in specialized equipment. The prices specified in the contract will make this investment profitable. After the investment is made, the importer's government may pass new health regulations which require the processor to make additional investments so that its confections can be exported. As the legislation was not anticipated when the contract was signed, the agreed prices do not reflect the additional costs. As the processor has already made a considerable investment in specialized equipment, it may wish to renegotiate the prices. The importer, which has not made any resource commitment, may feel no urgency to renegotiate. Negotiations will not take place on an equal basis. The contract did not anticipate the problem and is incomplete. Arbitration will provide a solution to the unforeseen problem, eliminating the possibility of a contract-threatening impasse.

Arbitration may be used to alter the conditions of a contract in cases when adhering to the original conditions would be to the detriment of both parties. Courts may not be allowed to alter contracts – only interpret the existing contract. For example, a price may be agreed in a contract, but the exporter's costs may increase dramatically as a result of some unforeseen circumstance. If the exporter keeps to the contract price it will go broke. The importer, however, may not be able to organize an alternative source of supply at short notice, and having the exporter cease production will be detrimental. The courts could only force the seller to honour the price specified in the terms of the contract. An arbitrator can be used to find a solution that is reasonable given the changed circumstances.

Conciliation may be used prior to arbitration. In other words, conciliation may be attempted as a first stage in the arbitration process. If the effort at conciliation fails, the dispute can be resolved through arbitration. The arbitration panel may be better informed of the problems faced by parties to a dispute as a result of the search for a mutually acceptable resolution of the problem through conciliation. This information can make it easier for the arbitrator to produce a reasonable decision.

Conciliation and arbitration may serve as useful alternatives when litigation is not an accepted part of business practice. In Japan, while litigation procedures exist, they are avoided because of the loss of 'face' associated with even an accusation that a contract has not been strictly honoured. Japanese firms are practised at finding mutually acceptable solutions. Western businesses put a great deal of effort into designing complete contracts. Using litigation to settle disputes is part of their business culture. If a Western firm finds itself in disagreement with a Japanese firm, it may attempt litigation in the Japanese courts. The Japanese firm's executives would lose face. Future business with the Japanese firm would be precluded, and other Japanese firms would probably not be willing to deal with the Western firm. On the other hand, Western firms may not have the skills required to arrive at a mutually acceptable arrangement with the Japanese firm. Conciliation or arbitration can provide a solution, particularly if it takes place at a mutually agreeable neutral venue outside Japan and the procedures are conducted with discretion. No loss of face will be involved, and a subsequent loss of reputation will be avoided by the Western firm. Clearly, the transactions costs are far less than in the case of litigation.

As arbitration, unlike litigation, can be conducted confidentially, technical secrets can be kept from competitors. Arbitration also allows firms to keep information secret from customers, the general public and the tax system. A firm may wish to prevent consumers from finding out about defects in its products. Companies may not wish to reveal financial difficulties to creditors. A firm may wish to avoid a loss of reputation that would reduce the value of its franchises to customers in foreign countries. Even if a suit in the courts is won, damage to a firm's reputation may arise from adverse publicity surrounding the case. The merits of the particular case may have nothing to do with the loss of reputation. Hence, firms will find arbitration preferable to the public scrutiny that an action in the courts allows.

The widespread use of arbitration in international transactions may simply be a reflection of the costs imposed by national courts because they are no longer a legal system suitable for business purposes. In particular, national courts – with their domestic mandate – may simply not be oriented to the efficient handling of disputes arising in international contracts. Businesses may simply be seeking to establish an efficient system of commercial law through the development of the institutions of international arbitration. Establishing an efficient system for litigation may no longer be possible on the national level because of the monopoly over the creation and interpretation of law given jurists by legislators. As with any monopoly, jurists may have an incentive to formulate laws and legal procedures that reduce the effort they must expend (**X-inefficiency**) and/or which enable them to extract monopoly rents. The monopoly price represents an increase in transactions costs for firms.

The absence of a jurists' monopoly in international law has allowed an efficient system for arbitration to develop. Given that there is an almost unlimited choice in the arbitration procedures and that there is a high degree of competition between the institutions that formally offer arbitration services, international arbitration is a low-cost method of dispute settlement.

Further, both the formal legal language used and the non-transparent procedures used in the courts require that lawyers be employed for even the simplest and most straightforward of disputes. Business people often have to spend considerable time and effort informing lawyers of technical complexities because they are not allowed to ask questions in court themselves. Arbitration removes these inefficiencies and the costs associated with them.

Even when the courts or the legislation underlying them does not have a national bias, the principles that form the basis of countries' legal systems differ. These differences can lead to a considerable degree of risk for firms wishing to enter into an international transaction. Legal scholars and national courts have not been able to reach agreement on matters relating to conflicts between nations' laws. While in some cases the parties to an international transaction may be able to choose which national law will apply to the contract, in many cases the question of which court will have jurisdiction cannot be determined when the contract is being drawn up. As the rulings of the courts will not be the same in different countries, members of the legal profession will not be able to give an unqualified answer to businesses regarding a contract's interpretation. It may not be possible to answer how damages will be assessed in the case of non-performance of contract obligations. The circumstances when revisions to contracts may be expected differ from legal system to legal system. In one national jurisdiction certain types of clause may be allowed, but they may not be allowed in another jurisdiction. The best a lawyer can do is to inform the firm of the difference and the likely consequences. Lawyers are not likely to be able to devise a contract that provides an equal degree of risk reduction in both jurisdictions. As a result, the prices firms eventually agree to in a contract will be less attractive (mutually beneficial) than if the level of risk could be harmonized. In some cases, no mutually acceptable price can be agreed and the transaction will be called off.

Arbitration allows the parties to choose a single set of rules. This decreases costs and, hence, increases the probability that a mutually acceptable contract price can be arrived at.

16.4 The institutions of international commercial arbitration

There has been a gradual evolution of international commercial arbitration. The process has become more formal. Although arbitration existed even in Roman times, it was in the twentieth century that it flourished. In part, the growth in the use of international arbitration is the result of the massive increase in the volume of international trade that occurred in the twentieth century. The increase in the demand for international arbitration services has led to the development of permanent institutions. The increased use of arbitration may also reflect the decline of colonialism in the latter half of the twentieth century. Colonialism acted to reduce the problems arising from differences in international laws in two ways. Firstly, it meant that one justice system was likely to apply to all commercial arrangements among the political units that made up a colonial empire. Secondly, direct trade between colonies of different nations was often discouraged. Trade between colonies and the colonial power was promoted instead. As a result, trade between different legal jurisdictions was reduced. The demise of colonial empires meant that trade links expanded between nations with different legal systems. Legal systems have also proliferated as the systems of justice in newly created states evolve independently.

The formalization of arbitration has been manifested in two ways. In the past, arbitration tended to be used on an ad hoc basis to resolve a dispute that had already arisen. It is common current practice, however, for parties negotiating a contract to make specific provision for international arbitration. In other words, arbitration is selected by firms in anticipation of disputes. This suggests that the general cost-effectiveness of international arbitration is accepted by firms conducting international business. Previously they would consider the merits of arbitration on a case-by-case basis.

Secondly, arbitration has been formalized through the development of generally accepted rules for procedures. These rules have been devised by international organizations or at permanent centres that offer facilities for arbitration. Rules for the procedures to govern international arbitration may be specified by firms without any reference to a formal centre where the arbitration will take place. In most cases, an international arbitration centre will allow firms wishing to avail themselves of its services to choose any set of arbitration rules they prefer. Firms can also choose to use a set of arbitration rules developed by an arbitration centre without using the services of the centre. The international organizations that have devised arbitration rules may also offer the services of a centre. The centre, however, is likely to allow a different set of rules to be used if it is the wish of the parties. This underlies the flexibility that characterizes the international arbitration system and contrasts with the rigid rules that are applied in the litigation systems of national courts. The formalization developing in international arbitration reduces business costs by providing procedural models for arbitration and specialized facilities. In other words, firms do not have to incur the costs of developing their own rules and finding a location with the mix of services that will maximize the efficiency of an arbitration.

While exact statistics on the pre-selection of international arbitration do not exist – because they are private contract information – the practice of including arbitration clauses is widespread and is promoted by many business associations. Arbitration is very common when the quality of the goods traded is easy to verify. It is less common when goods are complex, for example automobiles, apparel or electronics. This is probably because the complexity of the goods increases the costs of verifying quality, which in turn increases the cost of arbitrators' investigations. As a result, firms will have an incentive to work harder at arriving at a negotiated decision. The absence of the use of arbitration in an industry does not, however, imply that national courts are used as an alternative.

Many of the cases brought to arbitration centres are settled before the arbitrator reaches a decision. As arbitration is approached from a conciliatory rather than an adversarial perspective, the atmosphere at arbitration proceedings is much more likely to lead to a private settlement than when litigation is chosen.

Unless the domestic courts in a firm's country are willing to enforce awards, a firm entering into arbitration cannot be compelled to comply with the arbitrators' decision. David (1984) suggests that failures to comply with the rulings of international arbitrators are rare. Failure to abide by awards leads to loss of reputation and subsequent difficulties when contracts with other firms must be negotiated in the future. This increases a firm's transactions costs in the long run.

16.4.1 A choice of arbitration institutions

Arbitration is often arranged under the auspices of industry organizations concerned with particular commodities. More broad-based disputes can often be referred to chambers of commerce. In Britain, the Chartered Institute of Arbitrators was established in 1915. In the US, the American Arbitration Association was founded in 1926. The International Centre for Settlement of Investment Disputes between States and Nationals operates under the auspices of the World Bank. The Chamber of Commerce of Zurich is prominent in international disputes, as are the Netherlands Arbitration Institute, the Stockholm Chamber of Commerce and the London Court of Arbitration. These four institutions have well-publicized rules for arbitration procedures which firms can use if they choose. The Inter-American Commercial Arbitration Commission was chartered in 1933. Many major trading cities have centres that provide arbitration facilities.

Each arbitration centre has its own rules regarding the selection of who is eligible to be on the list of arbitrators. Some centres require arbitrators to pass examinations or to possess an independent technical certification. Often, however, no formal qualifications are required, and persons are added to the lists based on their reputations. In some cases, arbitrators can refuse to serve, while in other cases they agree to provide their services on demand when they agree to be added to the list. Persons remain on a list for a fixed period or they remain on indefinitely, depending upon the rules of the particular centre. Even if an arbitrator who is in demand finishes his or her term, many centres allow the parties to select arbitrators who are not on their list.

While arbitration proceedings are private, it is in the interest of firms engaging in international commerce to be able to identify high-quality arbitrators. As a result, a great deal of information is made available. A large number of academic journals and other publications are dedicated to the reporting and study of arbitration awards. Firms can study this information when they need to select an arbitrator. Parties to disputes will not be able to reach an agreement to appoint arbitrators who appear to be biased and will challenge arbitrators who they consider do not fit. If the list of arbitrators maintained by a centre has a large number of potential arbitrators whom parties consider unsuitable, the parties are free to choose an alternative centre for future contracts. As a result, arbitrators have an incentive to keep the quality of their arbitrations high.

The International Chamber of Commerce

The most prominent organization involved in offering international arbitration services is the International Chamber of Commerce (ICC), created in 1919. The ICC's only legal status is as an association registered under French law. It is, however, a federation of national organizations from more than 50 countries. These national organizations have the sponsorship of industry organizations and associations in their countries. The ICC has produced a widely accepted code for international arbitration and maintains a Court of Arbitration. The Court of Arbitration is appointed by the Council of the ICC. The United Nations has produced arbitration codes for those that do not wish to have their arbitrations subject to any commercial organization. The operation of the ICC, however, probably deserves closer examination, because it sets the standard against which other international arbitration organizations must compete.

The ICC's Court of Arbitration is located at the organization's headquarters in Paris. The Court of Arbitration does not itself settle disputes. The Court only confirms and selects arbitrators according to its Rules of Conciliation and Arbitration. In the case of arbitration, the preferred procedural choice is a single arbitrator mutually agreed to by the participants. The Court simply confirms the appointment. If the use of a single arbitrator is agreed to but the parties cannot agree on an arbitrator, the Court will make the appointment. The two parties have only 30 days to arrive at a mutually acceptable arbitrator.

If an arbitration tribunal is requested by the parties, then each party may nominate one arbitrator to be confirmed by the Court. The third arbitrator is appointed by the Court and chairs the tribunal. If one party fails to nominate an arbitrator the Court will appoint one. If the parties cannot agree on the number of arbitrators, the Court will appoint a sole arbitrator. If a decision to appoint a single arbitrator is challenged by one of the parties, the Court will judge whether the case is sufficiently complex to warrant a tribunal. The Court's decision is final. If a tribunal is approved the parties have 15 days to nominate their arbitrators.

For the arbitrators it appoints, the Court relies for nominees on lists of potential arbitrators maintained by the national committees which constitute the ICC. The rules state that sole arbitrators or chairpersons of tribunals cannot be citizens of the countries of the firms that are involved in the dispute. A firm is allowed to challenge the appointment of an arbitrator, but the Court judges the merit of the objection, and its decision is final.

Clearly, these rules provide firms with considerable flexibility while providing protection against national bias. The rules are also constructed to prevent opportunistic delaying tactics through a failure to respond to a call for nomination of arbitrators. It is in the interest of the national committees to maintain lists of capable, unbiased arbitrators, as firms can choose to use the services of a different arbitration court if they are not satisfied.

Selection of individuals for the lists of nominees for appointment as arbitrators varies among arbitration institutions, but competition has meant that, as a rule, they will have available individuals from countries other than the country that is home to the institution. Individuals from a large number of countries are normally included so that suspicion of national bias is removed. The right to challenge or refuse arbitrators is fairly universal, but the rules are constructed to prevent these rights being used opportunistically for the purpose of delaying the proceedings.

According to ICC rules, if recourse to arbitration by the ICC is explicitly written into a contract, then either party can ask for arbitration upon supplying evidence from the contract. If there is no mention of arbitration in the contract or if no particular arbitration body is specified in the contract, then either party can ask the ICC for arbitration. The other party will then be informed, but, if it does not agree that the arbitration should go ahead under the auspices of the ICC, the ICC will refuse to hear the case. Again the emphasis is on flexibility.

The rules allow firms to choose arbitration only when a problem actually arises. They allow firms to choose the appropriate arbitration body once the nature of the dispute is known. If the dispute relates to a question of product quality, for example, an arbitration system established by the industry organization concerned with the product can be used. Such specialized organizations are likely to have product experts on their list of potential arbitrators. They will be more efficient at arbitrating this type of dispute than more general ICC arbitrators. Of course, if either the use of arbitration or the choice of arbitration institution to be used for the arbitration is not pre-specified, a firm may be open to the refusal of the other party to agree to arbitration. It may also object to a particular venue. These trade-offs will have to be considered at the time the original contract is being negotiated. The greater the degree of mutual interest in continuing the business relationship, the more likely that the arbitration procedure will be kept flexible.

Any party to a contract can request arbitration from the ICC. If arbitration by the ICC has been pre-specified in the contract between two parties, then the defendant named in the case is informed of the claimant's request for arbitration and is provided with all documentation supplied by the claimant. The defendant must reply within 30 days and submit the basis of its case. It must also make any counterclaims at that time. The original claimant then has 30 days to reply to the counterclaims. Again, there is an emphasis on rigid time-tables to prevent the use of delay as a tactic.

If arbitration by the ICC was pre-specified in the contract between the two parties and one party refuses to submit to arbitration, then the arbitration will still take place. This protects the claimant from the defendant refusing to live up to the prior commitment to arbitrate. In this case, the Court of Arbitration appoints an arbitrator in place of the one that the defendant would normally nominate.

If one of the parties objects to the arbitration, the Court of Arbitration decides on the validity of the objection. The Court's ruling is binding. Even if the party does not agree with the Court's ruling, the arbitration will proceed. This may appear as a wasted effort if one side refuses to live up to its arbitration commitment. However, this strategy cannot be allowed to thwart the arbitration process. In any case, a firm's refusal to cooperate with the arbitration procedure itself may not mean that it will not abide by the arbitration ruling. More important, however, is that, by having the arbitration take place and a ruling given, the damage to the defendant's reputation is increased by forcing it into a position of having to formally refuse to abide by the decision. As the Court of Arbitration cannot actually enforce its rulings – unless the defendant's national courts have agreed to enforce the ruling – compliance relies primarily on there being the potential to damage the reputation of the company. If a firm refuses to abide by a ruling, then other firms are less likely to enter into contracts with the offender, because they will not feel that they are protected by the agreement to arbitrate. If the defendant were simply able to thwart the arbitration process by refusing to agree to arbitration, there would be no direct evidence of the defendant's wrongdoing. This would make the task of diminishing the firm's reputation more difficult. Without a judgment, the defendant could simply claim that it was not guilty and, hence, was refusing to participate in the arbitration because it saw no need for the proceedings. While the firm might be seen by some as automatically guilty by its refusal to submit to arbitration, others would still have doubts. It is also important that the claimant have its case heard to ensure that its reputation is not diminished by the defendant's public protestation of innocence. By increasing the transparency of the entire arbitration proceedings, its effectiveness is increased. This reduces the risks associated with international transactions.

The parties to the dispute may specify the country where the arbitration should take place. If they cannot agree, the Court of Arbitration will decide the country of arbitration. This provision relates primarily to the problem of preventing national bias. This is because, under ICC regulations, the parties to the dispute have three options regarding the rules governing the conduct of arbitration hearings. First, the parties can choose the procedural rules for arbitrations set out by the ICC. Second, the parties can choose any other rules for the conduct of arbitration proceedings that they can agree on. The ICC has no particular interest in promoting the rules of arbitration it has developed. Third, if the parties choose not to specify any set of rules for the arbitration, then the legal rules of the country where the arbitration will be held will apply. This allows the parties to choose a legal system with which they are both comfortable. It also ensures that there will always be a set of procedural rules available for any arbitration.

The arbitrator is given wide latitude in the procedural rules established by the ICC. The arbitrator is specifically empowered to be proactive – unlike the case with some judicial proceedings, where the judge simply applies rules of order and passively evaluates the case on the basis of the presentations of advocates. The emphasis is on the arbitrator being able to obtain, as quickly as possible, any information that will aid him or her in reaching a decision.

The arbitrator may call witnesses. As a result, only those considered relevant can be called. The arbitrator can appoint technical experts to provide information on product quality, on the quality of work undertaken as part of a contract and on the diligence of the parties in arranging for shipping and so on. The arbitrator can call upon legal experts to provide for the interpretations of points of law. The means by which witnesses and experts inform the arbitrator are not constrained by rules of evidence, cross-examination and so on.

Each party is allowed to submit its case in writing and provide all the documentation it feels is appropriate. The arbitrator is charged with attempting to decide the case based on the materials presented by the parties. This provides an incentive for firms to provide complete information to the arbitrator. Otherwise, the arbitrator may make the decision based on the information provided by only one side. Relying on written submissions to provide the basis of a settlement reflects an attempt to keep costs to the parties low. Expensive visits to neutral countries where the arbitration is taking place are avoided. This is an attempt to provide equal access to the arbitration process for all firms. Firms are often dissuaded from pursuing litigation in the courts simply because the costs of a court action are prohibitive. Of course, large firms or those in a stronger financial position can use the threat of a court action as a bargaining tactic. Arbitration seeks to minimize these types of tactical advantages. Either party to an arbitration, however, does have the right to request a hearing. Only the party who requests the hearing must attend. As the arbitrator controls the hearing process, its tactical use by one party is minimized.

If the arbitrator is unable to decide the case on the basis of the documents provided, a hearing may be scheduled. If one party fails to attend the summons of the arbitrator, the arbitration hearing will still proceed. This prevents a failure to attend from being used to strategic advantage.

Hearings are held in private. Hence, unlike the case with formal legal proceedings, the confidentiality of information is protected. Confidentiality is particularly important internationally where patent protection may be poor. This is clearly a procedure preferred by business that is not available in national courts, with their reliance on public scrutiny of proceedings and concerns relating to the public trust.

The parties can appear before the arbitrator themselves. This is stated explicitly in the ICC rules to emphasize that the proceedings are not based upon representation by counsel. The intent is that business people should not be intimidated by the process and that the less formal nature of proceedings will allow the arbitrator to obtain the information directly from those involved.

A party is also allowed to be represented by local agents whom it designates, thereby reducing travel costs.

The ICC rules regarding arbitration procedures state that the parties 'may also be assisted by counsel or solicitors' (United Nations, 1973, p. 83). The intent is clear: parties should represent themselves. Some firms, however, may be uncomfortable with the idea of making direct representations. Representation by counsel is encouraged in other rules of arbitration and represents an element of competition for the ICC.

Under the rules of the ICC, arbitration proceedings are expected to be concluded and a verdict reached within 60 days of the arbitrator having been appointed. Again, the stress is on keeping the time involved to a minimum. The arbitrator, however, is allowed to ask the Court of Arbitration for an extension of this period in complex cases. It is the arbitrator and not the parties that must seek the extension.

When a tribunal rather than a single arbitrator is being used, the award is based on the decision of a majority vote. If there is no majority, only then does the chairperson make the award. This means that the chairperson, appointed by the Court of Arbitration, cannot overrule in the case when the two arbitrators selected by the parties themselves agree on an award. This is in keeping with the notion that businesses themselves should know best and that the Court, through the arbitrator it appoints, should make the award only when all other avenues have been explored. Of course, if the arbitrators selected by the parties fail to agree, then the independent arbitrator makes the decision.

When an award is made by the arbitrator, it is submitted to the Court of Arbitration, which can alter the form of the award and, if it feels necessary, point out aspects of the case for the arbitrator's attention. The former simply ensures that awards will conform to legal or other conventions. The substance of the award, however, cannot be changed. This allows greater freedom to use individuals as arbitrators who have important technical knowledge but only limited knowledge of arbitration procedures and the associated legal requirements. Getting an informed decision in an arbitration is more important than the formal protection of rights. This flexibility is an overt attempt to prevent a group of individuals gaining a monopoly over arbitration institutions similar to that enjoyed by lawyers in the judicial system.

An arbitration award is final. When submitting to arbitration by the ICC, the parties waive all rights to appeal. This prevents an appeal process from being used strategically as a way of increasing costs for a party that is financially weaker. It also prevents the use of appeals as a delaying tactic. Other arbitration systems do allow for limited forms of appeal. The national courts in some nations, however, provide for the direct appeal of arbitration awards.

The Court of Arbitration attempts to ensure that, where possible, an award is enforced without comment by national courts. Many national court systems, however, refuse to surrender that prerogative, believing that to do so would undermine their monopoly on justice. The parties to the dispute also agree to 'carry out the award without delay' (United Nations, 1973, p. 83).

The arbitrator also assesses the costs arising from the arbitration procedure and apportions the costs between the parties. There is even a provision that allows the ICC to require that, prior to the actual arbitration proceedings, one or both of the parties deposit an amount sufficient to cover the cost of the arbitration with the ICC. Clearly the ICC itself is concerned with ensuring that it will get paid.

This in-depth examination of the ICC rules is provided to illustrate the types of costs that may arise in international commercial transactions. Obtaining an arbitration award appears to be fairly straightforward. The arbitrator considers the arguments and evidence provided by the parties to the dispute, invites in experts, considers their advice, arrives at a decision which apportions the blame and then makes an award. All of the additional complexity built into the procedures is either to prevent national bias being present in the decisions or to prevent the arbitration procedure itself from being used strategically to advantage by either party. While the ICC rules are simple, and simply stated, they are carefully constructed to minimize opportunism. Hence, they provide considerable insights into the types of opportunism that may be practised in international commerce.

16.5 Enforcement of arbitration awards by national courts

Those who offer international arbitration services are, however, cognizant of the risks associated with having to rely on voluntary compliance for restitution. As a result, there are ongoing attempts to have national courts recognize and enforce the awards of international arbitrations. Arbitration centres have made provisions for their arbitrations to be decided according to the principles, but not the procedures, of individual countries' laws. This can remove the potential for a conflict in legal principles. Conflicts over legal principles make it much more difficult for national courts to uphold arbitration awards.

While national governments have often been willing to enforce arbitration awards made by international arbitrators, they have been less willing to recognize the awards in the absence of the right to review the awards. If national courts wish to scrutinize the awards of international arbitrators, to some extent the purpose of choosing arbitration is defeated. The case will still end up in the courts. Further, review by national courts reintroduces the possibility of national bias into the proceedings.

On the other hand, the position of national courts is understandable. If they do not review the cases they are expected to enforce, they may be enforcing awards made on criteria that violate the principles of the law they are expected to uphold. This problem has meant that the relationship between international arbitration and national courts varies considerably among countries. The relationship tends to evolve slowly, with international arbitration institutions asking for more enforcement and less review, while national courts tend to give ground only grudgingly.

The Convention on the Recognition and Enforcement of Foreign Arbitral Awards (United Nations, 1959) came into force on 7 June 1959. Over 130 countries have signed the Convention. For the most part, the signatories will apply the rules of the Convention to arbitrations undertaken in any state that has signed the Convention. When signing the convention a country agrees to 'recognize arbitral awards as binding and enforce them . . . There shall not be imposed substantially more onerous conditions or higher fees or charges on the recognition or enforcement of arbitral awards . . . than are imposed on the recognition or enforcement of domestic arbitral awards' (United Nations, 1959, p. 38).

The Convention provides a number of conditions under which the state need not enforce an arbitration award. Most of these relate to cases where the court believes that the arbitration was carried out under a flawed procedure. Governments, however, can also refuse to recognize or enforce an international arbitration award if:

(a) The subject matter of the difference is not capable of settlement by arbitration under the law of that country; or
(b) The recognition or enforcement of the award would be contrary to the public policy of that country (United Nations, 1959, p. 38).

Clearly, considerable latitude is available for intervention by the national courts. As a result, most arbitration awards are not submitted to the national courts for enforcement. Voluntary compliance with the terms of an award remains the rule rather than the exception.

Within the European Union, the European Court has been established to act as a means to adjudicate disputes. Commercial disputes arising when contracting parties span two or more countries that are members of the European Union are included. The procedures of the Court are, however, cumbersome. Generally, direct appeal to the Court is not possible. A dispute must first be pursued through all levels of appeal in the domestic courts of a member state. Only then may the appeal be taken to the European Court. The Court can decide only if the decision violates laws of the European Union. The European Court relies on the national courts for enforcement. The entire process is very time consuming. Clearly, this is a legalist approach to dispute settlement and not particularly suited to the requirements of international commerce.

As with the other private institutions that evolved to facilitate international trade, international arbitration exhibits a great deal of flexibility in its forms and institutions. This allows firms engaging in international transactions to search out the particular arbitration system which bests suits their requirements. As a result, the transactions costs associated with the settlement of disputes will be kept low.

 REFERENCES

David, R. (1984) *Arbitration in International Trade*, Kluwer Law and Taxation Publishers, London.

United Nations (1959) Convention on the Recognition and Enforcement of Foreign Arbitral Awards, No. 4739. *Treaty Series*, Vol. 330.

United Nations (1973) Rules of conciliation and arbitration of the International Chamber of Commerce, in *Register of Texts of Conventions and Other Instruments Concerning International Trade Law*, Vol. II, United Nations, New York, pp. 77–85.

Summary of Section V

Any initial attempt to study the private sector institutions that have evolved to facilitate international commercial transactions is likely to quickly overwhelm the most inquisitive of minds. The sheer number, diversity and complexity of the institutions and how they interact with each other represent a closed and byzantine world which few outsiders comprehend. Even those on the inside seldom have an understanding of the wider system within which their particular institution operates. No discussion of this system can ever be complete. In Section V, an attempt has been made to lay out the major constraints faced by those who wish to engage in international transactions. A number of the major institutions that have evolved in the private sector to reduce the costs these constraints impose on firms are examined. A few are examined in depth to show the reader that details can be important. Small differences in the services provided by the institutions can considerably affect the viability of an international business deal. As these services are provided in the private sector, they are provided at a cost. Given the complexity of the system, firms wishing to use the services available face a large number of choices, which must be evaluated on the basis of the costs and expected benefits. As many of the benefits relate to the reduction of risk, evaluations will be particularly difficult.

Three major problems are examined:

1. the problems associated with ensuring payment, including problems associated with exchanging currencies;
2. the problems associated with physically moving a good between firms in two countries, including insurance;
3. the settlement of disputes in the absence of a supranational commercial legal system.

While these problems have been examined in turn, in reality they represent parts of a system that will govern any international transaction. The method of transport affects payment assurance through the nature of the documents required for collection. The bank guaranteeing a forfaiter may require that the parties to the transaction agree to insert a clause in the contract specifying arbitration of disputes concerning an exporter's performance. An insurance claim against damage in transport may be evidence required for an arbitration.

Acting in combination, these institutions may reduce the risks associated with international transactions to a greater degree than the sum of their individual contributions. The institutions often operate in layers, with the organization ultimately assuming the final portion of the risk being totally removed from the original transaction – having no interest in the goods or services actually transacted. The complexity of the system may lead firms contemplating entering international transactions to wonder how transactions are completed at all, yet without these institutions it is unlikely that many international transactions would take place. The risks would simply be prohibitive.

This suggests that the economic implications of these institutions are simple. They reduce the transactions costs associated with international commerce. Transactions costs in economists' models have been likened to friction in the models of physicists. The private institutions of international commerce simply act as lubricants to reduce friction. It is, however, difficult to measure their contribution to efficiency. It is interesting to note that governments have found them to be so efficient at reducing the costs of international transactions that they have found it necessary to invent and interpose their own brand of friction or transactions costs into the international trading system. These government-imposed transactions costs take a number of forms. In the face of low transportation charges, governments impose tariffs. In the face of private institutions that efficiently transfer funds between countries, governments impose currency restrictions. Restrictions are imposed on arbitration awards by national courts. Government red tape counteracts efficient exchange of the documents that facilitate the transfer of products between firms in two countries. If the private system were less efficient at reducing transactions costs, one suspects that there would be far less interference in international commerce by government. The efficiency imparted by the international commercial institutions allows the effects of changing comparative advantage to be transferred among countries very quickly – often far faster than governments are willing to tolerate. Protectionist policies have been the result.

The long struggle at the WTO and in other international forums has been undertaken in a period when the technology available to international commercial institutions has been relatively static. New technology is now becoming available to these institutions. The revolution in electronic communications technology makes possible the transfer of information and funds virtually instantaneously. This shortens the time required for verification, arbitration and even the physical transfer of goods. Governments already complain that they cannot control international movements of capital. Their ability to manage the economy is handicapped by instantaneous flights of capital. As information transfers become instantaneous, managers all over the world can react to the same signals at the same time. How governments respond to this increase in efficiency and, hence, a reduction in their ability to control events will affect the future functioning of international commercial institutions.

Firms wishing to enter into international transactions will also benefit from the electronic communications revolution. It will allow them to dispense with some international institutions, while they will become more reliant on others. If instantaneous visual transmissions between firms are inexpensive, disputes over quality will be reduced, because the exporter will be able to verify its product's arrival condition through high-definition pictures transferred electronically. Electronic sensors in individual containers allow the exact time of damage to be determined, greatly simplifying insurance claims. Banks can be directly accessed electronically, meaning the time it takes to arrange financing will be reduced. With better information, banks will be able to put together more favourable financing packages. The commercial world will become more integrated, reducing cultural and procedural difficulties. International transactions will become more common, and they will lose some of their distinctive character. The need for specialized institutions will remain, however, as long as nations retain a considerable degree of economic sovereignty.

The ability to act opportunistically will also be reduced with improved information flows. Circumstances that allow firms to act opportunistically arise because the costs of monitoring activities are too high or because of the time required to complete transactions. Both monitoring costs and time are being reduced because of the revolution in electronic information technology.

It is interesting to note that many economists who have had an interest in studying the international system felt that the transactions cost associated with international commerce could be safely assumed away. They did this to be able to concentrate on the 'friction' imposed on the international system by government – tariffs, subsidies, import quotas and so on. This suggests that the transactions costs are probably low, attesting to the efficiency of the institutions. Why economists did not devote more time and effort to the study of opportunistic activities by firms is less clear. After all, it would appear that most of the institutions of international commerce exist primarily to reduce the costs of opportunistic behaviour. There is little better proof than the very existence of the institutions to suggest that firms do act in an opportunist manner if an opportunity presents itself. If the international commercial system is to be better understood, far more research will be required on the ways firms actually behave.

Future trends in international trade and commerce

Introduction to Section VI

Both the number and the value of international commercial transactions are growing at an increasing rate. International business, in all its manifestations, is a major global growth industry. International trade in goods and services normally grows at a more rapid rate than the domestic economies of developed countries. While all areas of the world are exhibiting increases in international activity, it is the trade between developed countries that has been expanding the fastest. This suggests that their economies are becoming more closely integrated. Developing countries, with a few obvious exceptions, have also joined the global economy. Much of Africa, however, is the major exception, with poor infrastructure and poor governance.

Closer integration of national economies may be viewed by some with distaste. It is difficult, however, to ignore the growth – and development – potential arising from international commerce. Negotiations to liberalize trade follow a tortuous course as politicians struggle to satisfy those with vested interests in preserving a degree of economic isolation. Rumblings about the neo-colonial nature of the institutions of international commerce are still heard in some quarters. In spite of these difficulties, barriers to trade and commerce continue to decline. New trade agreements are being completed in record numbers. The EU accepts new members. The US and Canada have accepted Mexico – with its dramatically different economy – as a full trading partner. Some developing countries, including India, are unilaterally reducing trade barriers put in place over decades in the name of development strategies based on import substitution. These changes suggest increased opportunity for international business. The internet has greatly reduced the information costs associated with international commerce.

The major challenge for individual businesses is to determine how to best take advantage of the opportunities available to them. The answer to this complex question lies first and foremost in the people they employ. No matter to what degree new technologies reduce the cost of organizing international transactions and restrictions placed on international commerce by government are removed, doing business internationally will be more complicated than doing business at home. The continued integration of the world economy will mean two things. More individuals in any firm will be directly involved in international business, and a broader range of employees will be in direct contact with people having different business practices and cultures. Receptionists will have to deal directly with foreign business people, both on the phone and in person. As first impressions are extremely important, receptionists will need to be more sensitive to nuances of both spoken and body language – and not just in the office, but when they deal with video links on international communications. The electronics revolution will make it far more likely that production problems will be sorted out between supervisors on the production line in two countries rather than by cumbersome communication through a number of layers of management. Each supervisor must be better informed about the production technologies in use and the psychological profile of the person he or she is dealing with. The receptionist and the supervisor need a better standard of education, as well as additional training provided by the company.

Managers and executives will be far more likely to be directly involved in international business arrangements. It will be increasingly difficult to isolate export departments or international divisions from the rest of the firm. Instantaneous electronic communication will break down divisional barriers within firms. To be competitive, the export division will require that there be three-way direct communication between themselves, their production, engineering or finance divisions and the foreign firm with which they are negotiating.

International contacts are also likely to broaden to include more countries. Managers will have to deal with a much wider range of business cultures than in the past. This leads to questions regarding the type of education that will be appropriate for the executive of the future. The focus of most MBA programmes and undergraduate business degrees has been on providing managers with skills that will enable them to contribute to improving the internal performance of the firm. Their education has emphasized better planning, control and staff motivation. Great strides have been made through the widespread use of the principles of internal management. While internal management will always be important, as the international component of a firm's business increases, more of the gains in efficiency will come from reducing the costs associated with organizing international transactions. These cost savings will come primarily from reducing the friction created by the failure to correctly communicate across cultures.

As the electronic communications revolution reduces the technical difficulties associated with organizing international transactions, the costs associated with individuals failing to communicate will become more prominent. The rise of transnational corporations can be seen as a means by which the gains available from better internal management could be extended into international business. For the most part, transnationals simply transferred domestic management systems to coordinating activities in other countries. By imposing a uniform managerial structure, problems with cross-cultural communications were reduced. In essence, however, the cross-cultural interface was simply displaced further along the production and distribution chain. Of course, transnational corporations can seldom remove all cross-cultural contacts and have had to adapt their local organizations accordingly. One characteristic of transnational corporations is that their internal management systems will often differ to a considerable degree from those of the domestic firms in the countries within which they operate. The greater the degree of cultural differences, the more stark the contrast. While additional gains in efficiency are probably available from further extensions of better internal management practices transnationally, those gains will be limited. At some point the firm must interact with foreign business people or consumers. Cross-cultural differences will remain, and reducing their associated costs will become increasingly important.

Reducing the costs associated with the failure to communicate across cultures will require a different type of manager. A good manager will still need to be cognizant of the parameters that affect internal efficiency. As better internal management practices become matters of routine, the manager's role as an innovator and promoter of such practices will be reduced. This suggests a reorientation of managerial education toward the skills that will help reduce cross-cultural communication problems. A greater emphasis on language skills, cultural differences in business practices, tolerance of foreign approaches and, if possible, some direct foreign experience are suggested. A more liberal arts approach to executive education is indicated, but with a focus. A signpost may be provided by the curricula of the increasingly popular international MBA programmes. While some basic management skills are included in most curricula, the emphasis is on building cross-cultural understanding and tolerance. Finding a means to capitalize on the opportunities made available by those skills provides the programmes' focus. The best of these programmes encourage an international student body and job placements in foreign countries. It is interesting that many of these programmes have arisen outside state-funded education systems. Hence, they may be another manifestation of the private sector establishing institutions catering for the needs of international business in the absence of supranational publicly funded institutions.

Ensuring a successful future in international commerce will require a different orientation for many firms. Expanded opportunities will be available both to firms that wish to engage directly in international commerce and to those that specialize in providing the services which facilitate its undertakings. The economic question remains the same: how do institutions, both public and private, affect the efficiency of international transactions?

17
Facing the future

17.1 Disequilibrium and change

'Change' is the word which best describes the economics of international business. While the world economy is probably never close to equilibrium, the economic factors currently driving its evolution are more powerful forces for change than were seen in the last half of the twentieth century. Change will create opportunities for some firms engaged in international commerce. Opportunities will be reduced for others. The expansion of trade relations will never lead to all businesses being 'winners'.

The changes currently under way should lead to a net increase in trade and other international activities. International commerce will continue to be a growth industry. While expanding trade is often 'sold' on the basis of increasing export opportunities, over the long run every expansion of exports must be accompanied by an expansion in imports or investment abroad. The gains to society from increased trade do not arise from increases in exports. They arise from the movement of resources – raw materials, people and capital – from relatively inefficient uses to relatively efficient uses. Unfortunately, the movement of these resources does not take place instantaneously or costlessly. The expansion of trade will impose economic losses on those who own the resources employed in declining industries. Shareholders in these industries will suffer a loss in the value of their capital. Labour will become unemployed. These problems are unavoidable in an economy that trades. Of course, the owners and employees of businesses that are internationally competitive will prosper. Changing fortunes are the inevitable result of disequilibrium.

17.2 Resource mobility

Governments will always be faced with pressure from businesses and labour groups whose wealth and livelihood are threatened. This pressure can be dealt with in a number of ways. Governments can give in to the pressure of protectionists and intervene in the functioning of international markets in ways which slow down the rate at which resources leave an inefficient industry. Of course, this means that part of the nation's resources are inefficiently employed. Trade restrictions and other measures can prevent the exit of resources from an industry made uncompetitive by imports. These policies are often put in place 'temporarily' in the name of restructuring – to allow the industry to become internationally competitive again. The evidence suggests that attempts at restructuring are seldom successful. Even if they are successful, the costs will often far exceed the benefits to society.

Governments can also choose to ignore pleas for protection, take no action and allow industries to decline. Those who find themselves unemployed will be forced to rely on the support mechanisms of the nation's social welfare system. Of course, most governments will follow some mixture of policies as they weigh the importance of various interest groups and the welfare of the society as a whole. The role of politicians is to make the difficult trade-offs that give to some and take from others. Almost all changes in policy, including changes in trade policy, are choices concerning who will be the winners and who will be the losers.

Neither protectionism nor *laissez-faire* – non-interventionist – approaches to trade policy attack the root of the problem. The problem with the changes that arise from disequilibrium in the international economy is that resources do not move quickly and costlessly from declining to expanding industries. In some cases, where specialized capital is involved, there is little that can be done to increase its mobility. Owing to the increasing rate of technological change, a considerable proportion of **fixed capital** is obsolete in less than a decade. In the case of labour, however, it should be possible to develop policies which improve mobility, both between industries and, if necessary, geographically.

Keeping labour employed in declining industries by the use of protectionist measures or having people languish on various forms of social assistance for long periods is not efficient. Alternatives need to be found to assist those who lose as a result of changing international competitiveness. While most governments have policy initiatives that attempt to reduce labour's immobility, the majority of policy effort is directed at either protectionism or the social welfare system. Policies aimed at improving **resource mobility** have, in most cases, had only limited success. A greater investment in children's education will probably reap high rewards in the long run. However, far more thought and research into policies which will increase resource mobility will be required before effective policies are likely to arise. Economists who develop trade theory have added little to this debate (Leger et al., 1999). Most of the models that are used to examine trade problems make the assumption that resources move instantaneously and costlessly between sectors.

The fundamental question of resource mobility will become more important as the rate of change in the world economy accelerates. The major contributor to international disequilibrium is the increasing rate of technological progress. The individuals who can take advantage of these technological changes are those who can adapt quickly to acquire new skills which have a high degree of technical sophistication. In short, individuals need to have intellectual mobility. The more people a society has who are intellectually mobile, the greater the likelihood that they will prosper in the increasingly global economy. Nations that fail to create an intellectually mobile labour force will see their unemployment queues increase. The pressure for protectionism will rise.

Businesses need to lobby governments to make the investments in human capital required to ensure they will be able to take advantage of international opportunities. More importantly, firms will also have to provide additional training for their employees. Further, for those firms doing business internationally, there may need to be a reversal of the management strategy whereby contracting out is favoured over taking on permanent employees. The skills that are useful in reducing the costs associated with poor cross-cultural communications are likely to be specific to individuals. Success in reducing these costs will depend, to a considerable degree, on the establishment of ongoing relationships with foreign individuals. As a result, while the people who fix a firm's computer networks may be relatively interchangeable and, hence, the service can be purchased on contract, those who have developed working relationships with foreign businesses will not be interchangeable. It is probably not surprising that those firms that specialized in international transactions in the past had reputations as lifelong employers. The special relations with comprador families nurtured by the Hong Kong trading houses lasted over many generations. Japanese trading houses provided the model for Japanese lifetime employment policies. Conducting international business successfully in the future will mean approaching it from a long-term point of view.

17.3 Increasing diversity

Beyond the revolution in electronic communications technology, there are a number of major trends that are likely to foster the expansion of international commerce. The first is that, as incomes rise, consumers tend to wish to diversify the range of products they consume. Part of their craving for diversity will be supplied by foreign products. The variety of consumer products that are available nationally, but not yet internationally, is still enormous. Firms will find lucrative niche markets satisfying consumers' craving for the exotic.

While rising incomes allow consumers to better fulfil their quest for diversity, the internationalization of communications provides them with information about foreign lands and cultures. Increasingly, consumers have direct and indirect access to foreign programming transmitted by satellites. They watch television commercials for foreign products. They are made aware of new products and fads faster and in a much more visual way than in the past. The internet allows consumers direct, low-cost access to foreign suppliers, while the international capabilities of credit card firms and specialized internet payment firms facilitate payments for goods across international boundaries. International internet commerce is still in its infancy but opens up a whole spectrum of opportunities to expand international commerce – particularly the search for diversity. Government regulatory regimes are struggling to keep up with the international opportunities provided to firms by the internet (Boyd et al., 2003).

Consumers are also increasingly well travelled, meaning they experience foreign products first-hand. This tends to break down resistance to foreign products and leads consumers to seek them out when they return home. Trade is increasingly based on quality and product characteristics rather than on comparative advantage in relatively homogeneous industrial inputs. Predicting changes in trade flows becomes much more difficult.

Consumption of services is growing faster than the consumption of goods, While some services are tied to localized on-site delivery – restaurant food, car repairs, hairdressing – many are not. With access to modern communications technology, book editing can be undertaken anywhere in the world. Architectural drawings can be done on a computer as easily in Bombay as they can in Washington. Programs to control robotic production can be written in Vancouver, tested in Aberdeen and used in Tokyo. The distinction between products and services is becoming blurred. Is writing a new computer program production or a service? Is debugging that program still production?

Services based on human rather than physical capital – consulting, market research, management advice and even accounting – are ever more mobile. As the world becomes increasingly technical, the technology itself must be serviced. Trade in services will continue to increase. Trade in services is likely to require less transport and insurance than trade in goods. Problems associated with ensuring payment and the settlement of disputes will remain. As the quality of service is, in general, much more difficult to verify than the quality of goods, disputes are likely to increase.

Sourcing of components on an international basis is also likely to expand. Further integration of the global economy will result. Improvements to both the speed and the reliability of transportation have released manufacturing firms from reliance on local suppliers. Components can be bundled together into final products that are tailored to the preferences of local consumers. Some companies have become specialists at searching out the components that are available internationally and then bringing them together for assembly. Assembling components is a relatively simple procedure in many cases. This increases the weighting given the international procurement divisions of firms relative to their domestic manufacturing divisions. For those firms that are involved in international sourcing of components, reducing the costs associated with poor cross-cultural communications is imperative.

Few firms are, as yet, truly international. Companies remain identified with particular countries – even if their ownership may be truly international and their formal headquarters in a different country from that with which they are identified. While their international business has increased, they retain their national character. This national character is expressed primarily in managerial organization and ethics. The management of few companies can be considered truly multinational.

17.4 Developing countries

Firms in most developing countries have been less affected by the forces of change that are leading to increased international economic integration. Certainly, some components are sourced in developing countries. Exotic products are exported to satisfy the craving for diversity by consumers in rich countries. The fact remains, however, that a much smaller proportion of firms in developing countries engage in international commerce. Firms from developing countries are much less likely to instigate an international transaction than those in the developed countries. Trade between developed and developing countries is initiated by firms in developed countries seeking products or markets. Trade among developing countries, while growing, remains relatively small. A large proportion of this trade is organized and facilitated by firms headquartered in developed countries. Part of the reason is technological. Many firms in the developing world have not been able to finance the acquisition of modern electronic communications technology. Often they do not have staff well enough trained to utilize this technology effectively, and their governments have not provided the infrastructure required to support its use.

More important, however, many firms in developing countries do not have the resources to actively seek out international markets. The costs of market entry are too high to be financed out of current profits. Banks in developing countries will not provide financing for ventures with such slow pay-offs and high risks. In many cases, business practices are so different that firms find it impossible to overcome problems with cross-cultural communications. Business practices are, in part, governed by the commercial environment fostered by the government. Where contract enforcement is weak and other aspects of commercial law underdeveloped, business is conducted on a cash basis and remains based on family ties or long-standing personal relationships. Vertical coordination based on these business practices is very expensive in terms of managerial time and effort.

Firms in Western countries, where commercial law is well developed and enforced, have to a considerable degree substituted contracts for commercial relationships based on personal trust (Kerr, 1996). While it is possible to build relations based on personal trust when the number of other businesses being dealt with is small, it becomes impractical as the number of business contacts increases. The costs of building trust based on personal relationships increase greatly when that trust must be built with a business person in a foreign country. Travel cost alone can be prohibitive. In any case, firms in developed countries are likely to find the costs of building such relationships prohibitively expensive. They will prefer to deal with firms in other developed countries, which use contracts to organize the transfer of goods and services.

If developing countries are to benefit from the opportunities that will arise from the growth of international trade, their firms must become proactive participants in international commerce. Developed countries will continue to impose barriers on the imports of some products from developing countries. The market power that some transnational firms possess will continue to limit the ability of developing countries to capture all of the benefits available from trade. The major challenge for developing countries is, however, to reform their systems of commercial law. Without a secure commercial environment, the transactions costs associated with organizing international commerce will remain prohibitively high for all but a small minority of their firms. The insistence of developing countries that they receive 'special and differential treatment' – meaning that it is easier for them to implement and maintain protectionist measures – at the WTO is clearly detrimental to their long-run interests, as it prevents their firms from having to learn how to be internationally competitive.

The main growth area for international commercial activity is likely to be among the developed countries. The rapidly growing economies of the Asia-Pacific Rim are well on their way to becoming integrated into the international economy. China's integration into the international economy has made great strides, but it has not yet reached the norms associated with developed-country commerce – a process that will not be easy and is not likely to progress in a linear fashion (Kerr and Hobbs, 2001; Coase and Wang, 2012). India is also removing many of the barriers to trade and investment that have been an integral part of its long-term strategy of development based on self-sufficiency (Kerr et al., 2000; Khorana et al., 2010). The voluntary opening of two of the largest economies in the world has, however, added to the disequilibrium in the international system. It will take time for new market channels to be opened and for commercial opportunities to be identified and acted upon.

 REFERENCES

Boyd, S.L., Hobbs, J.E. and Kerr, W.A. (2003) The impact of customs procedures on business to consumer e-commerce. *Supply Chain Management*, 8(3), 195–200.

Coase, R. and Wang, W. (2012) *How China Became Capitalist*, Palgrave Macmillan, London.

Kerr, W.A. (1996) Managing risk and the organization of transactions: A perspective from the Pacific Rim. *Jurnal Manajemen Prasetiya Mulya*, 3(6), 1–7.

Kerr, W.A. and Hobbs, A.L. (2001) Taming the dragon: The WTO after the accession of China. *Journal of International Law and Trade Policy*, 2(1), 1–9, www.esteyjournal.com.

Kerr, W.A., Perdikis, N. and Hobbs, J.E. (2000) NAFTA and the 'New India', in *The Indian Economy: Contemporary Issues*, ed. N. Perdikis, Ashgate, Aldershot, pp. 37–57.

Khorana, S., Perdikis, N., Yeung, M.T. and Kerr, W.A. (2010) *Bilateral Trade Agreements in the Era of Globalization*, Edward Elgar Publishing, Cheltenham, UK and Northampton, MA, USA.

Leger, L.A., Gaisford, J.D. and Kerr, W.A. (1999) Labour market adjustments to international trade shocks, in *The Current State of Economic Science*, Vol. 4, ed. S. Bhagwan Dahiya, Spellbound Publications, Rohtak, pp. 2011–34.

18

Issues for the international trading system

18.1 Liberalization versus protectionism

While changing technology and the broadening of consumer tastes will provide commercial opportunities internationally, governments will continue to influence both which opportunities firms will be allowed to act upon and the manner in which this can be undertaken. The source of this influence will continue to be the trade accords governments negotiate with other countries and the regulations they unilaterally impose.

Trade liberalization is on the ascendancy as an official political ideology in most developed countries. While formal protectionism raises its head once in a while in developed countries, it is clearly no longer a major political force. Protectionism has lost favour as a legitimate intellectual alternative to trade liberalization. It has, instead, become associated directly with individual vested interests. This does not mean that politicians can always ignore the concerns of these vested interests. Hence, protectionism is currently applied on a piecemeal basis as a political response to particular concerns. The increasing reliance on contingency protection measures by the US, for example, allows requests for protection to be dealt with on a case-by-case basis. By making it easy for those seeking protection to file suits, the process is depoliticized to a considerable extent. The interim trade restrictions in US contingency protection procedures (and those in an increasing number of countries) provide a means by which intense pressure on politicians for protection can be dissipated. Individual vested interests are, however, finding it more difficult to have their concerns identified with the national interest. Even the Japanese rice import policy may be losing its credibility as one of the major guardians of the country's culture and morality. In general, however, agriculture in developed countries is an exception and remains closely associated with nations' welfare (Gaisford and Kerr, 2001).

The reasons why protectionism has lost its political legitimacy are complex. Part of the reason is the evidence itself. The success of the EU (despite the setbacks in the wake of the 2008 financial crisis), Japan's export-based economy and the relatively open economies on the Asia-Pacific Rim stand in sharp contrast to the stagnating economies following protectionist, closed-economy models.

Protectionism is also identified with direct government management of the economy. In the US and the UK, for example, there has been a movement away from big government and the welfare state, which to a greater or lesser degree affected economic policy in all developed countries. Trade liberalization was simply the international manifestation of the move toward deregulation and market forces. The demise of communism, with its emphasis on self-reliance, as an intellectual alternative to liberal trade policies is an additional contributing factor to the decline in the popularity of protectionism. The general reduction in the influence of labour unions, with their traditions of protectionism, has freed politicians from the need to listen as closely to their complaints.

Consumers have, for the most part, ignored pleas to buy American or buy British and instead purchased Toyotas, Samsungs and Toshibas without a shred of conscience. The choices of consumers have not gone unnoticed by politicians. In particular, politicians realized that voters could not be denied access to the latest foreign consumer gadgetry. The improvement in domestically produced products brought about by sharp foreign competition was also not lost on politicians.

The status quo is not acceptable as an alternative to liberalization. There was little support for leaving well enough alone when the Uruguay Round was being proposed. Expansion and closer cooperation are the bywords of the EU. NAFTA integration continues apace. Formal trade alliances are being proposed for the Pacific Rim. Many former command economies have been accepted for entry into the EU. In general, there is a momentum for change.

There are two major intellectual thrusts to the process of trade liberalism. One of the thrusts of trade policy is multilateralism. The other is for the development of regional trade organizations. They are not necessarily contradictory. When transformed by political energy into government policy, the end result can be the creation of institutions that move trade policy in opposite directions. Multilateralism is firmly rooted in the liberalization tradition. The enthusiasm for regional trade organizations is much more pragmatic and reflects the *art of the possible*. Multilateralism is sometimes perceived as a spent force, while great potential is seen in regional arrangements. This is particularly true since the WTO's Doha Round negotiations floundered for much of the first decade of the twenty-first century.

The political appeal of multilateralism, however, should not be underestimated. The vast amounts of political energy put into the Doha Round attest to its resilience. No major trading country seriously considered abandoning the WTO. In part, this is because the alternative – a total reliance on regional organizations – carries with it the unpleasant spectre of competition between trade blocs and protectionist beggar-thy-neighbour trade restrictions between blocs. Politicians fear that trade wars between blocs could be sufficiently destructive to wipe out many of the economic gains which have been made since the Second World War. This does not mean that there is not frustration with the multilateral systems and, at times, more emphasis given to regional or even webs of bilateral trading arrangements.

Trade blocs and multilateralism need not be incompatible. They share the common aim of trade liberalization. The WTO explicitly allows for regional trade organizations. The major problem with regional trade organizations is that making them work effectively can require a tremendous amount of political energy. Political energy tends to become focused on the problems of the organization. Further, there will be a need for political compromise among the countries in a regional trade organization. In some cases, accommodating competing national interests in a regional organization can be most easily accomplished by imposing costs on countries outside the regional grouping.

The EU provides excellent examples of the tendency to impose costs on non-members for the sake of internal harmony. The political energy required to keep the EU from self-destruction is enormous. The export subsidies of the Common Agricultural Policy are simply a means by which reforming the system of agricultural subsidies could be avoided. By exporting the surpluses at subsidized prices, costs are imposed on other agricultural exporters, which lost their markets. The inability to negotiate meaningful reforms to the Common Agricultural Policy eventually threatened the entire Uruguay Round and, again, is a major barrier to the conclusion of the Doha Round (Gaisford and Kerr, 2001).

One of the major proposals of the EU at the Uruguay Round was a relaxation of the principle of non-discrimination. This would have allowed selective imposition of trade restrictions on individual countries without the fear of multilateral retaliation. Being allowed to restrict the imports of selected countries would have reduced the cost of internal EU negotiations relating to access to sensitive markets.

The NAFTA contained elements that allow increased restrictions on car makers in other countries. These provisions eased the passage of the agreement through the legislatures of both countries. The difficulties which regional trade blocs face in achieving internal compromise are likely to increase as they expand the number of states they include. As a result, the trade concerns of non-members are more likely to be ignored. The final stages of the Uruguay Round negotiations became a search for compromise between the EU and the US. Other countries could only wait on the sidelines and hope the compromises reached did not significantly damage their interests. The 'backroom' nature of these negotiations led to a major confrontation over reform of the multilateral negotiating system at the WTO ministerial meeting in Seattle in 1999 and a commitment to reform the system at the Doha ministerial meeting in 2001 (Kerr, 2002).

Of course, the amount of political energy that is required to make even small amounts of progress at the multilateral WTO negotiations led to the interest in regional groupings in the first place. Much faster progress toward trade liberalization could be made when only a few countries were involved. Frustration with the slowness at the WTO negotiations provided one of the impetuses for the negotiations between the US and Canada that eventually led to the NAFTA. Additional countries wish to join the EU rather than waiting for multilateral negotiations. The Uruguay Round of GATT talks, with over 100 nations participating, took seven years to complete. There are over 150 countries involved in the Doha Round negotiations. If the issues were not so fundamentally important, it is unlikely that any agreement would have been reached at the Uruguay Round.

The major problem with multilateralism is that the number of participants involved makes the negotiating process nearly intractable. It is not clear how multilateral institutions might be reformed to increase efficiency. Any change that increases efficiency will require that states relinquish some of their sovereignty over trade matters. Most countries show little inclination to do this. As a result, regional trade organizations retain their appeal.

The extension of the existing GATT organization into areas of international commerce not concerned with trade in goods was a major accomplishment of the Uruguay Round. Since the inception of the GATT, the progress made in reducing tariffs has been considerable. Progress has been so great that only limited gains are likely to arise from the remaining tariff reductions, at least among the developed countries. Trade in services, international protection of intellectual property and government procurement now represent areas of international commerce where the removal of barriers exhibits the greatest potential for gains from trade. Liberalization in these areas, however, is likely to be difficult. These are also areas where the examples from regional trade organizations can provide a guide. This is because they have been able to make greater progress as a result of the smaller number of countries involved.

18.2 Trade in services

Liberalization in the areas of services is likely to be difficult, because the restrictions on trade in services are not often explicit border restrictions. They are, rather, integral parts of a country's domestic regulations. In some cases, it is possible to arrange for delivery of the service from the home country of the foreign service company – proofreading manuscripts or computer data entry. Few restrictions, however, limit this type of trade. Franchised services – where the service is provided to the standards of a foreign franchiser by citizens of the country importing the service – are also not heavily restricted. Problems may arise if the company selling the franchise is not able to send its employees to the importing country to provide training or to monitor the quality of the service. These problems are unlikely to greatly inhibit the franchising of services.

Far greater problems are likely to arise in the trade in services from the need to send employees to the importing country, even on a temporary basis. Problems with certification of professionals may also be important. The movement of people between countries has not traditionally been a trade matter but rather an immigration matter. Restrictions on immigration are, essentially, restrictions on the movement of one factor of production – labour. The forces of comparative advantage suggest that either goods or factors of production such as labour or capital should move to markets where they receive increased returns. Immigration policy is, hence, bound up in employment policy. Countries impose immigration barriers in the name of keeping unemployment down, of keeping wages up and of maintaining the fiscal integrity of their social welfare systems. Regardless of the validity of these arguments, nations will jealously guard their rights to control imports of labour.

Traditionally, the movement of labour between countries tended to be a permanent movement. The labour component of the trade in services is far more likely to be transitory. If the provision of the service requires a full-time labour commitment, then training a local employee would often be more cost-effective. The labour component of an imported service is unlikely to be based on a significant labour cost advantage. If the wages associated with the provision of imported services were significantly higher in the importing country, the exporter's employees could always better themselves by finding a means of immigrating, either legally or illegally. The exporter of the service would have high labour turnover costs.

While immigration policy is primarily concerned with long-term employment, it can be used effectively as a short-term trade barrier. The most obvious example of this is when an international contract involves the bundling together of both goods and services. As the technology embodied in goods has increased in complexity, both the requirements for servicing and the sophistication of that servicing have increased. Hence, when goods are sold, the contract often includes with it a long-term service component. Without a service agreement, the individual buyer would be forced into employing trained staff to repair the equipment purchased. It is often more efficient, however, for sellers to provide the service, because the cost can be spread over a large number of sales.

When tied combinations of goods and services are marketed internationally, government restrictions on the international movement of service people can adversely affect sales. While tariffs and other restrictions on the movement of the goods portion of the transaction may have been eliminated as a result of international trade negotiations, the movement of the personnel required to service the goods may still be restricted. Exporting firms must then be willing to establish service subsidiaries in export markets. This may mean costly duplication and compliance with regulations regarding local participation in subsidiaries, labour laws, social security and so on. The price of the entire package may be increased considerably and, hence, total sales reduced. These problems are likely to be particularly acute in the market entry stage, when the volume of sales cannot justify a full-time service organization in the importing country. Sending service personnel from the exporting country on a short-term basis may be the only cost-effective alternative. If this is not allowed, export markets will have to be forgone. Hence, finding mechanisms to reduce barriers to trade in services will become increasingly important as the technical complexity of exports continues to increase. The NAFTA, for example, includes special provisions for the short-run movement of personnel involved in servicing industrial goods.

Removing barriers to the trade in professional services is a complex topic. Doctors, lawyers, accountants, engineers and so on often have, as part of their mandate as professionals, the requirement to act as quality guarantors for those who use their services. Given the complexity of verifying quality, self-regulation by government-sanctioned professional organizations has been generally adopted. In most cases, professional organizations have the right of certification.

Certification procedures in different countries have evolved independently and, hence, vary considerably. The process of certification is often tied to and influences the education prospective professionals receive at university. Individuals who have been certified in one jurisdiction may be forced to incur considerable **switching costs** if they wish to have certification in another country. Given that they have a state-sanctioned monopoly over certification and, hence, entry into the profession, professional organizations have the opportunity to undertake rent-seeking activities. As the verification of quality can be exceedingly complex in professional services, it is difficult to determine when the standards for certification are necessary to guarantee quality for consumers and when they are used as barriers to entry for the purposes of rent seeking. In any case, as quality cannot be guaranteed absolutely, professional organizations will always be able to make the claim that their regulations reduce risks for consumers.

Imports of professional services are likely to be perceived as a threat by a professional organization that is using its certification powers for purposes of rent seeking. Certification may not be based on an examination, but rather on long-term processes involving education, supervised experience and socialization. Evaluation of the contribution of these aspects of certification for those trained in a different country can be very difficult. Formal certification examinations often only serve the purpose of a final check on professional competency – they can be used to fail candidates, but full certification relies heavily on the individual having passed all the previous steps in the process. Hence, it is probably not possible to design a single examination that can substitute for these long-term professionalization processes. Professional organizations sometimes attempt to devise special exams for foreign applicants. As these will inevitably be more demanding that those devised for domestic students – in an attempt to substitute for the professionalization process – they are open to charges of discrimination.

The problem of trade in professional services can be approached in a number of ways. Professional organizations in different countries can be asked to harmonize their regulations. This will mean protracted negotiations. Harmonization may also require the cooperation of educational institutions. The harmonization of the government regulations that affect the services will also be necessary. Overcoming determined opposition from professional organizations may be very difficult. It may be easy for professionals to enlist public support for their political battles. The trust they have built up can be used to unsettle consumers. References can easily be made to 'inferior' foreign standards when verification of standards is beyond the competence of individual consumers. Harmonization can be a long and difficult process.

One alternative is for the government to extend national treatment to individuals who have been certified by foreign professional organizations. National treatment means that individuals who hold foreign certification will have the same rights to practise their profession as those with domestic certification. This approach can succeed as long as quality differences are actually small and if foreign professional organizations are effective guarantors of quality.

The NAFTA and the EU have included elements of both harmonization and national treatment in their provisions for trade in services. The EU's provisions for the free movement of professionals need to be closely observed. Problems have arisen regarding the inability of professional organizations in other countries to, for example, verify the qualifications of dentists certified in Italy. A second alternative – establishing a supranational body to devise a common certification programme – has not generally been attempted because of the difficulty of structuring an examination which can evaluate the long professionalization process.

The problems associated with liberalizing trade in professional services can be likened to those associated with removing non-tariff barriers. Many non-tariff barriers arise from differences in domestic regulations put in place to protect the public interest. That the regulations also have an ability to restrict trade is an **externality** that can be used by vested interests to their advantage. As in the case of non-tariff barriers, there are political costs to removing the economic instruments useful to a professional's vested interests.

A **General Agreement on Trade in Services (GATS)** was reached as part of the Uruguay Round. The GATS is a parallel agreement to the GATT and is administered under the auspices of the WTO. All members of the WTO are signatories of the GATS. Any disputes arising in trade in services will be settled by the WTO. A broad range of services is covered, including investment, temporary movement of personnel and cross-border operations. The services provided by governments such as the police and education are not included.

A commitment to improve the transparency of regulations concerning services has been made by GATS members. Countries have agreed to open the services markets to varying degrees. Once a commitment has been made a country must, in principle, extend the concession to all other GATS members. There is a provision for exceptions, allowing discriminatory treatment to creep into the agreement. The exceptions were expected to be removed over time. Future negotiations are expected to reduce or remove restrictions on access such as limitations on the number of foreign providers of services, on the total value of services, on the number of transactions undertaken by foreign firms and on the number of employees foreign providers of services are allowed to hire. Over time, negotiations will take place regarding reductions to restrictions on the cross-border movement of people providing services, the harmonization of professional, technical and licensing standards and the control of trade-distorting subsidies in service industries. While commitments have been made to liberalize trade in financial services, maritime transport, telecommunications and international air flights, these services are treated as special categories.

The GATS, as yet, remains largely an agreement of intent. Its success will depend upon the concessions countries will grant in future negotiations. One strong clause in the agreement is that, while previously granted concessions may be withdrawn or modified after three years, compensation must be paid. If the parties cannot agree on compensation it will be awarded by arbitration.

18.3 Protection of intellectual property

The internationalization of protection for intellectual property is not fundamentally a trade issue. It was included in the Uruguay Round negotiations by developed countries so that it could be directly tied to concessions in the trade in goods and services (Kerr, 2000). The issue does, however, have a trade aspect. Products that use intellectual property as an input are often exported back to the country where the intellectual property originated. If the intellectual property has been used without full compensation being paid, it means that the low-cost imported product competes directly with the product of the firm that incurred the costs of developing the technology. As a result, incentives for companies that develop technology are adversely affected.

While intellectual piracy is not a new phenomenon, it has increased in importance as a result of the revolution in electronic technology. The proportion of a good's value made up by physical materials has fallen considerably. Computer chips are inexpensive to manufacture. The major component of their value is supplied by the intellectual effort incorporated in the chip's design. The flexibility that these chips give to product design means that industrial production is much less standardized than in the past. Further, the rate at which intellectual property is becoming obsolete is increasing. The fixed costs of developing intellectual property, as a consequence, have to be recouped from fewer and fewer sales. Given its increased importance, the incentives for using intellectual property without compensation have risen.

The more the unauthorized use of intellectual property takes place, however, the lower the returns to investing in such activities become (Boyd et al., 2003). The rate of technological change is reduced. Politicians in developed countries are concerned with sluggish growth in their economies. Protection of intellectual property has become an international issue in the same way that patent protection was once a public issue within national economies.

Resistance to increased international protection for intellectual property has come, for the most part, from developing countries. There are three reasons for this. First, as most intellectual property is developed in rich countries, they are able to maintain or increase their higher standard of living – an equity issue. Secondly, as patents are only a very crude instrument for providing for returns on investment, they also allow firms to extract monopoly profits. Thirdly, governments in some developing countries may not be able to effectively police the use of intellectual property.

As the proportion of the value of goods made up by intellectual property rises, a nation's economic prosperity increasingly depends on its ability to generate new technology. Most new intellectual property is developed in advanced economies. Part of the reason for this is that major corporations locate their research and development activities in their home countries. The much larger expenditures that developed countries can afford to make on education and publicly funded research are also important. In the view of some developing countries' governments, closing the development gap may simply not be possible without transfers of either human capital or the technology itself. As foreign assistance in these areas remains at levels far below what is required to close the gap, some governments in developing countries see the uncompensated use of intellectual property as the only means available to acquire the technology required for them to close the gap. While some governments openly espouse this view, others simply choose to ignore the unauthorized use of intellectual property.

Even if governments in developing countries accept the argument that those who invest in the development of new technology are entitled to a return on their investment, they find the mechanism used by developed countries to provide that return unacceptable. Developed countries want patent protection extended internationally. Further, they want developing countries to vigorously enforce patent protection. Patents endow the developer of new technology with the property rights to the use of the technology for a specified period. This allows the holder of the rights to act as a monopoly. Exercising monopoly power provides the basis for the return on the investment made in new technology. This means, however, that the returns actually received are not directly tied to the size of the initial investment. As a result, the rates of return on investment for developing new technology may exceed those required for a competitive return on investment.

The issue of a competitive rate of return for investments in research and development is complex, because it involves risk and risk spreading. The firms investing in research and development argue that rates of return on successful innovations must cover losses on other unsuccessful research ventures. Governments in developing countries, however, object to paying the monopoly rents that contribute to returns on investment that exceed competitive returns. This argument is particularly prevalent in the case of pharmaceuticals such as HIV/AIDS drugs and agricultural inputs such as seeds. Governments in low-income countries argue that their citizens are too poor to pay high prices for essential drugs and their farmers too poor to pay for high-priced inputs. As long as they are not involved in the development of new technology, they have little to lose from allowing their citizens access to low-cost domestically produced generic products. This is why developed countries have wanted discussions on intellectual property tied to other trade issues where they can exert some leverage.

Some developing countries may also feel that they are unable to expend the resources necessary to enforce intellectual property rights. Further, they may not have the capacity for effective enforcement (Kerr and Boyd, 2007). If they agreed to improved international protection for intellectual property, they might not be able to live up to their commitments. This would put them in violation of their international commitments and leave them open to withdrawal of trade concessions.

These are the fundamental issues that must be dealt with regarding protection of international property. For businesses that develop new technology, the lack of international protection increases the risks associated with those investments. Lowering the risk may take many forms, including direct transnational operations or vertical integration to better ensure control of the new technology.

International protection of intellectual property was a major concern of developed countries at the Uruguay Round. The negotiations concluded with a wide-ranging *Agreement on Trade-Related Aspects of Intellectual Property Rights, Including Trade in Counterfeit Goods* (TRIPS). The central theme of the agreement is that countries agree to enforce the property rights of other countries' firms and citizens. This commitment extends to patents, trademarks, films, sound recordings, computer software, integrated computer circuits, trade secrets, test data and the misuse of geographic indicators, for example labelling bottles of wine produced in Canada as originating in France. While the conventions covering different types of intellectual property vary, that the intellectual property of foreigners should receive the same protection as that given to the country's own nationals is the general principle applied. Further, the protection extended to one country's nationals must be extended to all other countries – the principle of non-discrimination.

With respect to patents, developing countries that did not have comprehensive patent protection had to enact legislation to cover those areas of technology not currently covered. They had ten years to complete the task. In terms of other aspects of the agreement, the least developed countries originally had 11 years to bring their legislation and practices into conformity with the agreement. This has been extended in some areas as a result of the Doha Round discussions. Other developing countries and former command economies had to conform within five years, while developed countries agreed to conform within a year. Hence, the agreement would appear to provide a considerable degree of protection for intellectual property rights. Enforcement will, however, be of paramount importance.

The agreement obliges member governments to provide procedures and remedies in their domestic laws to ensure that intellectual property rights can be effectively enforced. The procedures put in place must allow for judicial review. Excessive time delays and costs are not allowed. There is no requirement, however, that extra resources need to be dedicated to the enforcement of intellectual property rights or that enforcement should receive any priority. Countries with weak or ineffective judicial systems are still likely to have poor intellectual property rights protection (Kerr and Boyd, 2007).

The remedies which countries have agreed to put in place include injunctions, damages and the right of judicial authorities to order disposal or destruction of infringing goods. Countries are expected to provide criminal procedures and penalties for the most blatant abuses of trademark counterfeiting and copyright piracy. Clearly, in the negotiations an attempt was made by developed countries to have the problem of enforcement addressed. Enforcement, however, is ultimately dependent upon bureaucrats or the courts acting vigorously to identify and pursue infringements.

Under the agreement, a *Council for Trade-Related Aspects of Intellectual Property Rights* has been established within the WTO. Disputes are settled within WTO procedures. There is some evidence that the threat of trade sanctions for failure to protect intellectual property is not likely to be effective, calling into question the entire rationale for including the TRIPS in the WTO (Yampoin and Kerr, 1998; Gaisford et al., 2002).

18.4 Government procurement

Liberalization of government procurement procedures is another area where the potential for gains from trade is significant. Government involvement in national economies continues to increase, despite efforts in many countries to reverse the trend. Governments typically purchase in excess of a quarter of the goods and services sold in any year. For the most part, government procurement contracts have been reserved for domestic producers. If foreign firms are allowed to bid on government contracts, it is often under conditions that discriminate in favour of domestic firms.

In some cases, foreign bidders are excluded for legitimate reasons of national security. In most cases, the restrictions are the result of politicians giving in to pressure by lobbyists. Politicians have a role as the champions of the nation's products. They are often put in a difficult position when the government they represent is purchasing foreign goods and services. This inconsistency is not lost on opposition politicians and voters. Given that the goods and services purchased are often complex, explaining foreign purchases on the basis of strict commercial criteria to the satisfaction of voters is often difficult.

The result is that the goods and services purchased by government often enjoy near autarky levels of protection. Hence, the potential for gains from trade is probably significant. Opening up government procurement contracts to foreign bidders is likely to be difficult. Those politicians who perceive trade liberalization as being an engine for global economic growth will, however, promote liberalization – if for no other reason than the expected size of the potential gains.

The opening of procurement contracts to foreign bidders is likely to lead to a lively debate within political parties themselves. As suggested above, it will leave politicians open to criticism that they are abdicating their responsibility to champion domestic products. There are numerous examples of apparently trivial violations of their roles as champions of national products such as driving a foreign-made car or holidaying in foreign countries that have become major political issues. Fear of the effects of this form of criticism on a much larger scale may lead to considerable opposition to liberalization of procurement contracts. Further, the awarding of procurement contracts may be one of the ways political parties reward their supporters. Allowing foreign bidders will reduce the party's power base and, subsequently, resources. Resistance can be expected within the party if this is the case.

It will prove difficult to devise mechanisms for awarding contracts that will withstand international scrutiny. Governments have been at pains to devise bidding systems that allow criteria other than the lowest price to be considered in domestic sealed-bid auctions. In many cases, the perception of the ability of the firm to complete the project or to deliver on the quality specifications is as important to the decision to award the contract as the price. The problems created by the **winner's curse** phenomenon make reliance on bid price as the only criterion problematic at best (Cullen and Kerr, 1989). Making the allocation of government procurement contracts a sufficiently transparent process to overcome bidders' suspicions of bias has proved virtually impossible for purely domestic contracts. It will likely prove even more difficult when contracts are opened for international bidding and suspicions of national bias are endemic. New international institutions will probably be required to monitor government procurement procedures if liberalization takes place.

The NAFTA made specific provisions for the opening of government procurement contracts to firms in the other countries. This was done on the basis of reciprocity whereby each country agreed to open all contracts that exceeded pre-specified minimum values. Small contracts are still reserved for domestic firms. All three NAFTA countries are federations with multiple levels of government with constitutionally guaranteed powers. The Canadian provinces and the individual US states, as well as local governments in each country, have considerable economic independence. This includes control over their procurement processes. Attempting to have the agreement's procurement provisions extended to lower levels of government would have led to a constitutional challenge in Canada and the US. As it was a mutual problem, the procurement provisions were restricted to contracts of the national governments. This type of arrangement would not be suitable for countries with a more unitary government system, because it would mean that all contracts in the country with a unitary government structure would be open while a portion of a federation's contracts remained closed to international bidders. Wider acceptance of the liberalization of procurement contracts is likely to be subject to difficult negotiations.

While negotiations on government procurement were not formally part of the Uruguay Round, 12 countries – including the EU signing as one – signed an Agreement on Government Procurement in December 1993. The agreement will, however, be part of the WTO. Most developed countries including the US and Japan are party to the agreement, as well as Hong Kong and South Korea. Other countries are encouraged to join.

The basis of the agreement is the opening up of contracts over a certain size to bids from the other countries signing the agreement. The size of the contracts to be opened to foreign bids changes with the level of government involved. For national governments the threshold is US $176 000. It rises to approximately US $270 000 for states, provinces, departments and prefectures, while for utilities it is US $540 000. For construction contracts, it is US $675 000 000.

This system of thresholds leaves politicians considerable flexibility if they wish to exclude foreign bidders. Almost any contract can be rebundled into smaller units and separately tendered. In other words, if a contract is sufficiently large that foreign bids must be allowed under the terms of the agreement, it could simply be split into two (or more) smaller contracts and foreign bidders excluded.

The principles underlying the agreement on government procurement are transparency and national treatment. The signatories have agreed to widely disseminate information on contracts, including technical specifications, time limits, required documentation and submission procedures. Institutional arrangements are to be put in place for unsatisfied bidders to be able to challenge procurement decisions. Foreign suppliers and foreign goods and services must be given no less favourable treatment than domestic suppliers.

The agreement came into force at the beginning of 1996. Its wider success will, of course, depend on the number of additional countries that join over time.

18.5 Trade blocs

Liberalization of services and government procurement, as well as agreements over increased protection of intellectual property, will be much easier within regional groupings of countries than it will be in the multilateral forums of the WTO. As a result, regional groupings are likely to become increasingly influential and important regulators of international commerce. The danger is that these regional groupings may take on the characteristics of competing trade blocs. This will mean that, while trade barriers are coming down within the blocs, trade barriers between the blocs may remain in place. There is already considerable trade tension between the major focal points around which trade blocs will have to coalesce. The US and the EU are at loggerheads over some aspects of agriculture (Viju et al., 2012). The US and Japan are in conflict over access to Japanese procurement contracts and the Japanese distribution system. Japan and the EU battle over imports of Japanese cars and electronics.

If blocs are developing, countries must fear not belonging to a bloc. The worst-case scenario for a small country is having to go it alone in a world where trading blocs are building trade barriers around themselves. If trade blocs become the focus of political activity, the protection offered small countries by multilateral institutions will wane. The fate of Australia and New Zealand when Britain entered the EU is a lesson not lost on a few small countries. The safe course is to become a member of a bloc.

While countries such as Sweden, Austria and Finland perceived great benefits from being members of the EU, they also feared being left on the fringes of international commerce. As regional groupings expand, negotiations for the acceptance of new members will become more difficult and the terms of accession less favourable. Hence, it is better to attempt to join a group as early as possible. The scramble to join potential trade blocs will, of course, increase the economic power of the bloc. This will increase its ability to act independently. As blocs become larger they will also become more unwieldy. Additional political energy will have to be expended to progress internally. This will increase the likelihood that the trade concerns of other blocs and non-members will be ignored.

The potential for a third bloc on the Asia-Pacific Rim also exists. As yet, there is little evidence that it is in the process of forming (Yeung et al., 1999). One natural focal point is Japan, but other Asian nations appear to fear Japanese hegemony. Memories of Japan's last attempt at the formation of an economic bloc, its wartime Greater East Asia Co-Prosperity Sphere, may still be too sharp. Further, while growing rapidly, the markets of other Asia-Pacific Rim countries are not yet large enough to replace the US and Europe as Japan's major markets. China is a natural counterbalance to Japanese hegemony. If blocs in other parts of the world expand and increase in power, Asian countries may well find the will to follow suit (Yeung et al., 1999).

If true trade blocs arise, some developing countries will find themselves drawn into the sphere of influence of one of the blocs but without full membership. Others will be increasingly isolated. In both cases, their bargaining power over trade issues is likely to be decreased. Trade will not be their engine of growth.

While the increased speed at which trade barriers can be reduced when a small group of states cooperate is appealing, there is also great danger. While some disputes between blocs are to be expected and not likely to disrupt trade flows significantly, the spectre of full-blown trade wars between blocs is also possible. Trade among Japan, the US and the major countries of the EU exceeds that with their regional trading partners. This trade is also increasing rapidly. A full-scale trade war would be devastating to all the major economies. As a result, political effort will be required to prevent a further deterioration in relations (Viju and Kerr, 2011). The future is likely to see a seesaw between the forces of regionalism and the forces of multilateralism. If trading blocs begin to seriously conflict, multilateralism will ascend. Frustration with the slow progress possible through multilateralism will see renewed regional efforts.

18.6   Business input into trade issues

It will be important for businesses to watch closely the evolution of the international trading environment. Changes in trade regulations will provide opportunities. Falling barriers will open new markets. Change will also mean new threats from foreign competition. Increasing barriers will lead to opportunities to produce substitutes for foreign products. It will also mean that some markets will become closed. The opportunities from the reduction in barriers provided by regional groupings of states are likely to be easier to identify and act upon. The threats presented by competitors from within a bloc are also likely to be more vigorous. Information will be the key.

Regardless of the actions of governments, technological change will be the most important factor influencing future international commercial activities. Governments are likely to be able to act only after the fact in reaction to commercial realities. Given the current political acceptance of the *trade-led growth* thesis, firms which identify new opportunities that are constrained by trade barriers are likely to get a better hearing from government than those wishing to close off a competitive threat from foreigners.

Foreign non-tariff barriers may not be in place to protect any identifiable vested interest but may rather be put in place to regulate a situation that no longer reflects the commercial reality. The restriction remains in place only because of the inertia of government. Firms that find their opportunities constrained by such foreign regulations cannot be complacent. They will have to press their government strongly to negotiate with the foreign government for the regulations' removal. If the pace of technological change continues to accelerate, more redundant regulations that act as non-tariff barriers are likely to become evident. Firms seeking out international opportunities will be the first to identify these constraints. They will need to form much more of a partnership with government than in the past, when the major thrust of trade negotiations was the reduction of general-purpose trade restrictions – tariffs, import quotas and so on. Non-tariff barriers in the form of domestic regulations will be very diverse and less easily identifiable by governments. Industry must be prepared to take a more active leadership role. Further, the smaller-scale negotiations of regional groupings of states will make it easier to identify particular areas of business concerns than is the case with multi-lateral negotiations.

While one of the major assumptions of this discussion of the future has been that the influence of protectionists is on the wane, this does not mean that they have been vanquished. It does appear, however, that protectionists no longer have the ability to become identified with broad-based national inter-est. The poor showing of Canadian political parties which fought elections primarily over whether to sign and subsequently to 'tear up' the NAFTA, the difficult time had by most political parties opposed to their countries joining the EU, and the limited influence of those in the US advocating trade restrictions in the wake of the 2008 financial crisis attest to the protectionists' fading influence (Viju and Kerr, 2011). Those interested in protectionism, however, may also find themselves with new allies.

Environmental groups, frustrated with the rate of progress made on clean-ing up the environment in developing countries, have been attempting to have environmental issues tied to trade issues. This would enable more lev-erage to be applied to governments in developing countries (Kerr, 2001). The environmental groups have found willing allies among protectionists, who see lower environmental standards as unfair trade advantages (Kerr, 2010). While this line of reasoning is little more than the old cheap labour argument dressed up in a different guise, it has gained a degree of popularity. Certainly, the environmental record in developing countries is generally very poor and needs to be addressed. Tying it to trade issues, however, is not likely to lead to a significant improvement. It should be noted that along with poor enforcement of labour standards – the cheap labour argument – Mexico's less stringent environmental legislation was the major stumbling block to US approval of the NAFTA. The issue of labour standards applied in develop-ing countries to the production of goods imported into developed countries has become an increasingly important issue for some consumers in recent years – an issue distributors of such goods have had to deal with through the establishment of private standards and monitoring of foreign facilities (Bakhshi and Kerr, 2008). The convergence of interest between the protectionist instincts of businesses facing vigorous foreign competition and the environmental and consumer movements may wield considerable influence in the right circumstances.

Other special interests such as animal welfare groups and those concerned with endangered species may also wish to have their issues increasingly tied to trade sanctions (Hobbs et al., 2002). This increases their ability to influence events in other countries. The effectiveness of trade actions in influencing events in other countries was powerfully demonstrated when the European Union banned imports of seal products to protest against the methods used in Canada's seal hunt (Jhappan, 1994). While trade sanctions have been used to try to influence the behaviour of nations regarding aggression and human rights, the broadening of the spectrum of issues where trade sanctions can be applied may considerably influence future trade patterns and international commerce (Kerr, 2004).

Firms engaging in international commerce may have to be far more cognizant of the origins of the products they trade than in the past. While it may be relatively easy to identify when an endangered species is being used as an industrial input, it may be far more difficult to determine whether an imported input has been produced under environmentally acceptable conditions (Gaisford et al., 2001; Kerr, 2010). Firms engaging in international commerce that fail to take account of such factors may risk considerable loss of reputation through adverse publicity.

As the world economy continues to become more integrated, fewer and fewer firms will remain isolated from international commerce. Businesses are, however, able to influence considerably the economic environment in which they operate.

 REFERENCES

Bakhshi, S. and Kerr, W.A. (2008) Incorporating labour standards in trade agreements: Protectionist ploy or legitimate trade policy issue? *International Journal of Trade and Global Markets*, 1(4), 373–91.

Boyd, S.L., Kerr, W.A. and Perdikis, N. (2003) Agricultural biotechnology innovations versus intellectual property rights: Are developing countries at the mercy of multinationals? *Journal of World Intellectual Property*, 6(2), 211–32.

Cullen, S.E. and Kerr, W.A. (1989) International competitiveness and resource rents: Insights from the Canada–U.S. softwood lumber dispute. *World Competition Law and Economics Review*, 12(3), 25–39.

Gaisford, J.D. and Kerr, W.A. (2001) *Economic Analysis for International Trade Negotiations*, Edward Elgar Publishing, Cheltenham, UK and Northampton, MA, USA.

Gaisford, J.D., Hobbs, J.E., Kerr, W.A., Perdikis, N. and Plunkett, M.D. (2001) *The Economics of Biotechnology*, Edward Elgar Publishing, Cheltenham, UK and Northampton, MA, USA.

Gaisford, J.D., Tarvydas, R., Hobbs, J.E. and Kerr, W.A. (2002) Biotechnology piracy: Rethinking the international protection of intellectual property. *Canadian Journal of Agricultural Economics*, 50(1), 1–14.

Hobbs, A.L., Hobbs, J.E., Isaac, G.E. and Kerr, W.A. (2002) Ethics, domestic food policy and trade law: Assessing the EU animal welfare proposal to the WTO. *Food Policy*, 27, 437–54.

Jhappan, R. (1994) Animal rights versus aboriginal rights: Canada's aboriginal peoples and the European Community, in *The European Community, Canada and 1992*, ed. G.M. MacMillan, University of Calgary, Calgary.

Kerr, W.A. (2000) Is it time to re-think the WTO? A return to the basics. *Journal of International Law and Trade Policy*, 1(2), 99–107.

Kerr, W.A. (2001) The World Trade Organization and the environment, in *Globalization and Agricultural Trade Policy*, ed. H.J. Michelman, J. Rude, J. Stabler and G. Storey, Lynne Rienner, Boulder, CO, pp. 53–65.

Kerr, W.A. (2002) A club no more – the WTO after Doha. *Journal of International Law and Trade Policy*, 3(1), 1–9, www.esteyjournal.com.

Kerr, W.A. (2004) The changing nature of protectionism: Are 'free traders' up to the challenges it presents? *Journal of International Law and Trade Policy*, 5(2), 91–101.

Kerr, W.A. (2010) Environmental tariffs: Will they be captured by protectionists? *Journal of International Law and Trade Policy*, 11(2), 336–48.

Kerr, W.A. and Boyd, S.L. (2007) Piracy, property and productivity: The case for protecting the results of intellectual activity, in *Revitalizing Russian Industry*, ed. J.D. Gaisford, V. Mayevsky and W.A. Kerr, Nova Science Publishers, New York.

Viju, C. and Kerr, W.A. (2011) Protectionism and global recession: Has the link been broken? *Journal of World Trade*, 45(3), 605–28.

Viju, C., Yeung, M.T. and Kerr, W.A. (2012) The trade implications of the post-moratorium European Union approval system for genetically modified organisms. *Journal of World Trade*, 46(5), 1207–38.

Yampoin, R. and Kerr, W.A. (1998) Can trade measures induce compliance with TRIPS? *Journal of the Asia Pacific Economy*, 3(2), 165–82.

Yeung, M.T., Perdikis, N. and Kerr, W.A. (1999) *Regional Trading Blocs in the Global Economy: The EU and ASEAN*, Edward Elgar Publishing, Cheltenham, UK and Northampton, MA, USA.

Summary of Section VI

The pace at which change is taking place in international commerce is increasing. Part of the reason for this is the rapid rate of technological change in a key component to the costs of doing business internationally – electronic communications. An increase in both the quantity and the quality of information available to firms, as well as a reduction in the time it takes to transfer information, has improved the ability to identify new potential markets. More effective monitoring of transactions is also possible.

The rate of change is also increasing because governments in most countries have identified the liberalization of international trade as being important to improving the performance of their economies. A considerable momentum exists for the removal of trade barriers both multilaterally, despite the Doha Round impasse, and within preferential trade agreements. While those with vested interests in the status quo are still able to exert considerable pressure for protection, their efforts are less often identified with the broad national interest.

The progress in liberalization in preferential trade agreements has been more rapid recently than what has been the case at the WTO and helps to explain their current popularity. The success of the EU and NAFTA provides examples others wish to emulate. Their example is being followed in other areas of the world. From Australia and New Zealand to South America to Asia to Africa, new regional trade groupings are being formed and old ones resurrected. While 'free trade areas' have existed in many parts of the developing world for a considerable period, they were largely ineffective in the era when policies of import substitution and an expanding role for government in the economy were the popular ideologies. The new regional trade groupings are the result of initiatives from governments that are attempting to deregulate their own economies, including their trade policies. They may succeed where their predecessors did not. Their success will, however, be limited without better access to markets in at least one of the major developed economies.

Even though progress has been painfully slow at the WTO, multinational institutions remain a major force in trade policy. There is still more agreement among countries about trade issues than there is disagreement. While the disagreements surrounding agriculture and cultural industries receive the publicity, and may at times appear to threaten the entire multilateral system, agreement in a large number of other potentially difficult areas was achieved fairly easily in the Doha negotiations.

Governments also perceive that, for future large gains to trade to arise, liberalization will have to be applied in other areas – in particular trade in services and government procurement. Liberalization in these areas is being pursued both in multilateral and in regional trade organizations. The liberalization of services will be difficult because it will often involve the temporary movement of people. The liberalization of government procurement contracts will be difficult because of its direct influence on internal politics. Considerable progress in these areas has been made both by the EU and in the NAFTA. Their experience may prove valuable when attempts are made to extend liberalization in these areas to other countries. Reaping the full benefits of trade liberalization will also require government investment in reducing the costs of redeploying resources, particularly labour displaced as a result of liberalization.

The interaction between firms engaged in international commerce and trade policy makers is likely to increase in the future. With many of the formal barriers to trade removed, trade opportunities may be increasingly affected by non-tariff barriers. The formal barriers such as tariffs and import quotas were imposed by governments for the express purpose of restricting trade. They were visible targets for liberalization. Non-tariff barriers are less transparent and individually affect only a limited number of international commercial opportunities. Firms, in the process of investigating commercial opportunities, will encounter these restrictions. Often these restrictions will not have been imposed with the intent of impeding trade. Companies will have to work more closely with governments than in the past to help identify the constraints on their opportunities and to suggest solutions.

The economics of international business can be approached on two levels – trade between countries and international transactions between firms. Economists have traditionally focused on the former. Considerable insights are provided by trade theory models and from the understanding they provide regarding the effects of the trade policies used by governments. The challenge is to use those insights effectively to commercial advantage. It is also important for business people to understand the flaws in some commonly held theories. Only then can reasonable business responses to trade policy issues be formulated.

The study of the economic forces underlying international commercial transactions is less well developed. The current institutional arrangements available to facilitate international transactions can be explained as attempts by firms to reduce the costs associated with those transactions. The evidence suggests that the international institutions that have evolved to facilitate international commerce are efficient. It would appear, however, that many of these institutions have, as their primary *raison d'être*, reducing the risk of opportunist behaviour by parties to an international transaction. This suggests that economists need to spend more time studying how firms actually behave. Only then will better insights be gained into the interaction between trade policy and the other economic forces affecting the volume and organization of international transactions.

Exercise

While it is common to provide questions and exercises throughout a book, we have not done so. We believe that international trade and commerce needs to be approached as a system. Underlying economic forces, trade policies and international institutions, both public and private, together affect the choices firms make. We have decided to set only one exercise. *In light of what you have learned in this book, rewrite the executive's story that began the volume* (Chapter 1). Hopefully, you will have a better ending than Ryan.

Glossary

absolute advantage The ability to produce a good or service more cheaply than one's rivals.

ad valorem **tariff** A tariff which is expressed as a percentage of the price.

Appellate Body A body to which appeals to decisions regarding trade disputes between countries can be made.

asset specificity An investment which once made has no or very limited alternative use, for example purchase of specialized plant or machinery.

autarky A situation when a country is not participating in international trade.

aval A contract of exchange. A form of guarantee given by a bank or other party to enhance the value of a negotiable instrument.

balance of trade The difference between the value of visible exports and the value of visible imports. Thus a country may be in surplus or deficit on its visible transactions with one or all countries.

Baltic Exchange Freight-chartering exchange in the City of London.

bareboat charter A time charter under which the shipowner hires out only the ship, letting the charterer employ the master and crew, provide fuel and stores and bear all the cost and responsibility of operating the ship.

barter An agreement where goods and services may be exchanged for another specified set of goods or services. No currency is offered in exchange.

beggar-thy-neighbour Retaliatory trade policies designed to counteract other countries' trade restrictions. They usually lead to further retaliatory action which results in the reduction of trade volumes and benefits no one.

bilateral agreement An agreement between two countries.

black market	An illicit trade in goods.
Bretton Woods system	An agreement reached in 1944 among the finance ministers of 45 Western nations to establish a system of fixed exchange rates.
bulk cargo	Cargo consisting entirely of one commodity that does not need any packing, such as coal or wheat.
bulk carrier	A ship intended for carrying cargoes of loose materials, such as coal ore or grain, which are not packed in containers.
buy-back agreements	Agreements whereby a firm, with the aim of obtaining an order to supply a production facility such as a factory, agrees to buy a specified amount of the output of the plant when commissioned.
Cambridge School	A school of economic thought established by economists at the University of Cambridge in the United Kingdom.
capital	Assets which can be used in the production and distribution of goods and services, that is, capital equipment. Also the money value of real assets.
carrier of origin requirements	Requirements that imports be carried on ships or aircraft registered or owned by the country of destination or that exports be carried on the ships or aircraft owned or registered by the country of origin.
cartel	An association of independent entities that attempts to determine output, sales or prices so that members secure monopoly profits.
charter	A contract by which an owner agrees to hire a ship or aircraft to a person or organization known as the charterer.
c.i.f.	Cost, insurance and freight. In foreign trade contracts, the seller's price includes all charges and risks up to the point where the ship carrying the goods arrives at the port of destination. From that point the buyer accepts all costs and risks of unloading, lighterage and wharfing unless these have been included in the freight or collected by the shipowner when the freight was paid.

classical economics	A tradition of economic thought initiated by Adam Smith and developed by others.
closed economy	An economic system with little or no external trade.
command economy	An economic system where resources are allocated by a state planning authority.
Common Agricultural Policy (CAP)	An integrated system of subsidies and rebates applied to the agricultural sector in the European Union.
common market	A group of countries that agree to remove all barriers to trade among members, to establish a common trade policy with respect to non-members and to allow full mobility of factors of production.
community indifference curve	A locus of combinations of goods between which the community is, in some sense, defined as being indifferent.
comparative advantage	A situation where one country is more efficient than another in the production of two or more products but is relatively more efficient in the production of one of those products.
competitive advantage	A situation where a country has the ability to produce a good or service more cheaply than other countries owing to favourable factor conditions, successful related and supporting industries, appropriate firm strategies, structures and rivalry conditions, and favourable demand conditions.
comprador	An employee of a trading house or its exclusive agent, employed to foster personal business relationships and trust between traders, thus reducing the cultural clash between business people and encouraging trade.
conference	An association of shipping companies formed for the purpose of setting rates, routes and timetables.
confirmed credit	A letter of credit which a bank has made itself responsible for honouring.
conglomerate	A business organization generally consisting of a holding company and a group of subsidiary companies engaged in dissimilar activities.

consecutive voyage charter   A contract between the shipowner and charterer covering a specified number of trips.

constant returns to scale   The condition whereby an increase in the factors used in production by a given percentage leads to an increase in output by the same percentage. A doubling of inputs leads to a doubling of output.

consumer surplus   The difference between the market price and what a consumer would be willing to pay for a good.

containerized carriage   Goods being transported in a large metal case of standard shape and size. The standardization greatly helps in transporting the goods quickly and cheaply (dimensions: 2.4m × 2.4m × 6.1m or 12.2m).

contract of affreightment   An agreement between a shipowner and a shipper or owner of cargo to transport a specified quantity between ports over a specific period.

cost of search   The cost incurred by firms in attempting to identify new markets for their products.

countertrade   A form of barter in international trade where the buyer requires the seller to accept goods in lieu of currency.

countervailing duties   Import duties imposed on a commodity to offset a reduction of its price as a result of an export subsidy in the country of origin.

currency account   An account opened in a foreign currency which may allow a firm to avoid the costs and risks of exchanging currencies for each foreign business transaction.

customs union   A union among trading countries in which members dismantle trade barriers in goods and services and establish a common trade policy with respect to non-members.

decoupled subsidy   A level of subsidy paid to an organization or firm regardless of its level of output.

depression   A situation when output in the economy is below potential capacity for a prolonged period of time to damage another country's economy.

due process   The formal working of a fair legal action. The regular and orderly course of the law through the courts.

dumping	Selling goods overseas at a price lower than the exporter's home market price or at a price lower than the cost of production or both.
economic union	A union among trading countries that has the characteristics of a common market plus harmonized monetary policies, taxation and government spending policies, and uses a common currency.
economies of scale	Lower costs per unit made possible by operating on a large scale.
entrepôt	A centre at which goods arrive for subsequent trans-shipment.
equivalence	A situation where standards imposed on goods in one country are recognized as 'equivalent' to those imposed in another country.
exchange rate	The price or rate at which one currency is exchanged for another currency.
externality	A cost not fully accounted for in the price or by the market system.
factor intensity	The ratio of capital input to labour input used in the production of a good.
factoring	A means by which traders can receive immediate payment at a discount for goods sold from an intermediary known as a factor. The factor eventually receives payment from the purchaser.
false border trade	Trade in goods across border frontiers encouraged by an imbalance of sales taxes and excise duties in different countries, for example trade in alcoholic beverages between Britain (expensive, higher duty) and France (lower duty, cheaper).
f.a.s.	Free alongside ship/steamer price quotation. The seller's price where the goods are placed alongside the ship ready to be taken on board. The buyer must pay for the loading of the goods, *but*, if the ship cannot enter the port or tie up to the shore, the seller must arrange and pay for lighters.
fixed capital	Capital such as plant, machinery and buildings.
fixed costs	Costs which do not vary with output.
flexible exchange rate	An exchange rate determined by the market, where governments do not intervene to establish its value.

f.o.b.	Free on board price quotation. In foreign trade contracts the seller's price includes all charges and risks up to the point where the seller delivers the goods on board the ship named by the buyer at the named post of shipment. From that point, all risk and charges have to be borne by the buyer.
foreign direct investment (FDI)	The establishment or expansion of a firm's operations in a foreign country.
forfaiter	A specialist private firm which assesses the risk of foreign trade transactions.
forward exchange contract	A contractual form used by the money markets to fix an exchange rate for the future delivery of one currency for another.
forward rates	Contracts that provide for two parties to exchange currencies on a future date at an agreed exchange rate.
franchising	A form of licensing that allows a distributor or retailer exclusive rights to sell a good or service in a specific area.
free trade area	An association of countries that between them abolish import tariffs and quotas, export subsidies and other government measures designed to influence trade. Each country, however, maintains its own international trade measures vis-à-vis countries outside the association.
full employment	A situation in which everyone in the labour force who is willing to work at the market rate has a job.
futures market	A market where buyers and sellers of commodities or financial assets contract to exchange items at a specified price at a specified future date.
General Agreement on Tariffs and Trade (GATT)	The set of multilaterally agreed rules governing the trade in goods.
General Agreement on Trade in Services (GATS)	The set of rules that apply to trade in services. Negotiated in the Uruguay Round, its aim is to liberalize trade in services.
general cargo	Cargo consisting of various kinds of goods not of any particular kind; not full cargoes of a single commodity.

Greater East Asia Co-Prosperity Sphere	An economic bloc formed by Japan in the Second World War in an attempt to foster formal economic integration of Asian economies.
greenfield investment	An investment which creates an entirely new subsidiary or company.
harmonization	An agreement between nations to conform to a common set of regulations.
hedge	To counterbalance a present sale or purchase with a sale or purchase for future delivery as a way of minimizing loss due to price fluctuation. To make counterbalancing sales or purchases in the international market as protection against adverse movements in the exchange rate.
hegemony	Leadership, especially by one state.
horizontal integration (lateral integration)	The merger of two or more firms in the same business activity.
import quota	The quantitative limit placed on the importation of a specific commodity.
import substitution	A policy adopted by many developing countries that involves the systematic encouragement of domestic production of goods formerly imported.
income elasticity of demand	A proportionate change in demand brought about by a proportionate change in income.
indifference curve	A graphical representation of sets of different combinations of commodities which yield to the consumer the same level of satisfaction.
indivisible/lumpy cost	A production cost which is not divisible into smaller units.
infant industry argument	An argument in support of protection that tariffs should be imposed to protect an industry which is trying to get started. The presumption is that, once the 'infant industry' is established and technologically efficient, then the tariff barrier can be removed.
International Monetary Fund (IMF)	An intergovernmental body that oversees the operation of the international monetary system, and acts as a creditor to countries that find themselves in balance of payments difficulties.

irrevocable credits	Letters of credit which cannot be amended during the life of the credit except with the agreement of the beneficiary.
joint venture	A business formed by two or more companies or institutions to achieve a common goal.
Keynesian	Relating to a branch of economics associated with J.M. Keynes. Its main features are that aggregate demand plays a decisive role in determining the level of real output, and economics can settle at positions with high unemployment.
laissez-faire	The principle of non-intervention by government in economic affairs as proposed by classical economists.
Leontief paradox	A paradox indicated by Wassily Leontief's study of US trade that the US was exporting labour-intensive products. This was a paradox because of the general belief that the US was a capital-intensive country which should be exporting capital-intensive products.
limited option	Similar to an option except that currency has to be exchanged within a 30-day period beginning at a specified future date.
liner trade	Trade where a ship or ships make regular voyages on dates made known in advance between certain ports. Such a ship is the opposite of a tramp freighter, which keeps no regular route or timetable.
log rolling	A means of increasing the political power of disparate groups or individuals through cooperation to achieve mutually beneficial objectives.
Maastricht Treaty	The agreement signed in December 1991 in which European Community members agreed to a specific timetable and set of necessary conditions to create a single currency.
maquiladoras	Mexican factories that assemble goods for export to the United States.
marginal product	The output created by the employment of one additional unit of a factor of production.

marginal rate of substitution	The rate at which a consumer needs to substitute one commodity for another in order to maintain constant total utility from the commodities taken together, that is, the slope of an indifference curve.
marine underwriter	A person or firm that accepts marine insurance contracts.
Marshall Plan	Economic help given by the US mainly to countries in Europe to help rebuild their economies after the Second World War. The three-year plan was administered in the US by the Economic Cooperation Administration (ECA) and in Europe by the Organisation for European Economic Co-operation (OEEC).
mercantilism	A policy originating in the seventeenth and early eighteenth centuries aimed at increasing a nation's wealth and power by encouraging the export of goods in return for gold.
monetarism	A theory of macroeconomics which holds that money supply increases are necessary and sufficient conditions for inflation.
monopoly	A market in which there is only one seller.
most favoured nation (MFN)	The status granted to a trading partner which entitles it to the same privileges granted to other most favoured nations.
multilateral agreement	Agreement between a number of different countries.
multinational company or transnational corporation	A company or enterprise operating in a number of countries and having production or service facilities outside the country of origin.
national treatment	Foreign suppliers and foreign goods being given equitable treatment with domestic suppliers and goods.
neo-classical economics	A school of economic thought in the tradition of classical economics characterized by microeconomic systems constructed to explore conditions of static equilibrium.
niche market	A comparatively small segment of a market in which a company concentrates its efforts.

open accounts	A sort of trade credit that allows a buyer to purchase goods or services and pay for them within a specified period of time without the penalty of interest rates being charged.
open economy	An economic system in which the proportion of exports and imports to GDP is high.
opportunistic recontracting	See *post-contractual opportunistic behaviour (PCOB)*.
opportunity cost	Cost incurred by a firm by not undertaking an alternative strategy.
option	The right to buy or sell at a specified future date or within a specified period.
Organization of the Petroleum Exporting Countries (OPEC)	A cartel formed by the principal oil-producing and -exporting countries with the purpose of setting output quotas and raising prices.
patent	An exclusive right granted by a government to an inventor for a specified period.
per diem	Per day.
perfect competition	A market structure in which neither the buyer's nor the seller's individual decisions have an effect on the market price and output. Price and output are determined by the market.
post-contractual opportunistic behaviour (PCOB)	Purposeful renegotiation of an agreement for economic gain.
predatory pricing	Setting prices at very low levels with the aim of weakening or eliminating competitors or keeping out new entrants to a market.
price discrimination	The selling of the same good or service to different buyers at different prices.
primary products	The output of the agriculture, forestry, fishing and extractive industries.
principal–agent relationship	The relationship between a first party (the principal) and an agent employed by the principal to work on the principal's behalf. This involves delegation of some decision-making authority to the agent, which the agent might exploit to his or her advantage.

producer surplus	The difference between the price a producer receives for a good or service and what the producer would be willing to accept.
product differentiation	A way of distinguishing essentially the same products from one another by real or illusory means.
product life cycle	The four stages that a theory suggests products pass through: introduction, growth, maturity and decline.
production possibility frontier	A curve showing the various alternative combinations of two goods that a nation or community can produce by fully utilizing all of its resources.
protectionism	The imposition of tariffs or quotas to restrict the flow of imports.
real income	Money income adjusted for changes in prices.
recession	A sharp slowdown in the rate of economic growth.
regional trade association	An association formed by a number of countries in which mutual concessions on trade are agreed.
resource mobility	The relative ease or difficulty with which resources can be allocated or transferred from industry to industry or area to area.
returns to scale	The proportionate increase in output resulting from an increase in all inputs.
revocable credits	Letters of credit which may be amended at the option of the applicant.
Ricardian goods	Goods which require heavy natural resources, are climatically influenced or need unsophisticated labour inputs. Goods from extractive industries (coal, petroleum, minerals) or food, for example wheat and corn.
rules of origin requirements	Regulations which specify that a proportion of the value of the good sold in a country must have been added in that country.
second best	The best solution when the preferred solution – first best – is not available or unattainable.
senile industry	A once thriving industry which has lost its comparative advantage and is suffering decline.

serious prejudice	A concept introduced to prevent suits over minor trade distortions caused by the introduction of a subsidy.
shipbroker	A broker who acts as an agent for shipowners and shipping companies, arranging bill of lading contracts, charter parties and insurance, and finding cargoes and in some cases passengers. The shipbroker receives a commission as a percentage of the business he or she gets for the principals.
single voyage charter	A contract between the shipowner and charterer covering one trip only.
sogo shosha	A large Japanese trading company.
spot rates	Contracts that provide for two parties to exchange currencies with delivery in two business days.
state trading agencies	Organizations specifically authorized to make purchases and sales internationally by a government.
subsidiaries	Companies legally controlled by other companies.
subsidies	Payments by government to a firm or an industry in order to prevent its decline or in order to avoid an increase in the prices of its products or to enable its exports to compete more effectively on the international market.
sunk costs	Costs incurred in acquiring specific assets which have no or limited alternative use.
switching costs	The costs which will be incurred by a firm in changing production from one set of goods or services to another set of goods or services.
tariffication	The process by which quantitative restrictions such as quotas are converted to tariffs having equivalent effect.
tariffs	Taxes on imported goods and services levied by governments as a means of raising revenue and to act as barriers to trade.
terms of trade	The ratio of indexes of export prices and import prices.
time charter	A charter by which the ship or aircraft is hired for an agreed period of time, during which the charterer may use the ship as he or she wishes, paying

	a monthly rate of hire based on the deadweight tonnage of the ship. The ship is operated by the owners, but the charterer pays the cost of fuel and stores consumed during the period of the charter.
trade creation	The benefit accruing to a country when a group of countries trade freely amongst themselves but maintain barriers to trade with non-members.
trade diversion	The cost to a country when a group of countries trade freely amongst themselves but maintain barriers against lower-cost non-members.
trade liberalization	A policy aimed at the removal of tariffs or other trade barriers to encourage trade in goods and services.
trade-related investment measures (TRIMs)	Economic policies that restrict foreign companies in their operations, that is, restriction on ownership, repatriation of profits and so on.
trading bloc	A group of countries that agree to further links among themselves through trade in goods and services and the movement of capital across borders.
trading house	A company that specializes in arranging international transactions, for example Hutchison Whampoa.
tramp freighter	A ship travelling an irregular route scheduled only by demand conditions.
transfer pricing	The use of internal (as opposed to market) prices in large organizations for transactions between semi-autonomous divisions.
United Nations Conference on Trade and Development (UNCTAD)	A UN organization established to actively develop trade relations between developed and developing countries.
utility	The satisfaction derived by an individual from consuming goods or services.
variable levies	Taxes on goods that are not set at a fixed level but can vary according to world prices to keep the domestic price stable.

vertical integration   The placing of successive stages of production and distribution under the control of a sole enterprise. Firms can integrate forward towards retailing or backward towards the source of raw materials.

voyage charter   A charter by which the ship or aircraft is hired for a single voyage between agreed ports to carry a stated cargo at a fixed rate of freight. The owner bears responsibility for operating the ship and all expenses.

winner's curse   A situation where the highest bidder for a good or contract pays more than it is actually worth.

World Trade Organization (WTO)   The multilateral organization that administers the rules of trade agreed for goods, services and intellectual property, provides a venue for trade negotiations, reports on member states' compliance with trade agreements and settles disputes.

X-inefficiency   The discrepancy between the efficiency of firms as implied by economic theory and the efficiency level observed in practice (originated by H. Leibenstein).

Index